Creative Playgrounds and Recreation Centers

Revised edition

Alfred Ledermann and Alfred Trachsel

Frederick A. Praeger, Publishers

New York · Washington

The publishers wish to thank the architects, building owners, local authorities and institutions for all the information they supplied, and for their permission to reproduce drawings and photographs. Special acknowledgment is extended to Mr. Bernard Barenholz of Creative Playthings Inc., New York; Mrs. Anna Branzell, Stadsplankontoret Gothenburg; the editorial staff of Casabella, Milan; the Deutsche Städtetag, Cologne-Marienburg; Mr. Aldo van Eyck, Amsterdam; Mrs. Beate Hahn, Wolfeboro, New Hampshire; the National Playing Fields Association, London; Mr. Robert Nichols, Playground Associates, New York; the Pestalozzi Fröbel Society, Hamburg; the Royal Institute of British Architects, London; the Swiss Pro Juventute Foundation, Zürich; Mr. Max Siegumfeldt, Byplankontoret, Copenhagen; Mr. Amedee M. Sourdy, Park Department, Oakland, California; and to the Town and Country Planning Association, London.

Der Verlag dankt allen beteiligten Architekten, Bauherren, Behörden und Institutionen für die Überlassung von Bildmaterial, Plänen und Informationen. Zu besonderem Dank für Hinweise und Unterstützung fühlt er sich verpflichtet Herrn Bernard Barenholz, Creative Playthings Inc., New York; Frau Anna Branzell, Stadsplankontoret Göteborg; der Redaktion der Zeitschrift Casabella, Mailand; dem Deutschen Städtetag, Köln-Marienburg; Herrn Aldo van Eyck, Amsterdam; Frau Beate Hahn, Wolfeboro, New Hampshire; der National Playing Fields Association, London; Herrn Robert Nichols, Playground Associates, New York; dem Pestalozzi Fröbel Verband, Hamburg; dem Royal Institute of British Architects, London; der Schweiz. Stiftung Pro Juventute, Zürich; Herrn Max Siegumfeldt, Byplankontoret Kopenhagen; Herrn Amedee M. Sourdy, Park Department, Oakland, Calif; und der Town and Country Planning Association, London.

Published in the United States of America in 1959
by Frederick A. Praeger, Inc., Publishers
111 Fourth Avenue, New York, N.Y. 10003
Second edition, 1968
Copyright in Stuttgart, Germany 1959, by Verlag Gerd Hatje, Stuttgart
All rights reserved
Library of Congress Catalog Card Number: 68–31531
Printed in Germany
Translation into English by James C. Palmes and Ernst Priefert

Contents

Inhalt

Playground and Recreation Centre

By Alfred Ledermann, Pro Juventute Foundation, Zürich

"All nations play and they play remarkably alike."
Johan Huizinga

"Man only plays when he is human in the full sense of the word, and he is only completely human when he is playing."
Friedrich Schiller

I. Playing space for all

The modern city of asphalt does not tolerate a wild space where boys can play Robinson Crusoe, nor does it tolerate a quiet corner for the dreamlike play of smaller children. The tightly planned flats do not allow for children's noise; lanes and streets have become enemies of children. The streets no longer belong to the playing child and the adult pedestrian. The "homo faber", the working man, is the key-person for town-planners. The "homo ludens", the playing person, is left to the realm of the philosophers. A young father wrote: "Whoever has had to see his child carried home, because it ran into a car while playing on the road, defaced to such an extent that he could not recognise the beloved face which smiled at him daily, knows that it is worth while to do one's utmost to keep other children from a similar fate."
May this book rouse all who are willing to do their utmost to give back to the child its playing space. How quickly are we modern and clever grown-ups ready to dismiss the play of our children as an unnecessary waste of time, as mere fun, and how ready are we to measure everything according to its usefulness.
"What after all does mere play really mean when we know that in all the circumstances of man it is just play and only play which suits him completely?" Friedrich Schiller

Play is of decisive importance for the psychological development and the maturing of man. The consequences of insufficient possibilities for active and creative play clearly show results such as: poor imagination, nervousness, and irritability of children, waste of spare time and craving for entertainment, aggressiveness and rowdyism of many teen-agers. Of course, such psychological deviations of character have in most cases several causes and are the result of insufficient "warmth of the nest", wrong upbringing or unhappy family circumstances. But many of these wrong developments could be avoided or at least mitigated by means of an environment in which the child can wear out its joys and sorrows.

Especially in the early years of life play is one of the most important things. It is not wrong to call the years of infancy the playing age. But children of school age also want to play and they should do so even more extensively than we adults usually allow because, we say they are "too old". No one is ever too big or too old to play. It stimulates activity. The pathway to productive work is via play. While playing, the child develops skilful hands, agility, lively senses and a good-natured disposition, all of which are qualities needed later in life. Play is the surest guarantee for the healthy development of our children and is a valuable help in the upbringing of young people.
Does play belong only to the nursery, to the every-day life of youth? Has not also the adult a very special need of play and recreation in order to regenerate his intellectual powers? Modern city life weighs heavily on the nerves and health of mankind, more so than in former times. The high speed of work and often its monotony, as well as the rush of every-day life, are the causes of the impoverishment of man's inner life, if he is unable to find opportunities for a change and for renewing his strength. Rationalisation of work and automation mean more time to spare – (five-day week, earlier retirement age). From this arises the need for fresh opportunities for creative activity and appropriate utilisation of spare time. Otherwise the all-too-clever entertainment industry will absorb this free time and offer, as balance to hectic conditions of work, an equally hectic and noisy hubbub of amusement. The nervous routine of the city, the splitting up of family life and the passive wastage of time must be confronted by an environment of creative experience in order to strengthen the inner powers of the "asphalt-man" of the city and to fortify the bonds of the family.
Play and leisure, active spare-time occupation and creative work need space, playing space in the true sense of the word. Not only do cars need room for movement in order to pass each other, but children need space for playing as essentially as food and sleep. Will not our cities soon arrive at the point where space for playing is too restricted and friction becomes intolerable?
It is certainly time to admit the "human" elements of a town's organism, i. e. recreation and play centres, into the stark reality of our organically developed cities. It is a matter which town-planners and architects from all corners of the world have been demanding for a number of years.
In the realm of town planning, as it stands today, unfortunately the opinion often still persists that the problem of playing is simply dealt with under the heading "infants and toddlers' playing space". Children of school age, teen-agers and grown-ups find no consideration given to their different needs for play and recreation. The great significance of playing and of creative leisure for all age groups is not perceived. The toddlers' sand-pit is not being related to the family as a whole, nor to the community within the block of flats or neighbourhood. No wonder that the usual playgrounds become an easy, even if unintentional, dumping-place for parents who are tired of their children. Thus a further stone is added to the mosaic that reflects the disintegration of family life.

Thousands of towns and villages are at present in a stage of rapid expansion. New streets, dwellings, schools and factories are being built. It is extremely important to allocate and prepare there in good time sufficient play space and recreational facilities for all age groups.

II. Planning

If we face squarely the question of where this playing space should be located in the town or the village, we have to start from the consideration of the child and its play. To provide suitable play-spaces is not simply a task for building authorities and public parks departments. Play, and especially the play of infants, appertains to the home, the living room and the immediate surroundings of the house, but not to the playgrounds some distance from the home, however "wonderful", they may be.

Playing space at home.

The question of playing space must therefore be raised in the first instance in conjunction with the building of flats and housing estates. The room for playing (living room, children's corner, nursery or utility-room) is just as essential as the room for sleeping or for eating. Much is being done for physical hygiene in building homes. There are hardly any more dwellings being erected which do not provide washing and bathroom facilities. But in respect of provision for the hygiene of the inner life and for the maintenance of sound family life, there is still much to be done in designing dwellings and planning towns of the future.
Most of the flats built for families with children are too small and restricted. They often contain a sufficient number of rooms, but these are small, reduced to the minimum dimensions, "boxes" which provide the space required for furniture but not for human beings and their activities. And in addition to this we grown-ups cram the rooms full of furniture. Also the lightweight construction is the cause of much friction in many blocks of flats. If the children play in the flat, the neighbours complain. And yet, are not movement and noise an expression of the joy of living of our children? To suppress and prohibit them would result in a gradual psychological distortion. The children's rooms – especially in housing estates for large families – are only children's bedrooms but not play rooms. These longish rooms can take at best two small beds and a chest-of-drawers. Floor area for playing is hardly available. One could come to the conclusion that the life of the children only consists of sleep.
This is the reason why one should aim at a more sympathetic approach towards children and the family in the realm of housing. The problem of the playing child must be considered in the design stage; the family should find a nest and a living fellowship in its flat.
One of the most valuable playing places is the living room. Here the beginnings of play start with the smallest ones, at first in the cot, later in the play pen and the play corner. In every living room a play corner belonging to the infant alone

can be created by a skilful rearrangement of furniture. Here it should be allowed to do what it likes. Here is no need for a constant clearing up as on the living-room table, where one is always disturbed just when playing is most interesting. Here the child may build its first "cave" with boxes, chairs and pieces of cloth. In the play corner is the first home of the child, the home of his dream life, his inner life and one which he will never lose.

To create play corners and recesses should be a task at which architects, interior designers and parents work together. Furthermore in the basements of blocks of flats or one-family houses hobby rooms should increasingly be created and the drying rooms developed into playrooms for children.

Playing space in the open air.

A. For infants.

The playground for children under five years of age ought to be whenever possible immediately adjacent to the house as a "green enclosure", a place for play in the open, so that the mothers do not have to leave their work daily in order to accompany their children to the playground. They should be able to watch their little ones at play from the house. An infant feels "at home" only when it is allowed to play near its mother. One can almost compare this feeling of infants for the nest, the home, with the instinct of many wild animals for their particular home ground within the boundaries of which alone they only feel safe and secure. Even older children prefer to play in the vicinity of the home, in the surroundings which are familiar to them. At all events we should not lightly destroy the close link between the child and its immediate familiar environment. Inner unrest and rootlessness might be the consequences in later life.

Only on a farmstead does the small child retain his natural "run". There he is stimulated by a thousand things, in the stables, in the barn, with the small livestock, in the fields and in the woods. The farmer's child has his sphere of play near the home. He is in danger, however, of being torn too early from the land of childhood and put into the working routine of the grown-ups. Happy is that child who is introduced by understanding parents step by step, as he plays, into the working partnership of the family.

Most farm villages look different today from former times. Industrialisation leads to the erection in villages of housing estates and blocks of flats which look no different from those in towns; the families in these houses live like town people too. In addition, many villages have dangerous through-roads. This means that for the playing child exactly the same problems occur as in a town. To provide suitable play-space in the open air is therefore just as necessary as it is in every urban housing estate.

In contrast to the farm worker's child, a child in town mostly grows up in surroundings made for grown-up people. Hard asphalt, engine noise, hurry and polish make up that kind of world, which cannot be transformed into imaginative play. "It is therefore essential to aim at a network of infants' play-

grounds as near as possible to their homes in every town and in every village." The following suggestions can be taken into consideration:

Play-space in the back yard.

When designing blocks of flats, one has from the outset to allow for sufficient space between blocks, not only for the position of supports for washing lines and carpet-beating poles, but also for infants' play areas. The present tendency to have areas of grass between the blocks is very praiseworthy. Those grass areas should be accessible for play and recreational use and not, as is unfortunately so often the case, subject to every conceivable prohibition. An example of how it is possible, thanks to the initiative of individual landlords, to provide a well laid-out play-space between some blocks of flats is shown in the project illustrated on page 64.

In older neighbourhoods play areas are essential too but can usually only be made after clearance operations and the opening up of individual back yards into a communal space, whereby boundaries are eliminated and common cycle sheds, pram stores, etc. provided – a task which is extremely difficult to carry through psychologically and legally, under present conditions of ownership.

Copenhagen, the Danish capital, has found an interesting and exemplary solution for the problem. Every owner of a house which contains a minimum of eight flats is under legal obligation to provide a play-space. The tenants pay along with the rent a modest "play space-supplement". Copenhagen by this means has a large number of ideal house and yard play-spaces in the old city as well as in the suburbs. For examples see pages 48, 50, 58, 104.

The building laws of the city of Kassel require the provision of grass areas for linen bleaching and play-spaces in connection with dwellings before planning permission is granted. Such laws and regulations will be the only way in many places to obtain space for play in the densely built old quarters of a town.

Play-space in a housing estate.

When designing new housing estates a communal play space can be provided for at the planning stage in addition to individual gardens for each house; but up to the present day only very few building by-laws contain clauses to that effect. It should be a matter of course that with new housing estates not only the necessary allocation of space for access roads or garages should be required by law but also adequate play-space for children. For subsidised housing projects government subsidies should be granted only if sufficient play areas and recreational space in the open air are provided. An exemplary play-space in a housing estate is the infant's playground "Sonnengarten" (sun garden) in Zürich. (See pages 66–69). It was built as a result of the joint efforts of parents in a similar fashion to quite a number of others in Switzerland and the United States. We are convinced that such play-spaces are especially valuable, because such voluntary working groups afford a unique opportunity for bringing the anonymous city dwellers back into a community. Here an example of active

democracy can be realised similar to the unpaid labour of mountain peasants, who, by voluntary communal work, build flood and avalanche defences in order to protect their homes.

The kindergarten playground.

In order to obtain a large number of infants' play-spaces near the home, the network of private and co-operative house-and-yard and housing estate play areas should be extended through the incorporation of kindergarten playgrounds.

The playing ground of new kindergartens should be laid out as such, and developed from the outset as multi-purpose play-spaces, so that the grounds can be left to the children of the neighbourhood for playing in their free time. It is obvious that the kindergarten activity should not be disturbed by this.

The grounds of the existing kindergarten should be opened, whenever possible, to the uninhibited play of the children of the neighbourhood during the holiday periods and in the afternoons, when the kindergarten itself is closed. If need be, mothers should volunteer for the supervision of children.

At all events, there is no reason why in many towns and villages the kindergarten playgrounds should be closed outside kindergarten hours and thus hundreds of children should be faced with no alternative but to play on dangerous roads. With some good will it is certain that solutions can be found which are not detrimental to the educational value of the kindergarten activity, even when the ground is used otherwise.

The development of such areas for this dual purpose should undoubtedly be more diverse, more full of life. Most of the kindergarten playgrounds could be improved by being made more conducive to play. One is often tempted to believe when visiting a new kindergarten that the architect has given a lot of thought and imagination to the building but the surrounding grounds have been treated as of secondary importance. But much could still be done as the result of co-operation between architect, landscape designer and teacher in order to achieve real children's gardens, as for instance by providing a place for circle games, a small amphitheatre for puppet shows and fairy tales, play niches for games of fantasy, flower beds and other things.

B. Playgrounds for children of all age groups.

When children grow older, their range of play is extended beyond the home and its nearest environment. The schoolboy or girl in the so-called Robinson Crusoe age is out for discoveries. He or she no longer plays alone like the small child, but seeks playmates of the same age in order to compete with them in group games.

The older child prefers competitive games and sports, wants to be active, to build, to concentrate on things, to construct, to play at theatricals, to explore and to have adventures.

In order to satisfy all these wishes larger playgrounds are required than for smaller children. The play of older children is also more lively and noisier. For that reason the playground should not be too near houses.

The network of house, housing estate and kindergarten play-spaces should therefore be extended by a number of spacious grounds for older children, that is to say for children and young people. This applies equally to the village, the town and any built-up district. We do not believe that it is a happy solution to provide isolated play areas for the different age groups, such as for the 3 to 6-year-olds, the 7 to 12-and the 13 to 17-year-olds. Whenever possible, brothers and sisters of different ages should be allowed to play in the same grounds. Besides, the development of the desire for play does not often correspond with the psychological age groups. Why should not an older boy be allowed to burrow once again in the sandpit of the little ones, or a teen-age girl to play with a doll? Merely because they are really "too big and too old"? Those very games which we grown-ups consider unbecoming for the age group can be of particular value and necessary for the inner balance of the child.

Further, we do not believe that special and different play-grounds are required for school children and adolescents. It is a matter for the playground designer to arrange the individual areas in such a way that children, teenagers and youths can play games suitable for their respective age groups.

We would suggest therefore aiming at only three types of playground:

A. The infants' play-space near the home, in the form of a house-and-yard type, the housing estate and the kindergarten play area.

B. The playground for children of all age groups, where games mainly for older children, teen-agers and youths will be provided.

C. The playground and recreation centre for children and grown-up people.

The preparation and arrangement of these larger playgrounds for children of all ages can no longer be a matter for private initiative. Here the building authorities, the parks division, the educational and school authorities have to take the necessary steps. The public green spaces will have to be used principally for that purpose.

These larger playgrounds ought not to be too far away from home, but a quarter of an hour's walk should be the maximum distance for the older children. If the playground provides interesting possibilities for games, the older children will gladly take the walk: an urge to be away from home is usual at this age anyhow.

On the other hand we must resist the idea of providing one or two impersonal, super-size playgrounds on the outskirts of the town or village, far away from the dwellings. Playgrounds are meant to bring together children of one district who know each other from school or daily play. We do not need impersonal entertainment grounds with gambling or other slot machines, but playgrounds attached to a particular district where the same children meet together daily for group games and fellowship.

The following possibilities are available for such district play-grounds for all ages:

School playgrounds.

The open spaces of schools, the courtyards for the intervals between lessons, the playing fields and sports grounds should be designed more as multi-purpose playgrounds by the erection of suitable climbing structures, tubes for crawling through, balancing poles, horizontal bars specially designed for children, obstacle courses, sand areas and so on. Simple articles for play are also advantageous to the running of a school: the usually turbulent activity during the intervals would become quieter and therefore be more valuable psychologically and physically to the school children.

In addition, only those school grounds which are arranged in a manner which is full of life and suitable to children will be visited by them for playing during their free time. It is the welcome practice in some places to open school grounds and playing fields outside school hours, but these are usually rather boring and not sufficiently attractive to draw the older children away from the much more interesting streets. Quite apart from that, there is the childrens' fear of certain care-takers and officials whose pride it is to regard the school grounds under their care chiefly as objects to be kept tidy for the benefit of visitors.

In some countries, especially England and the U.S.A., schools and their grounds are already utilised as multi-purpose institutions for further education use (see pages 80–83). School buildings and their surrounding grounds should serve the interests of the community to a much greater degree in other countries too. Thereby the school would become once again an "open house", a cultural centre of the district, through the use – not only by the children but by the population as a whole – of its workshops, music rooms, gymnasia and class rooms as well as the grounds (see pages 150–151). Such schools with their various facilities for sports, music and practical hobbies would in the finest manner supplement the school-work within the meaning of Pestalozzi's demand: "Head, Heart and Hand." A school which offers young people opportunities for activity and play in their free time will become a familiar, beloved institution even to the weaker pupil and will foster a proper and positive attitude to the school. The fostering of community interests will again bring the school nearer to the children, their parents and the whole population of the district, a state of affairs which is specially welcome.

Play-spaces in sports grounds, open air swimming pools and private gardens.

Sports grounds should be transformed into public "multi-purpose grounds" for the free play of everyone; whereas the usual rule is that playing fields are reserved for a particular school or sports club which keeps watch in case unauthorised sportsmen appear on the scene. Access is strictly prohibited to unauthorised persons.

Very few non-organised play and sports enthusiasts have any suitable grounds where they can freely and spontaneously practise sports. As is well known, only a small percentage of young people and adults want to participate in organised exercises or join a sports club or association. They want to be free and not under any obligation. But many would be willing to have physical exercises or to take up some sports activity if they were given the opportunity for free play. Imagine the many places where badminton, table tennis, rugby, handball

and soccer are played; where school children and adolescents compete in all sorts of games and sports. We must not therefore in future, when planning sports grounds, give consideration only to the relatively small number of organised sportsmen or the huge mass of spectators of sports, but rather make allowance for the large number of unorganised young and older people who are keenly interested in sport and games.

Of course, such comprehensive sports grounds are subjected to heavy wear and tear and require intensive care. But if in the future only one single fatal accident can be prevented among youths playing football in the street, the provision of such grounds will have been worth while. Quite apart from that, they provide new possibilities for grown-up people to play with their children, as for instance when a father practises football with his boys.

In respect of public open-air swimming pools the designer has likewise attractive opportunities for the provision of grounds for free play. These grounds should not be furnished with the same type of equipment as ordinary playgrounds; they and their equipment should be planned and developed around the idea of water and water games, as was tried at Düsseldorf (see pages 90–91) or Grenchen (see page 89) with great success. Furthermore the swimming pools should be laid out in such a way that the surrounding areas can be used out of bathing season as public parks for people strolling and children playing during the spring, autumn and winter, as at Zürich, for example. In a number of towns there are extensive allotment gardens. Here too a communal play space for children should be provided, preferably by the tenants of the individual allotments.

The playground adjacent to a youth centre.

It is surprising and regrettable that with youth centres, "open door houses" and leisure-time houses, the surrounding grounds have hitherto been given hardly any attention, and most of these houses possess only ridiculously small and rudimentary open spaces and playgrounds. A well-furnished youth centre without equally well-laid-out open spaces is only half as valuable as a centre which can transfer a great part of its activities into the open air during fine weather.

Even the craftsmanship section of such a centre could, in the summer months, be moved into the yard in front of the work-shop, if the architect had thought of it when planning the centre. Enchanting possibilities occur in the arts section of the centre: open-air performances of theatrical plays, dances and singing, serenades under the open sky, not to mention the many types of games and sport which are the foremost activity of each youth centre during the summer. How many valuable possibilities are lost by youth centres which could win over the great mass of so-called passive young people who only play table tennis and stand around where a youth centre does not have play spaces out of doors. They could form a bridge by which many young people could be guided to creative activity. Hardly any youth centres which I was able to visit possessed sufficient and appropriately laid-out open spaces. It is the same with kindergartens; the architects seem to have exhausted themselves designing the building, and the more or less extensive grounds have received no attention.

The recreation centre at Zürich-Wipkingen, (see pages 130–139) serves as a good example of a youth centre and a playground which are complimentary to each other. Here the spare-time houses and recreation centres form a harmonious unit with the open spaces,and by that means play and handicraft or artistic activities, both in summer and winter, indoors and outdoors, constantly overflow into each other's territory. We believe that leisure-time centres with open spaces must be provided. That is to say, instead of so-called youth centres or "Houses-of-the-Open-Door" which only serve teenagers and children, recreation centres for people of all ages should be planned for every neighbourhood or village.

C. For children and adults.

The playground in the park – the play and recreation centre.

Public parks and green areas of towns and villages in our opinion perform not only the hygienic function of "lungs", but they form, in view of the present state of technical advance – traffic, hurry, tempo and "asphalt-civilisation" – indispensable oases of leisure, "mental and intellectual filling stations" for the whole population. Hardly any parks provide this additional amenity with their lawns, flower beds, neatly kept footpaths and signposts prohibiting this or that. Parks should to a far greater extent be accessible for the play and creative leisure of young and old and be laid out correspondingly. What a park playground can be like, is demonstrated by the "Isarauen", the public park area along the river Isar, in Munich (see pages 124–127), or by the Weißenburgpark in Stuttgart (see pages 120–123). Switzerland has pioneered in further developing the park playground into a combined recreation centre, with leisure-time buildings and open spaces complimentary to each other (see pages 146–149).
These centres for young and old which represent a mixture of leisure-time centres, playgrounds and public parks, form, so to speak, the last stone in the mosaic of play-spaces and similar recreational facilities within a town or village community. In the following section we should like to summarise briefly our proposals for town planners.

Ten proposals regarding town-planning.

A. Play spaces for small children:

1. For infants an extensive network of play-spaces must be provided near flats, houses, yards, housing estates and kindergartens.
2. The laying out of such play-spaces should be the responsibility of building authorities, educational authorities and public parks departments, private owners and building associations; such schemes should be subsidised by the state.
3. In the case of private and corporate housing projects numerous play spaces for infants should be provided near their homes; this could be achieved by appropriate by-laws, regulations, subsidies or voluntary efforts. Above all no housing estate should be planned or built without play spaces.

4. In the old congested quarters of towns play spaces can be provided by the demolition of rear buildings and throwing together of individual plots.

B. Play-spaces for all age groups:

5. For the play and spare-time activities of children and young people playgrounds must be provided near schools, at sports grounds and swimming pools, as well as in conjunction with youth centres and spare time houses.
6. When building schools, kindergartens, swimming pools, sports grounds and parks, the allocation of open spaces for multi-purpose use should be laid down at the outset in the schedule of requirements, or else special play areas should be added to the schedule. The equipment for these grounds should form part of that schedule just as much as do classroom, ancillary room or gymnasium fittings.

C. Play and recreation centres for young and old:

7. For the play and the creative leisure of young and old, public green spaces and parks should be laid out in such a way as to form play centres for the common recreation of all.
8. The respective authorities and parliaments should secure years in advance as a far-sighted measure the necessary land for green areas in every village, town and built-up locality, and prevent these from being used as building plots. Furthermore, appropriate bylaws or regulations for the protection of green zones should be issued.
9. For the future development of these green areas, plans should be worked out which ought to include school buildings, kindergartens, sports grounds, swimming pools, and above all playgrounds and recreation centres. If this plan is not drawn up in time, the result may be that some day green zones have been utilised in different ways leaving no space for play and recreation near the built-up areas.
10. Only when town-planners, architects and building authorities combine their efforts for this "general plan for play" with the same urgency as they approach traffic problems, will town planning become more humanised, a matter which is so urgently needed for the benefit of the young and the population as a whole.

III. Designing
Before we consider in detail how the above three types of playground (the small childrens' play space, the playground for all age groups and the play and recreation centre for young and old) should be designed and equipped, we have to mention first a few essential guiding factors which are of importance for the designing of all types of playgrounds. We base our considerations mainly on the experience which we have been able to gain from our own work on playgrounds.
These grounds (see pages 66–69, 70–73, 130–139) have been thought out, designed and equipped in close cooperation between educationists and architects, whereby constant critical observation of daily play clarified and consolidated our

educational experiences. Even if other playground designers find different solutions, to us it seems essential that when designing a playground, the child and its play must always be the first consideration, whereas with the recreation centre the adult and the family and their needs for play and recreation must rank first.

An educationist's ten stipulations for play:

1. Playgrounds must always be designed and equipped with their function for play foremost in mind.
This postulate appears to be self-evident, and yet, how many playgrounds there are (one feels tempted to say most of them) where the fittings are unsuitable, and the design merely planned around trees and shrubs which have been placed by a designer who has considered his task purely from the gardener's aesthetic point of view. We should not be surprised if the character of such grounds is as haphazard and casual as the character of some of the living rooms which we adults furnish without any imagination whatever. Noisy and nervous children's play is the consequence of playgrounds designed at random.
2. Architects, landscape designers and educationists, have to work together in order to produce good solutions to playground problems. Many an architect is in danger of practising architecture on playgrounds as art for art's sake with very original results to our adult eyes, but uninspiring and unchildlike to those who play. The landscape designer, on the other hand, is often aesthetically in love with his flora so that in the playground the main thing is not the play, but the trees and shrubs, the lawn and the flowers. Finally, the educationist is tempted to turn the playground into an institution for additional schooling of some kind.
Only open, honest discussion and co-operation between architect, landscape designer and educationist offer any guarantee of getting playgrounds which are pleasing from the architectural and landscape angle and at the same time – and this is the decisive factor – are both good for play from the teaching angle, and attractive to children. The child and its play, and not the architecture, must be the decisive factor in designing playgrounds.
3. The playground is not meant to be for passive entertainment. It must encourage active, spontaneous and creative play.
A conglomeration of gadgets for playing results only in an outdoor nursery. Let us not miss the opportunity to stimulate and develop imagination and activity at play, otherwise we cannot complain of the passive behaviour, craving for entertainment and craze for pleasure of so many young and older people.
4. More valuable than mechanical equipment for the playground are half-finished components and materials for play. Each kindergarten teacher endeavours to encourage active play in her children. In every lecture to parents one exhorts them not to spoil their children with ready-made mechanical toys. Playgrounds, however, are still largely dominated by inflexible contraptions which do not stimulate a child's imagi-

nation. A tree for climbing is more valuable than a roundabout, a sandpit more important than swings, materials for building and experimenting more valuable than table tennis. We do not mean to say that table tennis and swings should disappear from playgrounds, but we would like to recommend that more thought be given to active and creative play when choosing playground equipment.

5. Design and equipment of the playground must conform to the typical games of the particular age group for which the ground is intended.

A small child plays differently from one who goes to school. Girls prefer different games from boys of the same age. We should above all beware of providing merely play spaces for tiny children, and we must bear in mind the particular equipment for playgrounds for children of the Robinson Crusoe age and for teenagers. Even adults and elderly people, today more than in former times, need suitable areas for play and recreation.

6. The playground must offer a variety of possibilities for play.

Swings alone or a bare grass area for playing do not constitute a proper playground. To swing for hours is as dull as being amongst slot machines on a seaside pier. The playground should promote constructional and artistically playful activity in addition to stimulating action games, so far as the ground permits.

7. The design of the playground has to reflect the functions and movements of the different games.

The equipment of most playgrounds is still at the stage of the play "lumber room", a casual and haphazard array of gadgets. The casual equipment of a play area with all possible devices does not make a proper playground. In a living room we arrange the furniture so that it will serve us best according to the functions of the individual pieces.

It is most important that the designer of playgrounds should mould the whole area at his disposal into a real playground through appropriate distribution and functional equipment of the various subdivided areas for playing.

For example, the field for ball games should not be adjacent to the sandpit, as small children might be endangered through flying balls. Or a tree trunk for climbing should be on a sandy foundation but not – as frequently is the case – in the infants' sandpit. How easily can an older child jump down from the trunk onto a small one playing in the sand. In places where children of all ages play, the small ones who like to play dreamily by themselves must be kept away from the wilder games of the older children through appropriate landscaping devices.

8. Let us not forget the dreamy plays, the games in which children devote themselves to dolls and the like.

The playground should not cater exclusively for games in which large numbers or groups join. The child wants to be absorbed with itself at times; think of the girls impersonating grown-up people while playing with dolls. Play-niches and appropriate plants create the intimate "playrooms in the open air", necessary for such games. Vast open playgrounds are not childlike; they are noisy "games factories".

9. The architect and the landscape designer ought to "play" himself when designing the ground.

Playgrounds with natural or artificial hills, for example, are more popular with children than monotonous flat areas. A slide does not need to be placed unimaginatively in the centre of an open space, it could well utilise a slope and serve as an entrance to the playground. A sandpit does not need to be a square box. A ship-shaped sandpit, as often found in Denmark, Sweden and Great Britain, is surely more attractive to every child.

10. For the construction, equipment and maintenance of a playground the co-operation of parents and neighbours should be sought. The parents must be made aware that the playground is their concern. It should not be a new parking place for children, but on the contrary it should bring the whole family together by way of play and games.

A. The small children's play-space.

Children who are not yet of school age, i. e. children of the toddling, crawling and fairy-tale age, should have their own particular play space. In these play pits near home, whether they are in a backyard, attached to a housing estate or kindergarten, children of primary school age will want to stay there too. The design and equipment of small children's play-spaces will depend on the size and condition of the plot available and on the particular district. Otherwise the dividing line between this type of play-space and the playground for all age groups is naturally fluid. It is for the playground designer to picture the children and their needs and to form and equip the space accordingly. It would be an advantage, from the educational point of view, if the small children's play-space near home were based on the typical games of those youngsters and designed so intimately in scale that older children would find it less interesting and attractive. Naturally there should be a playground not too far away for children of all ages, where the older children can let off steam.

In order to find out how a small child's playground should be arranged in detail, we must first consider the child, how and with what he plays during the various stages of development up to his entry into school.

A child first starts to play in his cot. Here the baby one day begins his first playful movements. He discovers his hands and feet and plays with them. Later he finds that he can grasp things, and anything that comes near him is transformed into a plaything which must be touched, grasped and put to his mouth. Catching hold of a thing leads to recognising it. The child learns to sit up, he begins to crawl. The play pen, the floor of the living room and the play corner become his first playground and every day his world of play and experience is widening. He occupies himself with anything which is within reach.

As soon as he is able to walk he makes expeditions of discovery throughout the home and everything is examined and explored. With all this movement and activity the child exercises his body and limbs. At this age he does not yet play with other children. He is an individualist and even egoistic in his

play. Out of doors he prefers to play alone with sand and water, he climbs around everywhere or goes off on a "long trip" with his tricycle. In the years that follow, this type of play gradually changes into ball, circle and jumping games. Later on come competitive sports.

During his third and fourth years the child, who by now is in control of his body, begins to gain pleasure from all kinds of constructional games. Building blocks or wooden bricks are among the favourite toys, and the first attempts at painting and making things are undertaken. Out of doors sandcastles are built and with the help of old materials the most marvellous structures are erected. Of special value at this age would be large wooden blocks with which children could play out of doors in a sandpit.

Simultaneously with the desire for constructional activity, the three- and four-year-old child begins to imitate everything that is happening around him. They are the years of imagination when playing involves acting and a good deal of unreality. It is not surprising that this age is called the age of fantasy. In playing, the child transforms himself into different persons, animals or even objects. He changes his role constantly and can be father, mother, teacher, Red Riding Hood, wolf and many other things. The table in the room becomes a castle, a ship, a car or an aeroplane. Girls with their dolls play anything which they observe in their daily contact with mother. In playing these parts, the child develops and expands his emotional and mental powers. Games of imagination help him too, as he imitates grown-up people, to overcome his smallness. In his play he is liberated from all the burdens of his heart. Dolls, pictures and story books, material for disguising and acting, are coveted playthings of this age, not forgetting too the dearly beloved puppets. In these games of fantasy, the artistic activity of later life, amateur performances of theatrical plays and music and the visual arts, have their beginning.

From about the sixth year, games which are governed by rules and are played in conjunction with other children of the same age come into a child's life as novelties. Such games are circle and jumping games, marbles, catching and hide-and-seek games. In these games the child learns to submit to rules, he learns to win and to lose and to fit into a group.

Equipment.

A small children's playground should contain all the items which a child of the jumping, climbing and fairy-tale age needs for playing. The youngest ones, however, ought to be able to play near home. A sandpit in front of or behind the house is more valuable than a playground for small children serving a whole block of houses some distance away. Wherever space allows (with new blocks of flats, housing estates and kindergartens one has to allow for that in the design stage) a small children's playground should be provided containing the following divisions and play elements: 1. sand, 2. water, 3. a hard surface for "street" games, 4. grass land for playing and romping, 5. climbing equipment and movable devices, 6. walls for play surfaces and Wendy houses, 7. disused vehicles.

1. Sand.

Playing with sand is one of the most popular and most valuable occupations from the educational point of view. It serves especially to develop the imaginative and creative powers of the child. Sand is therefore the most important element for any small children's playground.

Most widespread is the use of a sandpit. Unfortunately, this is usually too small, just right for two dogs or cats, but not for several children at play. As the little ones do not want to sit still on one spot and make sand pies, but would rather build castles and tunnels, mazes of trenches and canals, they need more room than the usual small sandpits offer.

That is not to say that we want to go to the other extreme and create playgrounds with one single vast sandpit. Those of medium size for about ten to fifteen children are most appropriate. But why always of that boring square shape? And why only sand? Children do so like small tables made from parts of a tree, or of stone or concrete, on which they can bake their sand pies (see pages 42, 75).

In contrast to the sandpit, the piled-up heap of sand has the advantage of being cheaper, but it is only advisable where the provision of a sandpit would be too expensive. On the other hand the sand heap is more interesting to children than the sand in a pit when it is trodden hard and baked. There is still much to be done: a sandpit has to be maintained constantly, it has to be freshened up and filled regularly with new sand. The greatest variety for play can be achieved by a combination of sandheap and sandpit, i. e. a sandpit which is generously filled with sand at intervals.

On some Swiss playgrounds we have made experiments with a flat sand surface, where a part of the grounds was arranged as a wide plain of sand. A few lorry-loads of sand are poured onto this plain every spring, and in the course of the summer it is "worked out" by the children (see pages 70–73). We have found that sand plains of this type are less likely to be soiled by cats and dogs than the usual sandpits with their corners and hollows.

2. Water (drinking fountains, paddling pools, and paddling fountains).

Water is as much liked by small children as sand. They are especially delighted when they can play and "muck about" with sand and water at the same time. Of course, such fun often ends in tears because it cannot be had without leaving visible traces on clothes. If only mothers would dress their children appropriately for this kind of play, or better still undress them. Let them frolic to their hearts' content, and we can put the dirty happy little creatures into the bath in the evening. Every child must occasionally be able to splash and dirty himself. There is a reason for children's psychologists constantly pointing out the special importance of such play for mental development. Children who are given ample opportunities to play without inhibitions will rarely find it necessary in later life to seek outlets for their suppressed wishes and urges.

For playing with water, various possibilities can be considered:
In playgrounds where bathing facilities for small children are not wanted or are unsuitable, a little drinking fountain is sufficient, perhaps a simple concrete trough, a hollowed-out stone block or a tree trunk (see page 68). Here the children can fill their buckets with water or float their paper boats.

Two types of paddling pools are most widely used: the pool of even depth all over, with approximately 8 inches of water or the pool with a floor sloping gradually towards the middle, leaving the edges shallow, with the water in lively movement, as on a beach (see pages 88, 117, 136). Occasionally a paddling pool is combined with showers. Original solutions in the use of showers and fine drizzle jets can be seen at the Düsseldorf Water Playground (see pages 90–91), or at the Adventure Playground, Central Park, New York (see pages 96–99).

On some of the squares in Zürich, new kinds of paddling fountains instead of paddling pools have been tried (see page 73). One of these paddling fountains consists of approximately eight gaily painted concrete pipes of about six feet in diameter and of different heights. Water splashes over a coloured fountainhead from a jet into the highest basin and runs playfully over the periphery from one basin to the other down to the lowest one. The water level in the individual basins is approximately 4 inches; it is therefore without danger even for the smallest children. These paddling fountains have several advantages compared with paddling pools: the children are divided up into small groups by the different basins, which are more appropriate for their age than the noisy pool for everybody. Two or three children have their own "lake". The different heights of the basins, moreover, encourage fascinating gambols from one basin to the other. Furthermore the paddling fountain, because of its relatively shallow water level and the smallness of the basins, is less interesting to older children, so that the smaller ones can really bathe. In the spacious paddling pools the older children are always domineering and very often hinder or endanger with their wild games the quieter paddling of the small children. The paddling fountain has a further advantage in that, as a result of the constant flow of water, it does not become so easily polluted and therefore only requires a weekly cleaning out in contrast to the paddling pool, where a daily cleaning operation is necessary.

A combination of paddling pool and paddling fountain (see page 136) has also proved successful: it consists of a fair-sized paddling pool with a paddling fountain of five basins in one corner. In this way it is possible to combine the entire paddling equipment for small children and those of school age, without disturbing or endangering the former in the fountain basins. Even in cooler weather the pool can be left empty and only the paddling fountain filled with water.

3. Hard surfaces for street games.

It is a fact that our town children are "asphalt" kids who hardly know garden games but only play on streets. A playground consisting only of lawn is not enough to attract the children away from the street, as they cannot play on grass their accustomed everyday games such as hopscotch, marbles, hoops, ball games, riding tricycles and scooters. A playground without some hard surfaces or "play roads" and paved paths, which can serve as a substitute for roads, is insufficient. The hard surface must be kept clear of playground equipment so that action games are not hindered. All equipment, including walls for ball games, should be placed near the periphery.

4. Free-for-all playing field.

According to space available there should also be, in addition to the hard surfaces, a small or medium-sized free-for-all field for the various lawn games played with or without balls.

5. Equipment for climbing and action games.

For the elementary action play of the small child requiring courage such as climbing, crawling, leaping, balancing and swinging, appropriate equipment should be placed on soft lawn or sand. In respect of mechanical devices like roundabouts, the utmost caution is recommended. The various items of equipment are not only meant to entertain the children but to stimulate them to active play. Only articles of the best quality should be selected. Solidly built objects avoid accidents and save money in the long run. In that respect the following can be recommended:

Climbing tower (Sweden Tower, Altra Tower) and climbing tree.
A tree to climb, with big strong branches, turned on its side or built upright into the ground (see pages 72, 163) is more attractive to small children than a climbing tower made of tubular steel. However, a tubular steel tower has its charm especially when it is gaily painted in a way a child likes. Compared with the Sweden Tower (see page 92) with its rectangular criss-cross of poles, the circular and roofed-over Altra Tower developed in Switzerland (see pages 69, 73) has the advantages of a wider choice of possibilities for playing (climbing, swinging, sliding).
"Climbing arches" and "nets", "balancing poles" and "small scale horizontal bars" should be installed more frequently. In the last section of this book there is a list of well-designed climbing and action games equipment, among which the "Sand-Floh" equipment of Ulm (see pages 174–175) and a number of American tubular steel and concrete components for climbing and jumping games (see pages 168–169, 173) are mentioned. In the U.S.A., "play plastics" have been developed which can be used in a wide variety of ways (see pages 170–171). They serve at the same time as climbing towers, slides, crawling tunnels and horizontal bars.

Tunnels for crawling and climbing.
All parents know that small children especially like to creep into any kind of hollow space. How often do they disappear under some table. It shows their longing for a house suitable to their size, a home of their own, which they can take possession of and fill physically and psychologically. In addition to that, when exploring caves and channels there is the mysterious, the darkness which attracts children. We can respond to this elementary desire by providing crawl ducts, hollowed-out tree trunks, old barrels and similar receptacles.
Very suitable are also large concrete bowls and saddle-shaped

objects as used in America. They are either factory-made or can be poured in situ into moulds which can be hired for the purpose. (For examples see page 168.)

The crawl ducts should either be made in such a way that the individual concrete drums are closely joined together or with some distance between them so that the children do not wedge their feet when crawling. Often the colour schemes for such ducts are ill conceived. The duct is in the child's imagination an entity, an animal – perhaps a creeping beast, an elephant – or a house, a cave, a railway. We have to think of that when painting the duct.

It is wrong to paint pictures of a dog, a flower or a train on individual drums – the painting rather should emphasize the coherence of the whole thing.

Rope and tubular swings.

The rope and tubular swings should be placed away from the areas for action games and from the sandpit, so as to avoid accidents. Best of all is to put them in play niches which are sheltered by shrubs. There should always be several swings in order to avoid queueing up, pushing and quarrelling and to encourage exciting swing races. Instead of providing five or more rope swings, two or three could be substituted by a trapeze, rings, or a seat made of an old car tyre (see pages 55, 175). Such arrangements allow more varied and lively play and stop monotonous swinging for hours on end. Especially unsuitable, in our opinion, are swings which enable a whole gang of children to be swung by a single child, which is not a very positive or creative activity.

Slides.

Two problems are to be considered when a slide is erected. First the difficulty of finding a satisfactory material for the slide's surface and secondly the question of where to put the slide. We should take the slide away from the centre of the ground, where it looks lost and accidentally placed. We should rather place it on a hillside; it will not only give more fun but it is also less dangerous because the climb to it by the ladder is eliminated (see pages 72, 164).

Bollards and stools for leap-frog.

Short tree trunks, concrete bollards or similar objects facilitate a variety of jumping and adventurous games like leap-frog. At the same time they form seats or tables for the children (see pages 47, 64, 75).

6. Play partitions and Wendy houses.

For games which involve acting (father and mother, shop-keeping, theatre, puppet-show) space and opportunity must be available on every playground. For that reason more private play niches should be provided, with scenery partitions and Wendy houses so that a background is given to games of fantasy and impromptu acting. (For examples of Danish, German or Swiss playgrounds see pages 58–59, 104–105, 158–159.)

Partitions of wood or concrete with round or square-shaped holes and built-in asbestos-cement or slate panels are extremely useful. They form the right surface for pat-ball which

girls like to play. They can also be used for "hide-and-seek" and for crawling through. But mostly they serve as stage background, puppet stage and as walls for painting and drawing (see pages 147, 165).

On playgrounds without supervision small wooden houses of tent shape with two benches inside have proved successful (see pages 159–160). Especially girls like to play in them with their dolls or like to sit and dream and let their fantasy carry them away. On playgrounds with constant supervision whole hamlets can be built of a number of Wendy houses. This idea, which comes from Scandinavia (page 159) can be varied in such a way that besides small houses (furnished with garden table and chairs – all other items like dolls' crockery are brought by the children) there are miniature shops where display dummies are "for sale" (see page 136).

7. Old disused vehicles.

A disused car, an old tram-car or a ship are among the most adventurous toys for children who are growing up in this present technical age. Such "toys" exercise the necessary pull which draws children away from the far too interesting street. The individual vehicles, however, must be fitted up appropriately, otherwise they will constitute dangerous sources of accidents and serve older children, who have grown out of the age of fantasy, purely as objects for demolition. An old disused car, for example, should be painted up in gay colours, provided with wooden seats and have its roof strengthened. Bonnet and doors should be blocked on one side and removed on the opposite side. Most suitable seems to be a jeep or a lorry. In general, some caution is recommended when considering the provision of an old disused vehicle. On typical small children's playgrounds an improvised vehicle is usually sufficient, such as an aeroplane made of three trunks (see page 72).

Planning.

The unplanned placing of play equipment possibly facilitates certain games but it does not result in a good playground from an educational point of view. Only a purposeful grouping of the equipment and the right apportionment of the different play areas facilitate those games which correspond to the age of the children and awaken in them creative playing activity and pleasure in discovery, exploration and constructive work.

A small children's playground has a special charm when it allows for a definite sequence of games. What we mean is the relationship between the different areas, the arrangement of a definite sequence in the positioning of the equipment, the exploitation of the possibilities of the site – this is evident, for example, at the small children's playground in Zürich-Heiligfeld (see pages 70–73) or at the traffic playground in Zürich-Buchegg (see page 108).

Some further hints may perhaps stimulate future playground designers to seek some original solutions: A plot of land with contours is more attractive than a level one. Hills, play niches and hollows make the games varied and lively. A hill presents numerous possibilities – one can make a slide on it, tunnel

under it with ducts to creep through, place Wendy houses on the hill top or cut out steps on the slope to serve as amphitheatre seats, and all sorts of other things (for examples see pages 162–163).

Play partitions with holes in them and built-in slate or asbestos-cement panels are, as has been said, extremely useful for sketching and painting, for puppet shows and stage scenery, for climbing and romping about. In addition, these partitions form ideal boundaries between the different play areas.

Colours play an important part in a child's life. The painting of swings, crawling ducts and paddling fountains should therefore be colourful and cheerful but not childish.

The sandpit should be placed in a sheltered position away from turbulent action games and ball games. Furthermore it should not be too much in the shade (for quick drying after rain or disinfection of sand), and not in the bright sunshine either (danger of sunstroke for small children). There should always be a sufficient number of benches near the sandpit and elsewhere on the playground for mothers, who want to keep an eye on their young children.

The same care should be given to the placing and planning of lavatories: this subject, partly out of forgetfulness, partly because of financial considerations, is often neglected and yet the cleanliness of a playground is indivisibly linked up with the appropriate solution of this problem.

We have intentionally refrained from giving technical details such as the size and nature of sandpits and lawns for playing, the construction of swings, or possible ideal sizes for playgrounds. We would leave that to the publications already available on landscape designing. Besides, the playground planner is hardly ever confronted with an ideal site of ideal size, but rather with a haphazard area, from which he can only obtain the best possible results by a continual process of thinking and re-thinking.

B. The playground for all age-groups.

We understand by a playground for all age groups, as we mentioned before, a fairly large ground near a school, a stadium or a swimming pool, near a youth or leisure-time centre or a park. It is meant to serve especially school children and adolescents for active and creative play, but it ought to incorporate an area for smaller children too.

When considering the equipment of a place like this, we have to start from the different play needs of the various age-groups. Children of school age and adolescents like to play all sorts of action games and ball games, as do the smaller children, except that their games are rougher and require more room. Boys and girls of that age are by this time real sporting types. These are the ages of competitive and group games.

Earlier games of fantasy and acting give way at the school age to amateur theatricals, music and dancing. A special height of achievement is reached in constructional games: the sand-pit must be substituted by the "building site" and the workshop where children in the Robinson Crusoe age can develop their creative abilities to the full.

What is the position, however, with playgrounds for these age-groups? There are normally empty playing fields which only permit ball and action games. On these tedious acres youth cannot express itself freely, cannot reach after the adventurous, cannot satisfy its enthusiasm for handicraft and creative work. These are suppressed, only to appear later in adolescents and adults as dangerous rowdy behaviour. We have up to the present, when designing playgrounds for older children, given far too much consideration to physical athletic activities, at the expense of all others. All play involving creative work and artistic sensitivity, for which healthy school children yearn, has been forgotten.

A grass area for playing is easier to provide than a proper playground which ought to give school children diverse leisure-time activities, including constructional games and other hobbies. A ground of that nature must be equipped differently and demands, furthermore, in contrast to the playground for small children, full-time supervision by an educationist.

Equipment.

If site conditions permit, a district playground for all age-groups should incorporate the following:

1. Space for adventurous and constructional games, with workshops for leisure-time activities and other hobbies.
2. Open-air theatre with a building for communal games of an artistic nature.
3. Hard surfaces for ball and street games.
4. Lawn for sporting games.
5. Playground for small children.

1. Outdoor space for constructional activity with adjoining workshops.

The most important part of the playground for all age-groups is a rough grass area, if possible with shrubs and trees, for constructional activity, where boys and girls can erect huts and houses with old building materials or where they can go on some kind of journeys of discovery or adventure. At the periphery of the grass area work-tables should be placed (outdoor spare-time workshop) where all sorts of things can be carved, modelled or put together.

A two-roomed workshop should be available for children, adolescents and possibly even grown-ups for use during bad weather. One of the rooms with work-benches should be for noisier activities such as working in wood and metal or carving; the other room with tables for quieter work like modelling, textile printing and lino cutting. If financial resources allow, one would wish to build these workshops as permanent structures in the shape of a simple little house. At times one will have to be content with an old disused railway coach or tramcar, suitably equipped as a workshop. With playgrounds on school sites one would incorporate the workrooms of the school with the activities of the playground. They may be used during the day by the school for instruction in creative hobbies and during the evenings partly by young people (as a district youth centre), and partly by grown-ups (courses for creative hobbies for parents, pensioners, etc.).

2. Open-air theatre with buildings for games and community life.

An open-air theatre is one of the most important items of a playground for all age-groups. Through an appropriate layout, as for instance the arrangement of stepped seating cut into a slope of the ground and the erection of free standing walls as scenery requisites, a theatre-like atmosphere can be created. Thus children and young people are stimulated into building their own stage or puppet-show scenery. The stage should not be supplied as a finished product by the playground designer but, as with a playground for all age-groups, the furnishing of the buildings, workshops and community rooms should be undertaken by the children themselves.

The theatre space, which can be combined with the hard surface area, as was done on the Zürich-Buchegg playground (see page 146), serves the artistic and sensitive games of the children, like puppet shows and amateur performances, musical activity and country dancing, as well as circle and party games.

Whenever possible there should be one or more rooms for games and social activities, which present children, as well as grown-ups with an opportunity for party games, dances, theatrical performances, group meetings and film performances. In one of these rooms a library with reading space should be installed, where the children can not only obtain good books for reading on the playground (an antidote against the reading of trash), but where they can also borrow books to take home. These libraries are best managed by the same institution which looks after the public libraries' youth sections. Children, of course, should be encouraged to participate in the administration of the library.

The hobbies workshops and the building for communal activities form, as it were, a district leisure-time and youth centre.

3. Hard surface for street and ball games.

A hard surface area as well as paved paths and play streets should form part of a playground for all age-groups. Here all street games can be played, like riding scooters, stilt-walking, roller skating, hopping games, marbles, circle and ball games, volley balls, table tennis, "boccia", badminton. In areas with frequent rain, where the grass is constantly wet and slippery, hard surface areas are of special importance. During the frosty season the hard surface can be transformed into an ice rink for skating.

4. Playing field.

The playing field can be used for a variety of ball games such as football, basket ball and all the rest of the field games. It should not be just a large football field dimensioned according to Olympic rules and regulations for real international games, but it should be a meadow with trees and shrubs, so that small play areas are available where various groups of children can pursue their games simultaneously.

5. Playground for small children.

The older children must be able to take their small brothers and sisters to the playground. That is why an area must be set aside for smaller children, so that these can play without disturbing the older ones in their building activities or their artistic games or sports. This separate play while all are together enables the small children to be drawn gradually into the creative play of the bigger ones. Thereby the ideal transition from small children's games to the games of older boys and girls is achieved. Design and equipment of the playground for small children are identical in principle and in elements with those described in the preceding paragraph.

In contrast to the typical playground for small children (for which we recommend improvised vehicles, to stimulate the imagination, such as an aeroplane made of tree trunks) the playground for all age-groups ought to have a real car, a real aeroplane or a real tramcar. The older children, especially the boys, are fascinated by anything technical. They should be able to examine a vehicle of that nature close at hand and manipulate it. It is true that such vehicles are perhaps easily damaged or destroyed. But is this really always an act of wilful destruction? Is it not mostly a desire to penetrate into the interior, an exploration of the mechanism, a wish to get to know the whole thoroughly in the same way as we in our time took to pieces a clock, a bicycle or a wireless set? Moreover, this propensity for taking things to pieces can easily be transformed on the nearby building play-space into constructive activity. Our experience with such vehicles has shown that wanton destruction and misuse in most cases happened at night and could be attributed to adults and adolescents. This is a social and psychological problem which probably can never be solved completely. Abuses should, however, not tempt us to arrange playgrounds as simply and tediously as possible merely to prevent anything unpleasant happening. Every educational task – and here playgrounds are included – must reckon with positive and negative values and arrange matters accordingly.

Old disused vehicles serve also as "bridges", just as certain fascinating books prevent young people from reading rubbish and serve as a bridge towards books of literary merit. Similarly these old vehicles will entice from the streets juveniles who are nowadays mostly interested in things technical, and guide them towards creative play.

Design and Organisation.

We are aware that the playground for all age-groups as described above is an idealistic solution. We believe, however, that in the case of playgrounds for older children one has in future to depart more and more from the mere grass areas where only action games are possible. It is not for us grown-ups to complain about the passive attitude of so many young people, with their lack of interest, craving for pleasure, tendency to be mere spectators at games, and craze for gambling machines and rowdyism. So long as there are not sufficient grounds for older children and teenagers, where they can play in a creative way, there is no justification for complaint. The designer has to see that through an appropriate location of the individual elements the various games and activities merge naturally and without disturbance into one another.

This applies to the playground for smaller children just as much as to the one for all age-groups, which requires an area of at least 110,000 sq. ft., preferably of a hilly nature with shrubs and trees rather than a completely flat one.

A playground of that kind has to be planned, built and maintained by the authorities (public works department, parks department, etc.) in close co-operation with private local societies.

The municipality (town or village) should provide the land, arrange for the necessary building operations like levelling and fencing of the ground, build sanitary installations and erect the buildings (workshops and community rooms) and, if possible, give an annual grant to the private local society for the running of the playground (salary of supervisor, etc.).

The private supporters, the circle of "friends of the playground" or a similar association consisting of interested people and institutions (representatives of authorities, clubs of the neighbourhood, youth groups, people living nearby, parents and teachers) should take over the planning and supervision of the playground and support the playground leader. They should approach business firms in the neighbourhood for gifts of tools, sand, building materials, old vehicles and the like, also for money for purchasing equipment.

A playground of that type in any event needs a leader especially for the activities in the workshops and on the "building site". The leader must not be simply a supervisor but should be a personality with a gift for guiding children. He or she must understand how to stimulate children without mothering them too much, and how not to organise too many games or to entertain the children too much, but rather to awaken in them their own creative urge to play.

Men or women who are really fond of young people can be chosen as suitable leaders. Future teachers, university students, nursery teachers, youth leaders, students of sociology or those who have passed through arts and crafts schools are suited for this work. The decisive factor is not a certain technical training but rather an amiable personality. Usually one leader is not sufficient in the long run, but must be aided by other aspirants for similar work. Here valuable opportunities occur for prospective or qualified nursery teachers, students of teaching colleges, etc. to gain practical experience.

But the parents also, and above all the children themselves, have to be brought into active participation in the work of running the playground. It is the task of the leader to arouse their interest in the matter. At the Robinson Crusoe playgrounds in Zürich parents constantly offer their help voluntarily in looking after groups of children, doing creative work with them, modelling in clay or other materials, singing, etc.

In order to make a visit to a playground as attractive as possible to parents, particularly to mothers, deck chairs should be provided free of charge. Every playground ought to provide comfortable seats for grown-up people.

Children and young people should themselves build up and improve their own playing space. The playground for all age-groups will therefore never be entirely finished and will look different every year. Certain parts, especially the building yard, are not very beautiful to look at; but are aesthetic

criteria necessarily the most important standard for judging a playground? The playground should not only offer facilities for playing but it should be a medium of educating children through play towards mutual consideration and the team spirit. For example, children of each Robinson Crusoe playgrond in Switzerland form their own parliament, the "Robinson Council", as it were the local authority of the particular playground. The "Robinson Council" holds regular sessions, at which with the help of the leader all important questions of playground life are discussed in a democratic fashion, such as provision of materials, times of opening, keeping order, team tasks and any disagreements. To a large extent it is also the business of the children to see that the supply of building materials continues. They have to call on building firms in a proper way and say thank you for donations with drawings, theatrical performances, etc. Thus each of these playgrounds is a miniature democracy in which children through play grow into active and responsible citizens.

The Robinson Crusoe playground.

In quite a number of countries successful solutions for the playground for all age-groups are in evidence. There is, for instance, the "Skrammellegeplads" in Copenhagen (see pages 110–113), the Red Indian Playground at Mannheim (see pages 116–119) and others in Germany, there are the Adventure Playgrounds in the U.S.A. (see pages 96–99); and there are, of course, the Robinson Crusoe playgrounds in Switzerland; the one in Zürich-Wipkingen (see pages 130–139) was the first and is still nowadays a good example.

The idea of the Robinson Crusoe playgrounds developed from the Danish "Skrammellegeplads" and the post-war bombed site playing spaces which I saw in 1946 during my Children's Help work in the Ruhr district. I still remember the agonising question when I walked for the first time through the destroyed towns: "Is life still worth living among these ruins, improvised cellar accommodation and underground caves?"

Children gave me the answer, those "children of the debris", barefooted and in rags, but cheerfully climbing on the mounds of rubble which to an adult's eyes and heart seemed so cheerless, yet these children were playing full of delight with fragments of wreckage: playing spaces of refuse in the true sense of the word.

We certainly do not want to forget the other side of this romantic atmosphere of ruins: dirt and garbage, the danger of accidents and diseases. We do not want to belittle the material and psychological need of this post-war youth. One thing, however, these children possessed, namely playgrounds full of hazard and adventure.

Such playgrounds of debris were intentionally laid out by C. Th. Sørensen, the Danish landscape designer, in Copenhagen in 1943. He had observed, while walking through the city, how children were more fascinated in handling boards and demolition material on building sites than in playing with the ready-made equipment of his fine playgrounds. As a result of his observation he started the first "Skrammellegeplads" in Copenhagen (see pages 110–113).

This first example of a building play-site was later followed in various countries in either the same form or as Adventure Playgrounds. The Robinson Crusoe playgrounds are partly based on the Danish "Skrammellegeplads" but the Swiss solution affords a further decisive development and extension of the idea. In our opinion a building play-site in itself is as one-sided as a sports field. It is true that the former facilitates all the valuable building and constructional games, but it neglects all the artistic activities as well as the competitive and team games so necessary in youth.

The Robinson Crusoe playground, comprises all the other elements of a playground for all age-groups. It is not, as so often is unfortunately asserted in publications, merely a building play-site or a collection of old vehicles. It is a playground comprising all these elements, giving children and young people the greatest choice of creative games and activities. A few sentences from an issue of the "Robinson-Blatt" the periodical of one of the Zürich playgrounds which is edited largely by the children themselves, may give some insight into the nature of the Swiss Robinson Crusoe playgrounds.

"In Zürich-Wipkingen something has come into being again which can hardly be found in other cities: a community centre for the district, similar in spirit to the 'village tree' of old, which unfortunately even in rural areas is by now an item of the past. We think of a number of homely events like the 'egg-cracking' at Easter, the bonfires and the summer festivities at which parents and children have worked and played together. We must also mention the 'Robinson-Band' of the older boys which occasionally played for dancing, just as in remote olden days under the village tree. Equally famous was the children's Zoo, built by the children themselves who also looked after the small animals.

"That is why the Robinson Crusoe playground is not just a new possibility for parents to 'park' their children, neither is it an 'open air nursery' where one can be entertained. It is a proper spare-time centre for the whole district."

C. The play and recreation centre for old and young.

What is now needed is no longer just to set up in some urban area, or perhaps in a village, a playground for small children and to arrange in another corner a leisure-time workshop for teenagers, or a special workshop for the adults, and the pensioners somewhere else. This specialising on one particular age-group by the various institutions which are concerned with leisure-time activities in a particular place leads easily to a dispersal of the various elements beyond the confines of a playground. The result is the tearing apart of families in their leisure-time instead of bringing them together.

For that reason it is today an urgent task to revise and co-ordinate from the family and community angle all valuable spare-time efforts in every city, town and village. It is true that our youngest ones need play-spaces near the home because of the dangerous traffic in the streets. Playgrounds for children of all age-groups must, of course, be provided in each district, but the problems of leisure-time activity for adults demand new solutions. The rapid pace of work, the haste of everyday life, the mechanisation and monotony of working routine, the shortening of working hours and ever increasing free time cause the whole issue of leisure-time activitiy, play and re-creation for grown-ups to appear in an entirely new light. The city dweller requires a purposeful relaxation to preserve his sense of proportion. Old people and pensioners want to do something worth while with their leisure hours.

That is why we believe that the building authorities of our towns and villages should press emphatically for a realisation of the demand by modern planners for a humanising of town planning. The authorities will have to provide not only chil-dren's playgrounds but also play and recreational centres where parents and children, families and older people can spend their spare time, where from the mass of anonymous hurrying city dwellers a community of leisure, contemplation and play can again arise.

We know good solutions of such family and people's parks from examples in the U.S.A. (see page 129), where in our opinion, however, action games and sport prevail too much over facilities for creative, practical and artistic activities.

In Switzerland the attempt has recently been made to develop various parks into comprehensive recreational and play cen-tres for the population of a particular urban area. Such a communal centre as the one in Zürich-Buchegg (see pages 146–149) consists of the following:

1. Lawns with footpaths, seats, deck chairs and card tables for families and older people.
2. Playing fields for ball and garden games for old and young.
3. Playgrounds for small children.
4. A playground for all age-groups (Robinson Crusoe play-ground) with permanent buildings for social activities.

The buildings for social activities form, as it were, a district leisure-time centre with workshops, libraries for children and adults, as well as play and club rooms. These rooms are used by school children outside school hours and during holidays for all kinds of creative activities, play acting, reading, singing, music and games. In the evenings, the same rooms are open to teen-agers as a youth centre. In addition fathers and moth-ers can come there for evening classes in educational subjects or practical hobbies. In the library and the reading room young book-worms can find all they need, while older people are given opportunities to make use of their leisure hours.

The recreation centres above all encourage a deepening of the bond between parents and children. It is often said that the estrangement between parents and children in many cases is the result of the rush and speed of our time. The parents are no longer in a position to give time to their children. That may be so, but this phenomenon of estrangement may in part be due to the lack of opportunity nowadays on the parents' part to take any active interest in their children elsewhere than inside the home. In sharing play with their children, parents have new possibilities of companionship with them and of influencing their spiritual and physical development. An edu-cationist once said quite rightly: "He who wants to be a com-panion to the adolescent must have bent down to the child in the sandpit." The benefical influence of the recreation centre is, however, not limited only to parents and children but

extends also to grandparents, pensioners and old people in general who naturally have most time to spare. Recreation centres provide an ideal setting for reviving the natural rela-tionship between old and young. The opportunity of meeting old and young in a free and casual way, of observing them, of talking with them and of occupying oneself just as one pleases, cannot fail to have an effect on older people. Grandparents can mix with their children and grandchildren as participants in games, as story-tellers or as spectators. Pensioners find great pleasure in competing with young beginners in con-structional hobbies. Occasionally debating evenings can be arranged for old and young in order to promote mutual under-standing and to revive real family and public spirit.

The recreation centres with their diverse opportunities pre-vent an unhealthy specialisation. The young football fanatic may indeed follow his beloved sport to his heart's content. On the adjoining ground he may, however, discover his friends occupied with building or constructional hobbies and may soon be persuaded to join them. Or a small book-worm sees his sister playing theatre with others on their improvised stage and feels the urge to act what he has just read. And a morose individual at his hobby has not yet properly noticed that there are also books in the world, and then he discovers in the re-creation centre a library with all its treasures, and the wonder-ful world of reading is opened to him.

Thus the recreation centre with its manifold opportunities for play, hobbies and active leisure for all age-groups, its open-air theatre, its lawns for relaxing, its benches and footpaths, brings together the modern family which is torn apart during the day through profession and school. A world of creative experience for the strengthening of family bonds and the spiri-tual side of the "asphalt man" is the antidote to the nervous daily life of the city, the dissolution of family life, the entice-ments of the entertainment industry and the wasting of time.

IV. "Playground Charter"

1. The Planning of playgrounds – ten points for town-planners.

A. Playgrounds for small children.

1. For infants an extensive network of playgrounds should be provided adjoining flats, housing estates and kindergartens.
2. The provision of such playgrounds should be taken in hand by local authorities (building departments, school authorities, public park departments) and by private developers (building societies or individuals); these schemes should be subsidised and encouraged by the State.
3. In the case of private and co-operative building programmes the aim should be to provide as many playgrounds for small children as possible near houses and housing estates. Above all no housing estate should be built, or even planned, without provision for playgrounds.
4. With old houses it may be possible to gain play-spaces in courtyards through throwing adjoining plots together and demolishing ancillary buildings and other obstructions.

B. Playgrounds for children of all age-groups.

5. For leisure-time activity and play, children and young people should be provided with playgrounds which could be part of school premises, sports stadia and open-air swimming pools.
6. In the design stage of schools, kindergartens, open-air swimming pools, sports grounds and public parks, areas should be set aside from the very beginning for "multi-pur-pose use", or else specific playgrounds should be added to the schedule of requirements. The necessary equipment should be part of that schedule.

C. Play and recreation centres for old and young.

7. For play and creative leisure of old and young (children, families and elderly people) public green spaces and parks should be so modified that they become recreational centres.
8. The competent authorities and local councils should in due course, having long-term requirements in view, secure in every village, town or urban district, the necessary land for a green zone and prevent it from being gradually used up for buildings. Appropriate byelaws or regulations should further be issued for the protection of green areas.
9. A plan for the use of such green zones should be prepared not only embracing schools, kindergartens, sports grounds and swimming pools, but also providing especially for the inclusion of playgrounds and recreation centres in the whole lay-out. If this is not done in good time, all green zone land will one day be exhausted and no open ground will be found for play and recreation close to the built-up areas.
10. Only when town-planners and building authorities try to put such a master plan for leisure-time activity into practice as urgently as they do plans dealing with traffic problems, will town planning have achieved the higher degree of humani-sation essential for the population as a whole.

2. Design of playgrounds – ten points for the educationist.

1. Each playground must be designed and equipped from the point of view of its function, play.
2. The architect, the landscape designer and the educationist must work together in order to create good playgrounds.
3. The playground should not serve passive entertainment, but ought to stimulate active, independent and creative play.
4. More valuable than mechanical play-equipment are half-finished components and materials.
5. Design and equipment of the playground should be go-verned by the typical games of the respective age-group.
6. The playground should not be designed for certain ga-mes, but should afford opportunities for a variety of them.
7. In planning playgrounds the functions and movements of the various games should be taken into account.
8. The games of fantasy should not be overlooked.
9. Architects and landscape designers should themselves "play" a little while designing the grounds.
10. For designing, equipping and maintaining a playground, interested groups of people should cooperate.

Spielplatz und Gemeinschaftszentrum

Von Alfred Ledermann, Schweiz. Stiftung Pro Juventute,
Zürich

Alle Völker spielen, und sie spielen merkwürdig ähnlich.
Johan Huizinga

Der Mensch spielt nur, wo er in voller Bedeutung des Wortes
Mensch ist, und er ist nur da ganz Mensch, wo er spielt.
Friedrich Schiller

I. Spielraum für alle

Die moderne Asphaltstadt duldet keinen wilden Platz für Buben-Robinsonaden, keinen stillen Winkel für das verträumte Spiel der Kleinen. Die engen Mietwohnungen ertragen keinen Kinderlärm, und die Gassen und Straßen sind kinderfeindlich geworden. Sie gehören nicht mehr dem spielenden Kind und dem erwachsenen Fußgänger. Der homo faber bestimmt den Städtebau, den homo ludens überläßt man den Philosophen. »Wer es einmal erleben mußte«, schreibt ein junger Vater, »daß ihm sein Kind heimgebracht wurde, weil es im Spiel auf der Straße unter ein Auto rannte – so daß er nicht einmal mehr das liebe Gesicht, das ihn sonst täglich anlachte, erkennen konnte –, der weiß, daß es sich lohnt, sein Menschenmöglichstes zu tun, um andere Kinder vor dem gleichen Schicksal zu bewahren.« Möge dieses Buch alle, die guten Willens sind, aufrufen, das Menschenmögliche zu tun, um dem Kind seinen Spielraum wieder zurückzugeben. Wie rasch sind wir modernen und klugen Erwachsenen bereit, das Spiel unserer Kinder als überflüssige Zeitvergeudung, als bloße »Spielerei« abzutun und an alles und jedes den Nützlichkeitsmaßstab anzulegen. »Was heißt überhaupt bloßes Spiel, nachdem wir wissen, daß unter allen Zuständen des Menschen gerade das Spiel und nur das Spiel es ist, was ihn vollständig macht« (Friedrich Schiller).
Spiel ist für die seelische Entwicklung und Reifung des Menschen von entscheidender Bedeutung. Die Folgen ungenügender Möglichkeiten zu aktivem und schöpferischem Spiel zeigen sich heute deutlich: Phantasiearmut, Nervosität und Gereiztheit der Kinder, Freizeitvergeudung und Vergnügungssucht, Aggressivität und Rowdytum vieler Halbwüchsiger. Gewiß, solche seelischen und charakterlichen Verbiegungen können meist mehrere Ursachen und resultieren aus mangelnder Nestwärme, falscher Erziehung oder unglücklichen Familienverhältnissen. Aber manche dieser Fehlentwicklungen könnten vermieden oder gemildert werden durch eine Umwelt, in der das Kind seine Freuden und Nöte »ausspielen« kann.

Besonders in den ersten Lebensjahren gehört das Spiel zum Allerwichtigsten. Nicht umsonst nennen wir das Kleinkindalter das kindliche Spielalter. Aber auch das Kind im Schulalter will und soll spielen und zwar ausgiebiger, als wir Erwachsenen ihm meist zugestehen, weil es »dafür zu groß« sei. Für das Spiel ist keiner je zu groß oder zu alt. Spiel erzeugt Freude am Tätigsein. Der Weg zur sinnvollen Arbeit führt über das Spiel. Spielend erwirbt sich das Kind geschickte Hände, einen gewandten Körper, lebendige Sinne und ein reiches Gemüt – Eigenschaften, die es später im »großen Leben« braucht. Das Spiel ist der sicherste Garant für die seelische Gesundheit unserer Kinder und ein wertvoller Helfer in der Erziehung der jungen Menschen.
Gehört das Spiel nur in die Kinderstube, in den Alltag der Jugend? Hat nicht auch der Erwachsene für die Regeneration seiner seelischen Kräfte Spiel und Erholung ganz besonders nötig? Das moderne Stadtleben belastet Nerven und Gesundheit der Menschen viel stärker als früher. Das rapide Arbeitstempo, die oft sehr eintönige Tätigkeit im Beruf, die Alltagshetze lassen den Stadtmenschen seelisch verarmen, findet er nicht in seinen freien Stunden Möglichkeiten für einen Ausgleich und für die Aktivierung seiner brachliegenden Kräfte. Die Rationalisierung des Arbeitsprozesses und die Automation bringen mehr Freizeit mit sich (Fünftagewoche, frühere Pensionierung). Das erfordert neue Möglichkeiten zu schöpferischem Tun und sinnvoller Freizeitgestaltung, soll nicht die geschäftstüchtige Vergnügungsindustrie diese freie Zeit aufsaugen und die Berufshetze ablösen durch einen ebenso turbulenten Vergnügungsrummel. Der Nervosität des Stadtalltags, der Aufspaltung des Familienlebens und der passiven Zeitvergeudung muß eine schöpferische Erlebniswelt entgegengestellt werden, um die Gemüts- und Seelenkräfte des Stadt- und »Asphaltmenschen« zu stärken und die Familienbande zu festigen.
Spiel und Muße, aktive Freizeitgestaltung und schöpferisches Tun brauchen Platz, Spiel-Raum im tiefsten Sinne des Wortes. Nicht nur die Autos brauchen Bewegungsfreiheit, um aneinander vorbeizukommen. Auch das Menschenkind braucht Raum zum Spielen so nötig wie Nahrung und Schlaf. Sind nicht unsere Städte bald soweit, daß der Spiel-Raum zu eng und die Reibungen zu groß werden?
Es ist an der Zeit, die »humanen« Elemente des Stadtorganismus – die Erholungs- und Spielzentren –, wie sie Städtebauer und Architekten der ganzen Welt schon seit Jahrzehnten in ihren Planungen fordern, jetzt endlich auch in die Realität unserer gewachsenen Städte aufzunehmen.
Im heutigen Städtebau besteht vielfach leider noch die Meinung, das Spielproblem auf den einfachen Nenner »Kleinkind und Kleinkinderspielplatz« zu bringen. Das Kind im Schulalter, der Halbwüchsige und der Erwachsene mit ihren andersartigen Spiel- und Freizeitbedürfnissen finden keine Beachtung. Die große Bedeutung des Spiels und der schöpferischen Muße für alle Lebensalter wird nicht gesehen. Und der Kleinkinderspielplatz wird meist nicht in Zusammenhang gebracht mit der Familien-, der Wohn- und Hausgemeinschaft. Kein Wunder, wenn die üblichen Spielplätze – wenn auch unbeabsichtigt – lediglich eine bequeme Abstellmöglichkeit für kin-

dermüde Eltern ergeben und so ein weiteres Mosaikstück bilden im Zerstörungswerk an der Familie.
Tausende von Gemeinden befinden sich gegenwärtig in einem raschen baulichen Wachstum. Es entstehen neue Straßen, Wohnungen, Schulhäuser, Fabriken. Hier gilt es, rechtzeitig auch genügend Spiel- und Erholungsraum für alle Altersstufen freizuhalten und bereitzustellen.

II. Planung

Wenn wir uns konkret die Frage stellen, wo sich dieser Spielraum in der Stadt, im Dorf befinden soll, so müssen wir vom Kind und seinem Spiel ausgehen. Geeigneten Spielraum zu schaffen, ist nicht einfach eine Angelegenheit der Baubehörden und Gartenbauämter. Das Spiel, vor allem das Spiel der Kleinen, gehört ins Haus, in die Wohnstube und in die nächste Umgebung des Hauses und nicht auf wohnungsferne Spielplätze, seien sie noch so »schön«.

Der Spielraum im Heim.

Die Spielplatzfrage ist deshalb in erster Linie zusammen mit dem Wohnungs- und Siedlungsbau zu lösen. Der Raum für das Spiel im Haus (Wohnraum, Kinderecke, Kinderzimmer, Bastelraum) ist ebenso notwendig wie der Raum zum Schlafen und Essen. Für die körperliche Hygiene wird im Wohnungsbau heute recht viel getan. Es werden kaum mehr Wohnungen erstellt ohne Wasch- und Bademöglichkeiten. Für die seelische Hygiene, für die Gesunderhaltung der Familie, bleibt im künftigen Wohnungs- und Städtebau noch viel zu tun.
Die meisten Mietwohnungen für Familien mit Kindern sind zu klein und zu eng. Sie enthalten wohl oft genügend Zimmer, aber diese Zimmer sind enge, auf die knappsten Maße reduzierte Wohnkisten, in denen die Möbel, nicht aber die Menschen mit ihrem Leben und Treiben Platz finden. Und wir Erwachsenen stopfen dann überdies die Zimmer noch voll mit Möbeln. Auch die leichte Bauart führt in vielen Mietshäusern zu dauernden Reibereien. Spielen die Kinder in der Wohnung, so reklamieren die lieben Nachbarn. Und doch, sind nicht Bewegung und Lärm Ausdruck der Spiel- und Lebensfreude unserer Kinder, die zu unterdrücken und zu verbieten mit der Zeit schwerste seelische Verkrampfungen nach sich ziehen! Die Kinderzimmer selbst – und zwar auch in den Siedlungen für kinderreiche Familien – sind nur Kinderschlafzimmer, aber keine Kinderspielzimmer. Diese langen und schlauchförmigen Räume vermögen im besten Fall zwei Kinderbetten und eine Kommode aufzunehmen. Bodenfläche zum Spielen ist kaum vorhanden. Man könnte meinen, das Leben der Kinder bestünde nur aus Schlaf.
Es gilt deshalb, in erster Linie einen kinder- und familienfreundlicheren Wohnungsbau anzustreben, der das Problem des spielenden Kindes mit in seine Planungen einbezieht. Die Familie soll in ihrer Wohnung ein Nest und eine Lebensgemeinschaft finden.
Einer der wertvollsten »Spielplätze« ist und bleibt die Wohnstube. Hier beginnt das Spiel der Kleinsten, zunächst im Bettchen und im Stubenwagen, später im Laufgitter und in der

Spielecke. In jedem Wohnzimmer läßt sich durch eine geschickte Umstellung der Möbel eine Spielecke schaffen, die dem kleinen Spielkind ganz gehört. Hier darf es tun, was es will. Hier muß nicht ständig aufgeräumt werden wie auf dem Stubentisch – wo man stets gestört wird, wenn das Spiel am interessantesten ist. Hier darf es sich mit Kisten, Stühlen und Tüchern seine erste »Wohnhöhle« bauen. In der Spielecke ist die erste Heimat des Kindes, seine seelische Heimat, die ihm nie mehr verlorengeht.

Spielecken und Spielnischen zu schaffen, das sollte eine Aufgabe sein, an der Architekten, Innenarchitekten und Eltern gemeinsam arbeiten. Überdies sind in den Kellern der Miet- und Einfamilienhäuser vermehrt Bastelräume zu schaffen und die Trockenräume zu Spielzimmern für die Kinder auszubauen.

Der Spielraum im Freien.

A. Für Kleinkinder:

Der Spielplatz für die Kinder im vorschulpflichtigen Alter gehört als »grüne Stube«, als Spielraum im Freien wenn immer möglich unmittelbar zum Haus, damit die Mütter nicht täglich ihre Arbeit liegenlassen müssen, um ihre Kinder auf den Spielplatz zu begleiten. Sie sollten das Spiel ihrer Kleinen vom Haus aus beobachten können. Zudem fühlt sich das Kleinkind nur »zu Hause«, wenn es in der Nähe der Mutter spielen kann. Fast läßt sich dieses Nest- und Heimgefühl der Kleinkinder vergleichen mit dem Revierinstinkt mancher Wildtiere, die sich nur innerhalb ihres Territoriums, das sie mit ihren Duftmarken abgrenzen, sicher und geborgen fühlen. Selbst die größeren Kinder spielen mit Vorliebe in Wohnungsnähe, in der ihnen vertrauten Umgebung. Über diesem seltsamen »Instinktverhalten« des homo sapiens könnte man leicht ins Philosophieren kommen. Jedenfalls dürfen wir die starke Bindung des Kindes an seine nächste, ihm vertraute Umgebung nicht leichthin zerstören: seelische Bindungs- und Heimatlosigkeit für das spätere Leben könnten die Folge sein.

Einzig auf dem Bauernhof hat das kleine Kind für sein Spiel noch den natürlichen »Auslauf«. Da findet es tausend Anregungen im Stall, in der Scheune, bei den Kleintieren, in Feld und Wald. Das Bauernkind hat sein Spielreich in Wohnungsnähe; dafür läuft es allerdings Gefahr, zu früh dem Kinderland entrissen und in den Arbeitsprozeß der Erwachsenen eingeschaltet zu werden. Glücklich das Bauernkind, das von verständnisvollen Eltern Schritt für Schritt in die Arbeitsgemeinschaft der Familie eingeführt wird und nicht schon von klein an als Arbeitskraft einspringen muß.

Die meisten Bauerndörfer haben heute ein anderes Gesicht als früher. Die Industrialisierung läßt in den Dörfern Wohnsiedlungen und Mietshäuser entstehen, die nicht anders aussehen als die Häuser in der Stadt und in denen die Familien nicht anders leben als die Stadtbewohner. Zudem werden viele Dörfer von gefährlichen Durchgangsstraßen durchzogen. Hier stellen sich für das Spiel des Kindes genau die gleichen Probleme wie in der Stadt. Geeigneten Spielraum im Freien zu schaffen, ist daher ebenso notwendig wie in jeder städtischen Siedlung.

Im Gegensatz zum Bauernkind wächst das Stadtkind meist in einer unkindlichen Erwachsenenwelt auf. Harter Asphalt, Motorenlärm, Hast und Hochglanz bestimmen seine Welt, eine Welt, die man im Spiel nicht mehr gestalten kann. Es gilt deshalb, in jeder Stadt, in jedem Dorf ein möglichst dichtes Netz von Kleinkinderspielplätzen in Wohnungsnähe anzustreben, wobei folgende Lösungen in Frage kommen:

Der Haus- und Hofspielplatz.

Beim Bau von Mehrfamilienmietshäusern ist von allem Anfang an zwischen den Häuserblöcken soviel Fläche freizuhalten, daß nicht nur Wäscheständer und Teppichstangen aufgestellt, sondern auch Kleinkinderspielplätze angelegt werden können. Die heute übliche, lockere Bauweise der Wohnblöcke, mit Rasenflächen zwischen den Häusern, ist sehr zu begrüßen. Die Rasenstücke sind aber im Gegensatz zur leider weitverbreiteten Praxis nicht mit allen möglichen Verboten zu belegen, sondern als Spiel- und Erholungsflächen freizugeben. Wie es dank der Initiative privater Bauherren möglich ist, zwischen einigen Wohnblocks einen gut gestalteten Hausspielplatz anzulegen, zeigt etwa das auf Seite 64 abgebildete Projekt.

In den Altquartieren und bei Altbauten sind die hier besonders dringlichen Spielplätze meist nur durch eine Sanierung und Zusammenlegung von Hinterhöfen zu erreichen, indem die einzelnen Zäune niedergelegt und allenfalls gemeinsame Abstellräume für Fahrräder, Handwagen usw. errichtet werden, – eine Aufgabe, die bei den vorherrschenden Eigentumsverhältnissen psychologisch und durch Verordnungen außerordentlich schwierig zu lösen ist.

Die dänische Hauptstadt Kopenhagen hat dafür eine interessante und vorbildliche Lösung gefunden: jeder Hauseigentümer und jeder (private und genossenschaftliche) Bauherr, der ein Haus mit mindestens acht Wohnungen besitzt oder baut, ist unter Umständen gesetzlich verpflichtet, einen Hof- und Hausspielplatz zu erstellen. Die Mieter zahlen dafür mit der Wohnungsmiete einen bescheidenen »Spielplatzzuschlag«. Kopenhagen verfügt auf diese Weise in der Altstadt und in den neuen Wohnsiedlungen der Außenquartiere über eine große Zahl idealer Haus- und Hofspielplätze (Beispiele siehe Seite 48, 50, 58, 104). Auch die Bauordnung der Stadt Kassel verpflichtet die Bauherren, mit den Wohnflächen entsprechende Freiflächen für »Wäschebleichen, Spielplätze usw.« zu verbinden. Derartige Gesetzesbestimmungen und Verordnungen dürften vielerorts der einzige Weg sein, um in den dichtbebauten Altquartieren überhaupt Spielplätze zu bekommen.

Der Siedlungsspielplatz.

Bei neuen Wohnkolonien ist schon bei der Bauplanung zusammen mit den individuellen Hausgärten ein gemeinsamer Siedlungsspielplatz vorzusehen. Leider sind bis heute erst in einigen wenigen Baugesetzen und Bauverordnungen entsprechende Vorschriften enthalten. Es scheint uns selbstverständlich, daß bei neuen Siedlungen nicht nur der erforderliche Raum für Zubringerstraßen oder Garagen gesetzlich verlangt wird, sondern auch Bestimmungen zur Schaffung eines angemessenen Spielraums für die Kinder aufgenommen werden. Auch sind für Bauprojekte mit Familienwohnungen nur noch unter der Voraussetzung staatliche Geldzuschüsse zu gewähren, daß genügend Spiel- und Erholungsflächen im Freien geschaffen werden.

Als Beispiel eines hervorragenden Siedlungsspielplatzes kann hier der Kleinkinderspielplatz Sonnengarten in Zürich (siehe Seite 66–69) erwähnt werden, der ebenso wie eine ganze Reihe anderer Schweizer und amerikanischer Plätze in Gemeinschaftsarbeit der Väter entstanden. Wir sind überzeugt, daß solche Spielplätze besonders wertvoll sind, weil derartige freiwillige »Arbeitsgemeinschaften« eine einzigartige Gelegenheit bieten, die anonymen Stadtmenschen wieder zu einer Gemeinschaft zusammenzuführen. Hier kann ein Beispiel tätiger Demokratie lebendig werden ähnlich dem Fronwerk der Bergbauern, die in gemeinsamer freiwilliger Arbeit zum Schutz ihrer Heimstätten Wildbach- und Lawinenverbauungen errichteten.

Der Kindergartenspielplatz.

Um eine möglichst große Zahl von Kinderspielplätzen in Wohnungsnähe zu erhalten, ist das Netz der privaten und genossenschaftlichen Haus-, Hof- und Siedlungsspielplätze durch die Einbeziehung der Kindergartenspielflächen zu ergänzen. Die Freiflächen neuer Kindergärten sind so anzulegen und von allem Anfang an als »Mehrzweckspielplätze« auszugestalten, daß diese Anlagen den Kindern der Umgebung in der freien Zeit zum Spielen überlassen werden können. Selbstverständlich darf dadurch der Kindergartenbetrieb nicht gestört werden.

Die Freiflächen der bereits bestehenden Kindergärten sind, wenn immer möglich, an den kindergartenfreien Nachmittagen und in den Ferien für den freien Spielbetrieb der Nachbarkinder zu öffnen. Zur Betreuung der Kinder sind nötigenfalls Mütter als freiwillige Kindertanten beizuziehen.

Auf jeden Fall ist es kaum zu verantworten, daß in soundsovielen Städten und Dörfern die Kindergartenspielplätze in kindergartenfreier Zeit geschlossen und dafür Hunderte von Kleinkindern mit ihrem Spiel auf die gefährlichen Straßen angewiesen sind. Bei gutem Willen lassen sich bestimmt Lösungen finden, die dem pädagogischen Kindergartenbetrieb keinen Abbruch tun, auch wenn die Freiflächen anderweitig benutzt werden.

Die Ausgestaltung der betreffenden Areale muß dann allerdings vielfältiger, lebendiger und der Doppelverwendung angepaßt sein; den meisten Kindergartenspielplätzen würde ein spielfreudigeres Gewand ohnehin besser anstehen. Man ist beim Besuch neuer Kindergärten oft versucht zu glauben, die Phantasie der Bauherren und Architekten habe sich im Kindergartengebäude erschöpft und das Umgelände sei einfach als Nebensache behandelt worden. Dabei ließe sich in der Zusammenarbeit zwischen Architekt, Gartenarchitekt und Kindergärtnerin – etwa durch die Schaffung eines Reigenplatzes, eines kleinen Amphitheaters für Kasperlspiel und Märchenstunden, von Spielnischen für verträumte Spiele, von Blumenbeeten und anderem – noch so vieles tun, damit die Kindergärten zu wirklichen Kinder-Gärten werden.

B. Für Kinder aller Altersstufen:

Wenn die Kinder größer werden, greift ihr Spielbereich über das Haus und seine nächste Umgebung hinaus. Das Schulkind im sogenannten Robinsonalter geht auf Entdeckungen aus. Es spielt nicht mehr wie das Kleinkind vorwiegend für sich allein, es sucht gleichaltrige Kameraden, um sich mit ihnen in Gruppenspielen zu messen. Das größere Kind will Wettkampf- und Sportspiele, es will aktiv tätig sein, bauen, basteln, konstruieren, theaterspielen, etwas erforschen und »Abenteuer bestehen«.

Um all diese Spielwünsche zu befriedigen, braucht man größere Spielareale als für das Kleinkind. Das Spiel der großen Kinder ist auch bewegter und lauter. Man sollte deshalb die Spielplätze nicht allzunahe bei den Wohnungen anlegen.

Das Netz der wohnungsnahen Haus-, Siedlungs- und Kindergartenspielplätze ist darum in jedem Dorf, in jeder Stadt und in jedem Stadtquartier zu ergänzen durch eine Anzahl weiträumiger Spielplätze für die größeren Kinder, das heißt besser für die Kinder und Jugendlichen aller Altersstufen. Wir glauben nämlich nicht, daß es eine glückliche Lösung ist, für die verschiedensten Altersstufen, etwa für die 3- bis 6-, die 7- bis 12- und die 13- bis 17jährigen spezielle Spielplätze zu schaffen. Einmal sollten sich, wenn immer möglich, die verschiedenaltrigen Geschwister auf dem gleichen Spielplatz tummeln dürfen. Zum anderen entspricht die Spielentwicklung und das Spielbedürfnis des einzelnen Kindes oft nicht den kinderpsychologischen Altersstufen. Warum sollte etwa ein größerer Junge nicht wieder einmal im Sandhaufen der Kleinen wühlen oder ein älteres Mädchen mit der Puppe spielen dürfen, nur weil sie eigentlich dafür »zu groß und zu alt« sind? Können nicht gerade solche – wie wir Erwachsenen meinen – altersuntypischen Spiele für die seelische Gesundheit des betreffenden Kindes besonders wertvoll und notwendig sein?

Auch glauben wir nicht, daß für die Schulkinder und Jugendlichen oder Schulentlassenen spezielle und andere Spielgelände nötig sind. Es ist Sache des Spielplatzgestalters, die Anlage und die Einrichtung der einzelnen Spielplätze so vorzunehmen, daß die Kinder und Jugendlichen ihre verschiedenen Altersstufen gemäßen Spiele betreiben können.

Wir möchten deshalb vorschlagen, in der Spielplatzsystematik nur drei Spielplatzarten anzustreben:

1. den Kleinkinderspielplatz in Wohnungsnähe, in der Form des Wohnungs-, Haus-, Siedlungs- und Kindergartenspielplatzes;
2. den Spielplatz für Kinder aller Altersstufen, wobei hauptsächlich die Spiele der größeren Kinder und Jugendlichen Berücksichtigung finden;
3. das Spiel- und Gemeinschaftszentrum für Kinder und Erwachsene.

Die Bereitstellung und Ausgestaltung dieser größeren Spielgelände für Kinder aller Altersstufen kann nun nicht mehr Sache der privaten und genossenschaftlichen Bauherren sein. Hier haben die Baubehörden, die Gartenbauämter, die Erziehungs- und Schulbehörden das Notwendige zu veranlassen. Man wird hierzu vor allem die öffentlichen Grünflächen verwenden müssen.

Wenn diese Spielflächen auch nicht allzu weit von den Wohnungen entfernt sein dürfen, so bildet ein viertelstündiger Anmarschweg für die größeren Kinder keineswegs ein Hindernis. Bietet der Spielplatz interessante Spielmöglichkeiten, so nehmen die größeren Kinder diesen Weg gern auf sich: der Zug von zu Hause weg entspricht ohnehin diesem Alter.

Andererseits müssen wir uns aber hüten, in einer Stadt oder in einem Dorf einen einzigen oder einige wenige unpersönliche Mammutspielplätze – wenn möglich noch am Stadt- oder Dorfrand, fern von den Wohnhäusern – anzulegen. Auch diese Spielareale sollten die Kinder eines Stadtquartiers, die sich schon von der Schule oder vom täglichen Spiel her kennen, zusammenführen. Wir brauchen keine anonymen Unterhaltungsspielplätze und Spielmaschinerien, sondern Quartierspielplätze, auf denen sich täglich dieselben Kinder zu Spielgemeinschaften, zu Nachbarschaften zusammenfinden.

Zur Schaffung solcher Quartierspielplätze für alle Altersstufen kommen folgende Möglichkeiten in Frage.

Der Schulspielplatz.

Die Freianlagen der Schulhäuser, wie die Pausenhöfe, Spielwiesen, Turnplätze, sind vermehrt als »Mehrzweckspielplätze« auszugestalten durch Aufstellen geeigneter Klettergeräte, Kriechröhren, Balancierstangen, Kinderrecks, Hindernisbahnen, Sandflächen und anderes. Einfache Spielgeräte kommen auch dem Schulbetrieb sehr zugut: der übliche turbulente Pausenbetrieb wird ruhiger und damit für die Schulkinder seelisch und körperlich wertvoller.

Zudem werden nur lebendig und kindertümlich eingerichtete Schulanlagen von den Kindern in ihrer Freizeit zum Spielen aufgesucht. Die Öffnung der für das Kind eher langweiligen Schulanlagen und Spielwiesen außerhalb der Schulzeit – wie es erfreulicherweise mancherorts eingeführt ist – genügt nicht, um die größeren Kinder von der viel interessanteren Straße auf diese Plätze zu bringen. Ganz abgesehen von der Scheu der Kinder vor gewissen Schul-Hausmeistern und -Behörden, deren Stolz darin besteht, die ihnen anvertrauten Schulanlagen in erster Linie als Putz- und Demonstrierobjekte für Besucher zu betrachten.

In einigen Ländern, vor allem in England und Amerika, verwendet man bereits heute die Schulanlagen als »Mehrzweckanlagen« für Schule und Freizeit (siehe Seite 80–83). Die Schulareale, und zwar Schulhaus und Umgelände, sollten auch in den übrigen Ländern in viel größerem Maß ganz allgemein den Gemeinschaftsinteressen dienen. So würde das Schulhaus wieder zu einem »offenen Haus«, zu einem kulturellen Zentrum des Quartiers, indem die Schulwerkstätten, Singsäle, Turnhallen und Schulräume sowie die Freiflächen nicht nur den Schulkindern, sondern der ganzen Bevölkerung dienen (siehe Seite 150–151). Solche Schulanlagen mit den verschiedenen Möglichkeiten für das sportliche, musikalische und handwerkliche Spiel würden nicht zuletzt auch die Schularbeit aufs schönste im Sinn von Pestalozzis Forderung »Kopf, Herz und Hand« ergänzen. Und eine Schulanlage, die der Jugend für ihre Freizeit Spiel- und Betätigungsmöglichkeiten bietet, wird selbst dem schwächeren Schüler lieb und vertraut und erleichtert ihm so die richtige, positive Einstellung zur

Schule. Die Pflege der Gemeinschaftsinteressen bringt aber – und das ist besonders erfreulich – mit den Kindern auch deren Eltern und die ganze Quartierbevölkerung der Schule wieder näher.

Der Spielplatz in Sportanlagen, Freibädern und Familiengärten.

Die Sportanlagen sind in vermehrtem Maß als öffentliche »Mehrzweckanlagen« für das freie Spiel der Bevölkerung auszugestalten oder durch entsprechende Tummelwiesen und Spielplätze zu ergänzen. Der übliche Sportplatz ist der Schule oder dem Sportverein vorbehalten, die scharf darüber wachen, daß sich keine »wilden« Spieler einfinden: »Unbefugten ist der Zutritt strengstens verboten«.

Der großen Masse nichtorganisierter Spiel- und Sportfreudiger fehlen fast überall in unseren Städten und Dörfern geeignete Anlagen, wo sie frei und ungezwungen Sport treiben können. Nur ein kleiner Prozentsatz junger Menschen und Erwachsener will bekanntlich noch im organisierten Turn- und Sportbetrieb, in einem Klub oder Verein mitmachen. Man will frei sein und keine Verpflichtungen eingehen. Viele wären aber sehr wohl für eine körperliche und sportliche Betätigung zu haben, wenn ihnen Gelegenheit zu freiem Spiel geboten würde. Wo wird nicht überall Federball, Tischtennis, Völkerball, Handball und Fußball gespielt! Wo messen sich nicht Schulkinder und Jugendliche in allen möglichen Kampf- und Sportspielen. Wir dürfen deshalb in Zukunft bei der Planung von Sportanlagen nicht nur von der relativ kleinen Zahl organisierter Sportler und der Riesenmasse der Schausportler ausgehen, sondern sollten vielmehr die große Zahl der unorganisierten, spiel- und sportfreudigen jüngeren und älteren Leute berücksichtigen.

Gewiß, solche Sportanlagen sind einer rascheren Abnutzung unterworfen und bedürfen einer intensiveren Wartung. Aber wenn in Zukunft nur ein einziger Jugendlicher weniger beim Fußballspiel auf der Straße dem Unfalltod zum Opfer fällt, so hat sich die Schaffung solcher Sportplätze gelohnt. Ganz abgesehen davon, daß sich auch den Erwachsenen auf solchen Sportplätzen neue Möglichkeiten des gemeinsamen Spiels mit ihren Kindern ergeben, so wenn etwa ein Vater mit seinen Buben Fußball spielen kann.

Bei der Gestaltung öffentlicher Freibäder ergeben sich für den Gestalter ebenfalls reizvolle Möglichkeiten, diese Anlagen dem freien Spiel besser zu erschließen. Vor allem sind die mit den Bädern verbundenen Freiflächen und Spielplätze nicht mit den gleichen Geräten einzurichten wie die gewöhnlichen Spielplätze. Warum werden diese Areale und Spielgeräte nicht ganz vom Wasser und von den Wasserspielen her entwickelt, wie dies in Düsseldorf (siehe Seite 90–91) oder Grenchen (siehe Seite 89) mit Erfolg versucht wurde? Zudem sollten die Freibäder in vermehrtem Maß so angelegt werden, daß die Grünflächen außerhalb der oft sehr kurzen sommerlichen Badesaison im Frühjahr, Herbst und Winter ganz allgemein als öffentliche Quartierparkanlagen den Spaziergängern und spielenden Kindern offenstehen. In Zürich zum Beispiel sind in dieser Beziehung recht interessante Lösungen gefunden worden.

In vielen Städten gibt es größere Areale von Klein- und Familiengärten (Schrebergärten). Auch hier sollte, wenn immer möglich, am besten von den Pflanzlandbesitzern selbst in freiwilliger Arbeit, ein gemeinsamer Spielplatz für die Kinder angelegt werden.

Der Spielplatz beim Jugendhaus, beim »Haus der offenen Tür«, beim Freizeithaus.

Es ist eigentlich überraschend und bedauerlich, daß bei den Jugendhäusern, Freizeithäusern und Häusern der offenen Tür dem Umgelände bis heute kaum Beachtung geschenkt wird und daß die meisten dieser Häuser nur lächerlich kleine und rudimentäre Freiflächen und Spielplätze besitzen. Meines Erachtens ist ein gut eingerichtetes Jugendhaus ohne gleich gut und vielseitig gestaltete Freiflächen nur halb soviel wert wie ein Jugendhaus, das in der schönen Jahreszeit einen großen Teil seiner Tätigkeit in das Freie verlegen kann. Selbst der handwerkliche Jugendhausbetrieb könnte im Sommer hinaus ins Freie, etwa auf den Werkstättenvorplatz verlegt werden, hätte der Architekt bei der Planung des Hauses daran gedacht.
Und welche reizvollen Möglichkeiten ergeben sich erst recht auf dem musischen Sektor: Freilichttheateraufführungen, Tanz- und Reigenspiele, Serenaden unter freiem Himmel. Gar nicht zu reden von den vielen Spiel- und Sportarten, die im Sommerbetrieb eines jeden Jugendhauses im Vordergrund stehen. Wieviel wertvolle Möglichkeiten zur Gewinnung der großen Masse der sogenannten passiven Jugendlichen, die nur Tischtennis spielen und herumstehen, entgehen einem Jugendhaus, das über keine Spielflächen und -ecken im Freien verfügt, doch diese Einrichtungen bilden die Brücke, die manche Jugendlichen über das freie Spiel zu einer aktiv-schöpferischen Tätigkeit hinzuführen vermöchte. Kaum eines der Jugendhäuser, die ich besuchen konnte, besitzt genügend und zweckmäßig gestaltete Freiflächen. Es verhält sich hier ähnlich wie bei den Kindergärten: die Bauherren und Architekten scheinen sich erschöpft zu haben in der Gestaltung des Hauses, so daß dem zufällig vorhandenen, mehr oder weniger großen Umgelände bedauerlicherweise keine Beachtung mehr geschenkt wurde.
Als Beispiel für die wechselseitige Ergänzung von Freizeithaus und Spielplatzgelände mag die Freizeitanlage in Zürich-Wipkingen gelten (siehe Seite 130–139). Hier bilden die Freizeit- und Gemeinschaftsräume zusammen mit den Freiflächen eine harmonische Einheit, wobei Spielbetrieb und handwerkliches oder musisches Freizeitschaffen sommers wie winters im Innenraum und im Freien ständig ineinander überfließen. Im übrigen glauben wir, daß heute an Stelle von Jugendhäusern, Häusern der offenen Tür, welche nur den schulentlassenen Jugendlichen und vielleicht noch den Kindern dienen, vielmehr »Freizeithäuser mit Freiflächen«, das heißt Spiel- und Gemeinschaftszentren für alle Altersstufen, für jung und alt eines Stadtquartiers, eines Dorfes geschaffen werden sollten, wie sie im folgenden unter C. geschildert werden.

C. Für Kinder und Erwachsene:

Der Spielplatz im Park, das Spiel- und Gemeinschaftszentrum (Freizeitanlage).
Die öffentlichen Park- und Grünanlagen der Städte und Dörfer haben unseres Erachtens nicht nur die hygienische Funktion von »Lungen«, sie bilden beim heutigen Stand der Technik, des Verkehrs, der Hast, des Tempos und der »Asphaltkultur« unentbehrliche Oasen der Muße, »seelische Tankstellen« für die ganze Bevölkerung. Dieser erweiterten Funktion entsprechen die wenigsten Parkanlagen mit ihren Rasen, Blumenbeeten, Spazierwegen und – Verbotstafeln. Die Parkanlagen sollten in weit größerem Maß dem Spiel und der schöpferischen Muße von jung und alt erschlossen und dementsprechend ausgestaltet werden. Welche Möglichkeiten sich für die Einrichtung von Parkspielplätzen bieten, zeigt das Beispiel der Münchener Isarauen (siehe Seite 124–127) oder des Stuttgarter Weißenburgparks (siehe Seite 120–123). In der Weiterentwicklung des Parkspielplatzes zur kombinierten Freizeitanlage (Freizeithaus und Freifläche) hat die Schweiz Pionierarbeit geleistet (siehe Seite 146–149).
Mit diesen Gemeinschaftszentren für jung und alt, welche eine Kombination von Freizeithaus, Spielplatz und öffentlichem Park darstellen, schließt sich der Ring der Spiel- und Erholungsräume innerhalb einer Stadt oder Dorfgemeinde. Im folgenden möchten wir unsere Wünsche an die Städteplaner kurz zusammenfassen.

Zehn städtebauliche Wünsche:

A. Kleinkinderspielplätze.

1. Für das Spiel des Kleinkindes ist ein möglichst großes Netz von Wohnungs-, Haus-, Hof-, Siedlungs- und Kindergartenspielplätzen anzustreben.
2. Die Anlage solcher Spielplätze ist von Behörden (Baubehörden, Schulbehörden, Gartenbauämtern) und Privaten (Baugenossenschaften und privaten Bauherren) in die Hand zu nehmen, wobei diese Bestrebungen finanziell durch staatliche Subventionen zu fördern sind.
3. Beim privaten und genossenschaftlichen Wohnungsbau ist durch entsprechende Gesetze, Verordnungen, Subventionsbedingungen oder freiwillige Vereinbarungen die Schaffung einer möglichst großen Zahl von Haus-, Hof- und Siedlungsspielplätzen für die kleinen Kinder anzustreben. Vor allem sollte keine Siedlung für Familien mehr geplant und gebaut werden ohne Spielplätze.
4. In den Altquartieren können allenfalls durch Auskernung und Zusammenlegung von Parzellen Hofspielplätze gewonnen werden.

B. Spielplätze für alle Altersstufen.

5. Für das Spiel und die Freizeitgestaltung der Kinder und Jugendlichen aller Altersstufen sind Schulspielplätze, Spielplätze in den Sportanlagen und Freibädern, bei den Jugend- und Freizeithäusern zu schaffen.

6. Beim Bau von Schulhäusern, Kindergärten, Gartenbädern, Sportplätzen, Parkanlagen ist im Bauprogramm von allem Anfang an die Verwendung der Freiflächen als »Mehrzweckanlagen« vorzusehen oder es sind dem betreffenden Bauprogramm spezielle Spielplätze anzugliedern. Die hierzu notwendigen Spielgeräte und Einrichtungen sollten genauso in das Raumprogramm einbezogen werden wie Schulzimmer, Nebenräume oder Turngeräte.

C. Spiel- und Gemeinschaftszentrum für jung und alt (Freizeitanlage).

7. Für das Spiel und die schöpferische Muße von jung und alt (der Kinder, Familien und älteren Leute) sind die öffentlichen Grünflächen und Parkanlagen so auszugestalten, daß sie zu Spiel-, Erholungs- und Gemeinschaftszentren für die ganze Bevölkerung werden.
8. Die zuständigen Behörden und Parlamente haben rechtzeitig und auf weite Sicht in jedem Dorf, in jeder Stadt, in jedem Stadtquartier das notwendige Land als Grünzone zu sichern und von der Überbauung freizuhalten. Ferner sind entsprechende Gesetze oder Verordnungen zum Schutz der Grünzonen zu erlassen.
9. Für die Grünzonen ist ein Nutzungsplan aufzustellen, der nicht nur Schulbauten, Kindergärten, Sportplätze, Bäder umfaßt, sondern vor allem auch Spielplätze und Gemeinschaftszentren in die Gesamtplanung mit einbezieht. Geschieht dies nicht rechtzeitig, so ist eines Tages alles Grünzonenland benutzt und in der Nähe der Wohnhäuser kein freies Land mehr für Spiel und Erholung zu finden.
10. Erst wenn die Stadtplaner, Städtebauer und Baubehörden diesen »Generalplan für das Spiel« ebenso ernsthaft zu verwirklichen suchen wie die aktuellen Generalpläne für den Verkehr, dann wird der Städtebau die so dringend notwendige Humanisierung erreicht haben zum Wohle der Jugend und der ganzen Bevölkerung.

III. Gestaltung

Bevor wir im einzelnen untersuchen, wie die genannten drei Spielplatztypen (der Kleinkinderspielplatz, der Spielplatz für alle Altersstufen und das Spiel- und Gemeinschaftszentrum für jung und alt) gestaltet und eingerichtet werden sollen, seien zunächst einige wesentliche Richtlinien genannt, die für die Gestaltung aller Spielplätze von Wichtigkeit sind. Dabei gehen wir weitgehend von den Erfahrungen aus, die wir mit unserer eigenen Spielplatzarbeit sammeln konnten. Diese Plätze (siehe Seite 66–69, 70–73, 130–149) sind in enger Zusammenarbeit zwischen Pädagoge und Architekt geplant, gestaltet und eingerichtet, wobei ständige kritische Beobachtungen des täglichen Spiels unsere spielpädagogischen Erfahrungen klärten und festigten. Mögen andere Spielplatzgestalter andere Lösungen finden, wesentlich scheint uns zu sein, daß die Errichtung eines Spielplatzes das Kind mit seinem Spiel, beim Gemeinschaftszentrum der Erwachsene und die Familie mit ihren Spiel- und Erholungsbedürfnissen den entscheidenden Maßstab abgeben.

Zehn spielpädagogische Wünsche:

1. Jeder Spielplatz muß von seiner Funktion, vom Spiel her eingerichtet und gestaltet sein.

Dieses Postulat scheint selbstverständlich zu sein. Und doch, bei wie vielen Spielplätzen – fast sind wir versucht zu behaupten bei den meisten – richtet sich die Gestaltung und Ausrüstung nach den in der betreffenden Stadt üblichen industriellen Spielgeräten und andererseits nach den Bäumen und Sträuchern, die der nur unter gartenästhetischen Gesichtspunkten an seine Aufgabe herangehende Gestalter pflanzt. Wir dürfen uns nicht wundern, wenn die Spielatmosphäre dieser Plätze ebenso zerfahren und zufällig ist, wie die Wohnatmosphäre in manchen Zimmern, die wir Erwachsenen phantasielos möblieren. Lärmige und nervöse Kinderspiele sind die Folge solcher vom Zufall gestalteten Spielplätze.

2. Architekt, Gartenarchitekt und Pädagoge müssen zusammenarbeiten, um vorbildliche Spielplatzlösungen zu schaffen.

Mancher Architekt läuft Gefahr, auf den Spielplätzen Architektur als l'art pour l'art zu betreiben. Eine vielleicht für unsere Erwachsenenaugen recht originelle, aber nüchterne und unkindliche Spielarchitektur ist das Ergebnis. Der Gartenarchitekt wiederum ist vielfach ästhetisch verliebt in seine Flora, so daß auf den Spielplätzen nicht das Spiel, sondern die Bäume und Sträucher, der Rasen und die Blumen die Hauptrolle spielen. Und der Pädagoge endlich ist versucht, aus dem Spielplatz eine Erziehungsanstalt zu machen. Nur eine ehrliche, offene Diskussion und Zusammenarbeit zwischen Architekt, Gartenarchitekt und Pädagoge scheint uns die bestmögliche Gewähr dafür zu bieten, daß Spielplätze entstehen, die architektonisch und gärtnerisch ansprechend und zugleich – und das ist das Entscheidende – spielpädagogisch und kindgemäß sind. Das Kind mit seinem Spiel und nicht die Architektur sind maßgebend für die Gestaltung von Spielplätzen.

3. Der Spielplatz darf nicht der passiven Unterhaltung dienen. Er muß das aktive, selbsttätige und schöpferische Spiel fördern.

Eine Ansammlung von Spielgeräten ergibt leicht einen »Spielsalon im Freien«. Verpassen wir nicht die Gelegenheit, im Kleinkind- und Schulkindalter die Spielphantasie und die Spielaktivität anzuregen und zu entwickeln, sonst dürfen wir uns nicht beklagen über die Passivität, Unterhaltungs- und Vergnügungssucht vieler Halberwachsener und Erwachsener.

4. Wertvoller als mechanische Spielgeräte sind unfertige Spielelemente und Spielmaterialien.

Jede Kindergärtnerin bemüht sich, in ihren Kindern die Spielaktivität zu fördern. In jeder Elternschule ermuntert man die Eltern, ihre Kinder nicht mit fertigen, mechanischen Spielsachen zu verwöhnen. Die Spielplätze hingegen sind immer noch weitgehend beherrscht von starren Spielgeräten, die der kindlichen Phantasie kaum Anregung bieten. Ein Kletterbaum ist wertvoller als ein Karussell, ein Sandhaufen wertvoller als Schaukeln, Bau- und Bastelmaterial wertvoller als Tischtennistische. Wir möchten damit keineswegs sagen, daß Tischtennis und Schaukeln von den Spielplätzen zu verschwinden hätten. Wir möchten aber empfehlen, bei der Auswahl der

Spielgeräte und Spielelemente eine spielpädagogische Wertskala anzuwenden zugunsten des aktiven und schöpferischen Spiels.

5. Gestaltung und Einrichtung des Spielplatzes muß sich nach den typischen Spielen der betreffenden Altersstufe richten, für die er bestimmt ist.

Ein Kleinkind spielt anders als ein Schulkind. Die Mädchen haben zu bestimmten Zeiten andere Spielwünsche als die gleichaltrigen Jungen. – Vor allem dürfen wir nicht nur Spielplätze für Kleinkinder schaffen, sondern müssen auch zweckmäßig gestaltete Spielareale für die Kinder im »Robinsonalter« und für die Jugendlichen einrichten. Selbst die Erwachsenen und die älteren Leute brauchen heute mehr als früher geeignete Areale für Spiel und Erholung.

6. Der Spielplatz darf nicht einseitig sein, er muß vielfältige Spielmöglichkeiten bieten.

Schaukeln allein oder eine leere Spielwiese machen noch keinen Spielplatz. Stundenlanges Schaukeln ist nicht weniger stumpfsinnig als der Automatenrummel in einem Spielsalon. – Der Spielplatz muß, sofern es das Gelände nur irgend zuläßt, außer den Bewegungsspielen auch Konstruktions- und musische Spiele ermöglichen.

7. Die Gestaltung des Spielplatzes hat auf die Funktionen und den Bewegungsablauf der verschiedenen Spiele zu achten.

Bei der Spielplatzausrüstung ist man vielerorts noch im Stadium der spielpädagogischen »Gerümpelkammer«, der zufälligen und regellosen Aufstellung von Geräten steckengeblieben. Die »Zufalls-Möblierung« eines Spielplatzes mit allen möglichen Geräten ergibt noch keinen Spielplatz. In einer Wohnstube stellen wir ja auch die Möbel so auf, daß sie uns entsprechend ihren Funktionen am besten dienen.

Es ist die wichtigste Aufgabe des Spielplatzentwerfers, das ihm zur Verfügung stehende Areal durch eine zweckmäßige Ausstattung und Verteilung der verschiedenen Spielelemente zu einem wirklichen Spielplatz zu »gestalten«.

So darf zum Beispiel das Feld für Ballspiele nicht direkt neben dem Sandplatz liegen, damit die Kleinen nicht durch die fliegenden Bälle gefährdet werden. Oder ein Kletterbaum gehört, wenn auch auf eine Sandunterlage, so doch nicht – wie man dies leider immer wieder sieht – in den Sandplatz der Kleinen. Wie leicht springt ein größeres Kind vom Baum auf ein Sandkind herab. Auch sind auf den Plätzen, auf denen Kinder aller Altersstufen spielen, die Kleinkinder, die gerne verträumt für sich allein spielen, durch eine entsprechende gartenarchitektonische Gestaltung von den wilderen Spielen der Großen zu trennen.

8. Vergessen wir nicht die verträumten Spiele, die Spiele der Hingabe.

Der Spielplatz darf nicht nur Gruppen- und Massenspiele zulassen. Das Kind will sich auch im Spiel bisweilen auf sich zurückziehen; denken wir nur an die Mädchen mit ihren Rollen- und Puppenspielen. Spielnischen und eine entsprechende Bepflanzung schaffen die dafür notwendigen intimen »Spielstuben im Freien«. Die offenen Mammutspielplätze sind unkindlich. Es sind lärmige »Fabrikhallen des Spiels«.

9. Der Architekt, der Gartenarchitekt soll bei der Gestaltung des Platzes selbst ein wenig »spielen«.

So sind zum Beispiel Spielplätze mit natürlichen oder künstlichen Hügeln bei den Kindern beliebter als eintönige, flache Spielareale. Eine Rutschbahn braucht nicht langweilig mitten auf dem Platz zu stehen, sie kann auch an einen Hügel angelehnt werden und als Zugang zum Spielplatz dienen. Eine Sandfläche muß auch nicht immer und für ewige Zeiten eine quadratische Kiste sein, ein Sandschiff, wie es in Dänemark, Schweden und England gerne verwendet wird, ist sicher anziehender für jedes Kind.

10. Für den Bau, die Gestaltung und die Betreuung des Spielplatzes sind, wo immer es geht, die daran interessierten Bevölkerungskreise (vor allem die Eltern und Anwohner) zur Mitarbeit heranzuziehen.

Die Eltern müssen spüren, daß es sich beim Spielplatz um ihre Sache handelt. Der Spielplatz darf nicht eine neue »Abstellgelegenheit für Kinder« ergeben, er sollte im Gegenteil die ganze Familie im Spiel zusammenführen.

A. Der Kleinkinderspielplatz.

Unter einem Kleinkinderspielplatz verstehen wir einen Spielplatz für Kinder im vorschulpflichtigen Alter, also für Kinder im »Hock-, Kletter- und Märchenalter«. Auf diesen wohnungsnahen Spielplätzen in der Form von Haus-, Hof-, Siedlungs- oder Kindergartenspielplätzen werden sich meist auch Kinder der ersten Schuljahre gerne aufhalten. Die Gestaltung und Einrichtung jedes Kleinkinderspielplatzes wird sich nach der Größe und Beschaffenheit des zur Verfügung stehenden Grundstückes und nach dem betreffenden Einzugsgebiet richten. Im übrigen sind die Übergänge vom Kleinkinderspielplatz zum Spielplatz für alle Altersstufen naturgemäß fließend. Es ist Sache des Spielplatzgestalters, sich im konkreten Fall die Kinder und deren Spielbedürfnisse vorzustellen und den Platz entsprechend zu formen und auszurüsten. Allerdings wird es spielpädagogisch von Vorteil sein, wenn der wohnungsnahe Kleinkinderspielplatz jeweils so auf die typischen Kleinkinderspiele ausgerichtet und so intim gestaltet wird, daß ihn die größeren Kinder weniger interessant und anziehend finden. Selbstverständlich muß sich dann aber in nicht allzugroßer Entfernung ein Quartierspielplatz für Kinder aller Altersstufen befinden, auf dem die größeren Kinder ihre Spielwünsche befriedigen können.

Wenn wir uns klarwerden wollen, wie ein Kleinkinderspielplatz im einzelnen einzurichten ist, so haben wir davon auszugehen, wie und womit das Kleinkind in seinen verschiedenen Entwicklungsstufen bis zum Schuleintritt spielt.

Das Spiel des Kindes beginnt in seinem Bettchen. Hier fängt der Säugling eines Tages mit seinen ersten Spielbewegungen an. Er entdeckt seine Händchen und Füßchen und spielt mit ihnen. Später merkt er, daß er mit seinen Händchen greifen kann, und alles, was in seine Nähe kommt, wird zum Spielding, das betastet, ergriffen und in den Mund geführt sein will. Das Ergreifen führt zum Begreifen. Das Kind lernt sich aufrichten, es beginnt zu kriechen und zu krabbeln. Es beschäftigt sich mit allen Dingen, deren es habhaft wird. Das Laufgitter und die Spielecke werden zu seinem ersten Spielplatz, und immer mehr dehnt sich die Spiel- und Erfahrungswelt aus.

Sobald es gehen kann, unternimmt es Entdeckungsreisen durch die ganze Wohnung und alles wird untersucht und erforscht. Mit diesen Bewegungs- und Funktionsspielen übt das Kleinkind seinen Körper und seine Glieder. Es spielt in diesem Alter noch nicht mit anderen Kindern; es ist ein Individualist, sogar ein kleiner Spielegoist. Im Freien beschäftigen sich die Kleinen am liebsten für sich allein mit Sand und Wasser, klettern überall herum oder begeben sich mit ihrem Dreirad auf »große Fahrt«. In den folgenden Jahren gehen diese Bewegungsspiele allmählich über in Ball-, Reigen- und Hüpfspiele und später in die sportlichen Wettkämpfe.

Im dritten und vierten Lebensjahr beginnen die Kleinen, die jetzt ihren Körper schon gut beherrschen, Freude an allen möglichen Konstruktionsspielen zu bekommen. Bauklötze gehören zum begehrtesten Spielzeug, und die ersten Mal- und Bastelversuche werden unternommen. Im Freien entstehen Sandburgen, und aus altem Material werden die wunderlichsten Bauwerke errichtet. Besonders wertvoll wären für dieses Alter große Bauklötze, mit denen die Kinder auch im Freien, in ihrem Sandplatz, spielen könnten.

Gleichzeitig mit den Konstruktionsspielen fängt das drei- und vierjährige Kind an, alles nachzuahmen, was es um sich herum erlebt. Es sind die Jahre der Rollen- und Phantasiespiele. Nicht umsonst nennt man dieses Alter das Phantasiealter. Das Kind verwandelt sich im Spiel in Menschen, Tiere und Dinge. Es wechselt unablässig seine Rollen, es »ist« einmal Vater, Mutter, Lehrer, Rotkäppchen, Wolf und vieles andere mehr, der Stubentisch wird zum Schloß, zum Schiff, zum Auto oder zum Flugzeug. Die Mädchen spielen mit ihren Puppen alles, was sie im täglichen Zusammensein mit der Mutter erleben. In diesen Rollenspielen entwickelt und entfaltet das Kind sein Gemüts- und Seelenleben. Die Phantasiespiele helfen ihm auch – indem es die Großen nachahmt, Vater und Mutter spielt – über seine Kleinheit hinwegzukommen. Es befreit sich im Spiel von allem, was sein Herz belastet. Puppen, Bilder- und Märchenbücher, Requisiten zum Verkleiden und Theaterspielen sind begehrte Spieldinge dieses Alters, nicht zu vergessen die heißgeliebten Kasperlfiguren. In diesen Phantasiespielen nimmt die musische Beschäftigung des späteren Lebens, das Theater- und Laienspiel, das Musizieren und das künstlerische Schatten, ihren Anfang. Dafür läßt sich »spielend« das Interesse wecken.

Etwa vom sechsten Lebensjahr an treten neu in das Kinderleben die Regel- und Gemeinschaftsspiele mit gleichaltrigen Kameraden, also Reigen-, Hüpf- und Kreisspiele, Murmeln-, Fang- und Versteckspiele. Mit diesen Gruppenspielen lernt das Kind spielend sich Regeln unterzuordnen, es lernt zu gewinnen und zu verlieren und sich in eine Gemeinschaft einzufügen.

Einrichtung.

Ein Kleinkinderspielplatz sollte all die Elemente enthalten, die ein Kind im »Hock-, Klettor- und Märchenalter« für sein Spiel braucht. Die Jüngsten müßten allerdings in Wohnungsnähe spielen können. Ein Sandhaufen vor oder hinter dem Haus scheint uns wertvoller als ein noch so vielseitig eingerichteter Kleinkinderspielplatz für ein ganzes Wohnquartier, der eine Viertelstunde entfernt liegt. Wo immer der Platz es zuläßt (bei neuen Mietshäusern, Wohnkolonien und Kindergärten ist von allem Anfang an dafür zu sorgen), ist ein Kleinkinderspielplatz zu schaffen, der folgende Teile und Spielelemente aufweist: 1. Sand, 2. Wasser, 3. Hartbelag für »Straßenspiele«, 4. Spiel- und Tummelwiese, 5. Kletter- und Bewegungsgeräte, 6. Spielwände und Spielhäuschen, 7. Ausgediente Fahrzeuge und Geräte.

1. Sand:

Das Spielen mit Sand gehört zu den beliebtesten und pädagogisch wertvollsten Beschäftigungen und dient in ganz hervorragender Weise dazu, die Phantasie und die schöpferischen Kräfte des Kindes zu entfalten. Sand ist deshalb das wichtigste Element für jeden Kleinkinderspielplatz.

Am meisten verbreitet ist der »Sandkasten«. Leider meist in Miniaturausgabe, gerade recht für zwei Hunde oder Katzen, aber nicht für das Spiel mehrerer Kinder. Da die Kleinen nicht immerfort auf einem Fleck sitzen und Sandkuchen formen wollen, sondern mit besonderem Vergnügen Burgen und Tunnels bauen, Grabenlabyrinthe und Wasserkanäle anlegen, brauchen sie Platz, mehr Platz, als die üblichen Sandkisten bieten. Das heißt allerdings nicht, daß wir ins andere Extrem verfallen und Spielplätze mit einem einzigen Mammutsandkasten einrichten wollen. Sandkasten mittlerer Größe für etwa zehn bis fünfzehn Kinder scheinen uns am zweckmäßigsten zu sein. Und warum immer die langweilige quadratische Form – und warum nur Sand? Die Kinder haben so gerne Tischchen aus Baumstücken, Stein oder Beton, auf denen sie ihre Sandkuchen backen können (siehe Seite 42, 75). Der aufgeschüttete »Sandhaufen« hat gegenüber dem Sandkasten einmal den Vorteil, daß er billiger kommt. Er ist aber nur anzuraten beim kleinen Hausspielplatz, wo das Anlegen eines Sandkastens zu kostspielig wäre. Zum anderen ist der Sandhaufen für die Kinder interessanter als der oft festgetretene und zusammengebackene Sand im Sandkasten. Da wird noch viel gesündigt: ein Sandkasten muß laufend unterhalten, aufgefrischt und regelmäßig mit neuem Sand nachgefüllt werden. Die vielseitigsten Sandspiele gestattet nach unserer Erfahrung eine Kombination von Sandhaufen und Sandkasten, also ein Sandkasten, der periodisch reichlich mit Sand aufgefüllt wird.

Auf einigen schweizerischen Plätzen haben wir Versuche mit einer Sandfläche gemacht, wobei ein Teil des Spielplatzes als weites Sandareal ausgebildet wurde. Auf diese Sandfläche werden jedes Frühjahr ein paar Autoladungen Sand geschüttet, der dann von den Kindern im Lauf des Sommers »verarbeitet« wird (Beispiel siehe Seite 70–73). Wir haben dabei die Erfahrung gewonnen, daß solche Sandflächen weniger durch Hunde und Katzen verunreinigt werden als die Sandkasten mit ihren Ecken und Vertiefungen.

2. Wasser (Trinkbrunnen, Planschbecken, Planschbrunnen):

Wasser ist bei den Kleinen ebenso beliebt wie Sand. Besonders entzückt sind die Kinder, wenn sie gleichzeitig mit Wasser und Sand spielen und »dreckeln« können. Gewiß, solche Sand- und Wasserspiele gehen nicht ohne sichtbare Spuren ab und enden meist mit Tränen. Wenn doch nur die Mütter ihre Kleinen für dieses Spiel entsprechend an- oder besser ausziehen würden. Stecken wir die glücklichen Schmierfinken am Abend einfach in die Badewanne, und lassen wir sie doch nach Herzenslust toben. Jedes Kind muß gelegentlich planschen und dreckeln können. Nicht umsonst weisen die Kinderpsychologen immer wieder darauf hin, wie wichtig gerade solche Spiele für die seelische Entwicklung sind. Kinder, denen Gelegenheit geboten ist, sich auszuspielen, werden es im späteren Leben kaum nötig haben, unterdrückte Wünsche und Triebe auszuleben.

Für das Wasserspiel kommen verschiedene Möglichkeiten in Frage:

Auf Plätzen, auf denen Badegelegenheiten für die Kleinen nicht erwünscht oder unzweckmäßig sind, genügt ein kleiner Trinkbrunnen, etwa ein einfacher Zementtrog, ein ausgehöhlter Findling oder ein ausgehöhlter Baumstamm (Beispiel siehe Seite 68). Hier können die Kinder ihre Sandeimerchen mit Wasser füllen oder ihre Papierschiffchen schwimmen lassen.

Als Planschbecken sind zwei Formen am gebräuchlichsten: das überall gleich tiefe Wasserbecken mit einem Wasserstand von etwa 20 cm oder das nach außen allmählich seichter werdende Becken, in dem das Wasser »wie am Strand« in lebendiger Bewegung ist (Beispiele siehe Seite 88, 117, 136). Gelegentlich wird das Planschbecken mit Duscheinrichtungen kombiniert. Welche originellen Lösungen beim Aufstellen von Brausen und Sprühdüsen möglich sind, zeigen der Düsseldorfer Wasserspielplatz (siehe Seite 90, 91) oder der New Yorker Adventure Playground im Central Park (siehe Seite 96–99).

Auf einigen Plätzen in Zürich wurden an Stelle der Planschbecken neuartige Planschbrunnen ausprobiert (Beispiel siehe Seite 73). Ein solcher Planschbrunnen besteht aus etwa acht bunt bemalten, verschieden hohen Betonrohren von etwa 2 m Durchmesser. Das Wasser sprudelt über einen farbigen Brunnen-Turm als Springbrunnen in das höchste Becken und läuft als Wasserspiel rundherum von einem Becken zum anderen bis zum niedersten. Der Wasserstand in den einzelnen Becken beträgt etwa 10 cm, ist also selbst für die Kleinsten ohne jede Gefahr. Diese Planschbrunnen haben gegenüber den Planschbecken mehrere Vorzüge: einmal werden die Kinder durch die verschiedenen Becken in kleine Spielgruppen aufgeteilt, die ihrem Alter besser entsprechen als das lärmige Massenbad. Zwei, drei Kinder haben ihren eigenen »See«. Die verschieden hohen Becken ermöglichen zudem reizvolle Hüpfspiele von einem Becken zum anderen. Ferner ist der Planschbrunnen wegen des relativ niederen Wasserstandes und der Kleinheit der Becken für die größeren Kinder weniger interessant, so daß wirklich die Kleinen zum Baden kommen. In den weiträumigen Planschbecken dominieren stets die kräftigeren Schulkinder und verhindern oder gefährden mit ihren wilden Wasserspielen sehr oft das stillere Planschen der Kleinen. Der Planschbrunnen besitzt zudem noch den Vorteil, daß er wegen des ständigen Wasserlaufs weniger rasch verschmutzt und deshalb wöchentlich nur einmal geputzt werden muß im Gegensatz zum Planschbecken, das einer täglichen Reinigung bedarf.

Sehr bewährt hat sich auch eine Kombination von Plansch-becken und Planschbrunnen (siehe Seite 136), die aus einem größeren Planschbecken besteht, in dessen einer Ecke ein Planschbrunnen mit fünf Wasserbecken eingebaut ist. Auf diese Weise ist es möglich, die ganze Planschanlage für die Klein- und Schulkinder zusammenzufassen, ohne daß die Kleinsten in den Brunnenbecken gestört oder gefährdet wären. Auch kann bei kühlerem Wetter das Becken leer gelassen und nur der Planschbrunnen mit Wasser gefüllt werden.

3. Hartbelag für »Straßenspiele«:

Unsere Stadtkinder sind nun einmal »Asphaltkinder«, die kaum mehr Rasenspiele, sondern nur noch Straßenspiele kennen. Ein reiner Rasenspielplatz vermag die Kinder nicht von der Straße wegzuziehen, da sie auf dem Rasen die ihnen geläufigen Alltagsspiele wie Hüpfen, Murmeln, Reifeln, Ball-spiele, Dreirad- und Rollerfahren nicht betreiben können. Ein Kleinkinderspielplatz ohne Hartfläche und Hartbelagsplatz, straßen und Plattenwege, die als Straßenersatz dienen, ist ungenügend. Der Hartbelag muß von Spielgeräten freigehalten werden, um die Bewegungsspiele nicht zu behindern. Die Geräte gehören ebenso wie die Spielwände an den Rand.

4. Spiel- und Tummelwiese:

Je nach den Platzverhältnissen sollte außer dem Hartbelag auch eine kleinere oder größere Spiel- und Tummelwiese für die verschiedensten Rasen- und Tummel-, Reigen-, Kreis- und Ballspiele vorgesehen werden.

5. Kletter- und Bewegungsgeräte:

Für das elementare Bewegungs- und Mutspiel der Kleinen wie Klettern, Kriechen, Hüpfen, Balancieren, Schaukeln sind auf weichem Rasenboden oder auf einer Sandunterlage entsprechende Spielgeräte aufzustellen. Gegenüber mechanischen Geräten wie Karussells ist größte Zurückhaltung am Platz. Die einzelnen Geräte sollten die Kinder nicht nur unterhalten, sondern zu aktivem Spielen anregen. Auch sind nur Geräte bester Qualität zu wählen. Solide Geräte vermeiden Unfälle und sparen auf die Dauer Geld. Als Spielgeräte kommen unter anderem in Frage:

Kletterturm (Schwedenturm, Altraturm) und Kletterbaum.

Ein Kletterbaum, mit großen starken Ästen, umgelegt oder aufrecht stehend eingegraben (Beispiele siehe Seite 72, 163), ist für die Kleinen meist anziehender als ein Kletterturm aus Stahlrohr. Doch hat auch ein Stahlrohrturm, besonders wenn er kindgemäß bemalt ist, durchaus seine Reize. Gegenüber dem Schwedenturm (Beispiel siehe Seite 92) mit seinen sich rechtwinklig durchkreuzenden Stäben hat der in der Schweiz entwickelte runde und überdachte Altraturm (Beispiele siehe Seite 69, 73) den Vorzug größerer Vielfalt an Spielmöglichkeiten (Klettern, Schwingen, Rutschen).

Auch »Kletterbögen«, »Kletternetze«, »Balancierstangen« und »Kinderrecks« sollten mehr verwendet werden. Im letzten Abschnitt dieses Buches sind eine Reihe guter Kletter- und Bewegungsgeräte zusammengestellt, unter denen die Ulmer Sandflohgeräte (siehe Seite 174–175) und verschiedene ame-rikanische Stahlrohr- und Betonelemente für Kletter- und Hüpfspiele (siehe Seite 168–169, 173) besondere Erwähnung verdienen. In Amerika wurden auch sehr vielseitig verwendbare »Spielplastiken« entwickelt (Beispiele siehe Seite 170–171), die zugleich als Klettertürme, Rutschbahnen, Kriechröhren und Hangelgeräte dienen.

Kriech- und Kletterröhren.

Daß die Kleinen sich besonders gern in jedem Hohlraum verkriechen, wissen alle Eltern. Wie oft verschwinden unsere Jüngsten unter irgendeinem Tisch. Es zeigt sich darin der Wunsch, ein ihrer Körpergröße angepaßtes Haus, ein eigenes Heim zu besitzen, das sie körperlich und seelisch zu erfassen und auszufüllen vermögen. Dazu kommt beim Erforschen von Höhlen und Röhren das Geheimnisvolle, Dunkle, das die Kinder lockt. Diesem elementaren Spielbedürfnis können wir durch Aufstellen von Kriechröhren, ausgehöhlten Baumstämmen, alten Fässern und ähnlichen Behältnissen entsprechen. Auch Betonschalen und sattelförmige Elemente, wie sie in Amerika serienmäßig hergestellt oder in geliehenen Formen am Platz selbst gegossen werden (Beispiele siehe Seite 168), sind sehr geeignet.

Die Kriechröhren sind entweder ganz dicht aneinander anzu-schließen oder mit so großem Abstand zwischen den einzelnen Röhren zu placieren, daß die Kleinen bei ihren Kletterversuchen nicht die Füße einklemmen. Auch bei der Bemalung der Röhren wird viel gesündigt. Die Röhre ist für die kindliche Phantasie ein Ganzes, ein Tier – etwa ein Tatzelwurm, ein Elefant – oder ein Haus, eine Höhle, eine Eisenbahn. Daran müssen wir beim Bemalen denken! Es ist falsch, auf die Kriechröhren einen Hund, eine Blume oder eine Eisenbahn als einzelne Bildchen aufzumalen.

Seil- und Balkenschaukeln.

Die Seil- und Balkenschaukeln sind abseits von den Flächen für Bewegungsspiele und vom Sandplatz aufzustellen, um Unfälle zu vermeiden. Am besten werden die Schaukeln in abgetrennte Spielnischen placiert, die durch Büsche geschützt sind. Stets sollten mehrere Schaukeln Verwendung finden, um das Schlangestehen, Drängeln und Streiten zu vermeiden und den Kindern das spannende Wettschaukeln zu ermöglichen. An Stelle von fünf oder mehr Seilschaukeln können auch zwei oder drei durch ein Trapez, durch Ringe oder einen Schaukelsitz aus einem alten Autoreifen ersetzt werden (Beispiele siehe Seite 55, 175). Solche kombinierten Geräte gestatten ein vielseitigeres und lebendigeres Spiel und verhindern das stumpfsinnige stundenlange Schaukeln. Vor allem scheinen uns die sogenannten Wikingerschaukeln keine sehr glücklichen Spielgeräte darzustellen, weil sie leicht dazu verführen, daß sich eine ganze Anzahl Kinder von einem einzelnen schaukeln läßt, eine nicht gerade sehr aktive und schöpferische Tätigkeit.

Rutschbahn.

Zwei Probleme sind beim Aufstellen einer Rutschbahn zu bedenken: erstens die Schwierigkeit, ein befriedigendes Material für die Rutschfläche zu finden und zweitens die Standort-frage. Nehmen wir die Rutschbahn doch heraus aus der Platzmitte, wo sie wie zufällig und verloren steht, lehnen wir sie besser an einen Hügel. Das macht den Kindern nicht nur mehr Spaß, es ist auch ungefährlicher, weil dadurch der Aufstieg über die Leiter wegfällt (Beispiele siehe Seite 72, 164).

Hüpfsockel und Hüpfhocker.

Baumstrünke, hohe und niedere Betonsockel oder ähnliche Elemente ermöglichen vielseitige Hüpf- und Mutspiele wie das Bockspringen. Zugleich geben sie Sitzgelegenheiten für die Kinder oder Sand- und Spieltische ab (Beispiele siehe Seite 47, 64, 75).

6. Spielwände und Spielhäuschen.

Für die Rollenspiele der Buben und Mädchen (Vater und Mutter, Verkaufen, Theater, Kasperltheater) muß auf jedem Spielplatz Raum und Gelegenheit vorhanden sein. Daher sind, abseits von den Spielflächen und Geräten für die lauten Bewegungsspiele, intime Spielnischen vorzusehen mit Spielwänden und Spielhäuschen, damit das verträumte und nicht nur das bewegte Spiel zu seinem Recht kommt (Beispiele von dänischen, deutschen oder schweizerischen Spielplätzen siehe Seite 58–59, 104–105, 158–159).

Spielwände aus Holz oder Beton mit runden und quadratischen Durchbrüchen und eingesetzten Eternit- oder Schieferplatten sind äußerst vielseitige Spielgeräte. So dienen sie den Mädchen für ihre Wandballspiele. Auch werden sie verwendet für Verstecken, Fangen und zum Durchkriechen. Ganz besonders aber müssen sie herhalten als Theaterkulissen, als Kasperlbühne und als Mal- und Zeichenwände (Beispiele siehe Seite 147, 165).

Auf Plätzen ohne Spielplatzleitung haben sich offene Holzhäuschen in Zelthüttenform mit zwei Kinderbänken an den Längswänden gut bewährt (Beispiele siehe Seite 159–160), in die sich vor allem die Mädchen zu Rollen- und Puppenspielen gerne zurückziehen.

Auf Spielplätzen mit ständigem Spielplatzleiter können ganze Dörfchen aus mehreren verschließbaren Spielhäuschen angelegt werden. Diese Idee, die aus Skandinavien kommt (Beispiel siehe Seite 159), läßt sich in der Weise variieren, daß neben den Wohnhäuschen (ausgestattet mit einem Kindergartentisch und -stühlen, alles andere wie Puppengeschirr wird von den Kindern mitgebracht) einzelne Häuschen als Kaufläden eingerichtet werden, in denen Schaufensterattrappen zu kaufen sind (Beispiel siehe Seite 136).

7. Ausgediente Fahrzeuge.

Ein ausgedientes, richtiges Auto, ein alter Tramwagen oder ein Schiff gehören zu den abenteuerlichsten Spielgeräten der Kinder. Solche Geräte ziehen die Kinder, die in der heutigen technischen Welt aufwachsen, am ehesten von der interessanten Straße weg. Die einzelnen Fahrzeuge müssen jedoch entsprechend hergerichtet werden, sonst ergeben sich gefährliche Unfallquellen und dienen den größeren Kindern, die über das Phantasiealter hinausgewachsen sind, lediglich als Demolierobjekte. Ein ausgedientes Auto zum Beispiel ist bunt zu bemalen, mit Holzsitzen zu versehen und das Dach ist zu verstärken; Motorhaube und Türen sind auf der einen Seite zu blockieren und auf der anderen Seite zu entfernen. Am besten geeignet scheint ein Jeep oder ein Lastauto zu sein. Ganz allgemein ist beim Aufstellen ausgedienter Fahrzeuge einige Vorsicht angezeigt. Auf typischen Kleinkinderspielplätzen genügt meistens ein improvisiertes Fahrzeug, etwa ein Flugzeug aus Baumstämmen (Beispiel siehe Seite 72).

Gestaltung.

Das planlose Aufstellen von Spielgeräten ermöglicht wohl einzelne Spiele, ergibt aber noch keinen spielpädagogisch guten Spielplatz. Erst eine vom Kinderspiel her bedingte, sinnvolle Gruppierung der einzelnen Spielgeräte und die richtige Verteilung der verschiedenen Spielflächen ermöglicht den Kindern die ihrem Alter entsprechenden Spiele und weckt in ihnen schöpferische Spielaktivität und Freude am Entdecken, Erforschen und Gestalten.
Ganz besonders reizvoll wird ein Kleinkinderspielplatz dann, wenn er als Ganzes, als Komposition, eine bestimmte »Spieldramatik« besitzt. Was darunter zu verstehen ist – das Schaffen eines Beziehungsspiels zwischen den verschiedenen Platzelementen, das Herausarbeiten einer bestimmten Folge in der Aufstellung der Geräte, das Ausnutzen der Möglichkeiten, die das Gelände bietet – das sei ersichtlich am Beispiel des Kleinkinderspielplatzes in Zürich-Heiligfeld (siehe Seite 70–73) oder des Verkehrsspielplatzes in Zürich-Bucheggg (siehe Seite 108).
Einige weitere Hinweise vermögen vielleicht zukünftige Spielplatzgestalter anzuregen, eigene »spielerische« Schöpfungen und Lösungen zu suchen: Ein modelliertes Gelände ist reizvoller als ein ebener Spielplatz. Hügel, Spielnischen und Mulden ergeben erst ein vielseitiges und lebendiges Spiel. Reiche Möglichkeiten bietet vor allem ein Hügel – man kann eine Rutschbahn anlehnen, ihn mit Kriechröhren untertunneln, auf der Kuppe Spielhäuschen aufstellen oder in die Böschung Sitzstufen einlegen für ein Amphitheater und was sonst noch alles (Beispiele siehe Seite 162–163).
Spielwände mit Durchbrüchen und eingelegten Schiefer- oder Eternitplatten sind außerordentlich vielseitige Spielelemente: zum Zeichnen und Malen, als Theaterkulissen und Kasperltheater, für Kletter- und Tummelspiele; auch ergeben sie ideale Abgrenzungen für die verschiedenen Spielflächen.
Farben spielen im Leben der Kinder eine wichtige Rolle. Die Bemalung der Schaukeln, Kriechröhren, Planschbrunnen sollte deshalb bunt und fröhlich, aber nicht kindisch sein.
Der Sandplatz ist immer geschützt und abseits von den turbulenten Bewegungs- und Ballspielen anzulegen. Er sollte ferner nicht allzusehr im Schatten (rasches Trocknen nach dem Regen, Desinfektion des Sandes), aber auch nicht in der prallen Sonne (Sonnenstichgefahr für die Kleinen) liegen. Beim Sandplatz sind jeweils genügend schattige Ruhebänke für die Mütter zu errichten. Überhaupt gehören auf die Kleinkinderspielplätze ausreichend Bänke, da die Mütter ihre Jüngsten beim Spiel beaufsichtigen wollen.
Das gleiche gilt für die Toiletten: diese Frage wird, zum Teil aus Vergeßlichkeit, zum Teil aus finanziellen Erwägungen,

vielfach vernachlässigt; und dabei steht und fällt die Sauberkeit eines Spielplatzes mit einer zweckmäßigen Lösung dieses Problems.
Im übrigen haben wir bewußt darauf verzichtet, technische Einzelheiten anzugeben, etwa über die Größe und Beschaffenheit von Sandflächen und Spielwiesen, über die Konstruktion von Schaukeln oder über etwaige Idealgrößen für die Spielplätze. Wir möchten das den bereits vorhandenen gartenarchitektonischen Publikationen überlassen. Außerdem steht dem Spielplatzgestalter meist kein Idealgelände zur Verfügung, sondern ein zufälliges Areal, aus dem er nur in immer neuen Überlegungen das Bestmögliche herausholen kann.

B. Der Spielplatz für alle Altersstufen.

Unter einem Spielplatz für alle Altersstufen verstehen wir, wie schon gesagt, ein größeres Spielgelände beim Schulhaus, in einer Sportanlage oder einem Freibad, bei einem Jugend- und Freizeithaus oder in einer Grünanlage. Es dient vor allem dem aktiven und schöpferischen Spiel der Schulkinder und Jugendlichen, muß aber auch Spielelemente für die Kleinkinder enthalten.
Bei der Einrichtung eines solchen Platzes haben wir wieder von den verschiedenen Spielbedürfnissen der betreffenden Altersstufen auszugehen. Die Kinder im Schulalter und die Jugendlichen betreiben wie die Kleinkinder mit besonderer Freude alle möglichen Bewegungs- und Ballspiele, nur sind ihre Spiele wilder und benötigen mehr Raum. Auch sind die Buben und Mädchen in diesem Alter schon richtige Sportler. Es sind die Jahre der Wett- und Gruppenspiele.
Die früheren Rollen- und Phantasiespiele gehen im Schulalter über in das Theater- und Laienspiel, in das Musizieren und Tanzen. Einen besonderen Höhepunkt erreichen jetzt die Konstruktionsspiele: der Sandplatz muß abgelöst werden durch den Bauplatz und die Bastelwerkstatt, wo sich das abenteuerliche und handwerkliche Spiel der Kinder im »Robinsonalter« und das schöpferische Freizeitschaffen der Jugendlichen ausleben kann.
Wie ist es nun aber mit den Spielplätzen für diese Altersstufen bestellt? Es sind meistens leere Spielfelder, die einzig Ball- und Tummelspiele zulassen. Auf diesen langweiligen Plätzen kann sich all das, was in den Jugendlichen an gesunden Kräften, an frischen Sinnen für das Elementare und Abenteuerliche und an echter Begeisterung für das Handwerkliche und Schöpferische lebendig ist, nicht freisetzen, es bleibt verdrängt, um später einmal bei den Halberwachsenen und Erwachsenen etwa als gefährlicher Rowdytum zum Vorschein zu kommen. Wir haben bis heute bei der Ausgestaltung von Spielplatzanlagen für größere Kinder und Jugendliche allzusehr nur die körperliche und sportliche Betätigung berücksichtigt und all die schöpferischen, handwerklichen und musischen Spiele vergessen, nach denen gerade das gesunde Schulkind und der Jugendliche hungern.
Eine Spielwiese ist organisatorisch allerdings bequemer als ein Spielplatz, der den Schulkindern und Jugendlichen die verschiedensten Freizeitbeschäftigungen bis zum Bauen und Basteln ermöglicht. Ein solcher Platz muß anders eingerichtet

sein und erfordert zudem im Gegensatz zum Kleinkinderspielplatz eine vollamtliche pädagogische Leitung und Betreuung.

Einrichtung.

Wenn es die Platzverhältnisse zulassen, so sollte ein Quartierspielplatz für alle Altersstufen aus folgenden Teilen und Spielelementen bestehen:
1. Bau- und Werkplatz mit Freizeit- und Bastelwerkstätten für das handwerkliche und abenteuerliche Spiel.
2. Freilichttheater mit Spiel- und Gemeinschaftsbau für das musische Spiel.
3. Hartbelag für Straßen- und Ballspiele.
4. Spielfeld für das körperliche und sportliche Spiel.
5. Kleinkinderspielplatz.

1. Bau- und Werkplatz mit Bastelwerkstätten.
Der wichtigste Teil des Spielplatzes für alle Altersstufen ist ein Stück Wiese, wenn möglich mit Büschen und Bäumen, der wilde Bau- und Werkplatz, auf dem die Buben und Mädchen mit Werkzeug und altem Baumaterial nach ihrer Phantasie Hütten und Häuser bauen oder auf irgendwelche Abenteuer und Entdeckungsreisen ausgehen können. Am Rand des Bauplatzes sind Werktische aufgestellt (Freizeitwerkstatt im Freien), an denen alles mögliche geschnitzt, modelliert und gebastelt werden kann.
Für die handwerkliche Beschäftigung der Kinder, Jugendlichen und wenn möglich auch der Erwachsenen an Schlechtwettertagen im Sommer und in den Wintermonaten, sollte ein Werkstattbau mit mindestens zwei Werkstatträumen vorhanden sein. Der eine Werkraum mit Hobelbänken dient den »lauten« Basteltechniken wie Holz- und Metallarbeiten oder Schnitzen, der andere mit Werktischen den »stilleren« Tätigkeiten wie Modellieren, Stoffdrucken oder Linolschneiden. Je nach den Bedürfnissen und finanziellen Möglichkeiten wird man diese Werkstätten in der Form eines soliden Stein- oder eines einfachen Barackenbaues erstellen. Unter Umständen kann man sich auch damit helfen, daß ein ausgedienter Eisenbahn- oder Tramwagen als Werkstatt eingerichtet wird. Bei Spielplätzen auf einem Schulgelände wird man die Werkräume des Schulhauses in den Spielplatzbetrieb mit einbeziehen können. Sie werden je nach den Gegebenheiten tagsüber von den bastelfreudigen Kindern, an den Abenden teils von den Jugendlichen (Quartier-Jugendhaus), teils von den Erwachsenen (Bastelkurse für Eltern, für Pensionierte und so weiter) benützt.

2. Freilichttheater mit Spiel- und Gemeinschaftsbau.
Das Freilichttheater gehört zu den wichtigsten Bestandteilen eines Spielplatzes für alle Altersstufen. Durch eine entsprechende Gestaltung, etwa das Anlegen von Sitzstufen an eine Böschung und das Aufstellen von Spielwänden als Kulissen läßt sich eine Theateratmosphäre schaffen, welche die Kinder und Jugendlichen reizt, je nach Bedarf selbst eine Bühne oder ein Kasperltheater zu bauen. Die Bühne sollte nicht vom Spielplatzgestalter fix und fertig geliefert werden, wie ja überhaupt auf dem Spielplatz für alle Altersstufen möglichst vieles

an der Einrichtung der Bauten und am Innenausbau der Werkstätten und Gemeinschaftsräume von den Kindern und Jugendlichen selbst übernommen wird.

Der Theaterplatz, der unter Umständen mit der Hartbelagfläche kombiniert werden kann wie auf dem Spielplatz Zürich-Bucheegg (siehe Seite 146), dient dem musischen Spiel der Kinder, dem Kasperl- und Laienspiel, dem Musizieren und Tanzen, den Reigen- und Gesellschaftsspielen.

Dazu gehören, wenn immer möglich, ein oder mehrere Spiel- und Gemeinschaftsräume, welche den Kindern, Jugendlichen und je nach Bedarf auch den Erwachsenen an Schlechtwettertagen im Sommer und in den Wintermonaten tagsüber und in den Abendstunden Gelegenheit geben für Gesellschaftsspiele, Tanz- und Theaterveranstaltungen, Gruppenabende und Filmvorführungen. In einem dieser Räume sollte eine Bibliothek mit Lesestube eingerichtet werden, wo die Kinder und Jugendlichen nicht nur guten Lesestoff für den Spielplatz (ein Gegenmittel gegen das Schundlesen) holen, sondern auch nach Hause ausleihen können. Diese Bibliotheken werden am besten von der gleichen Institution betrieben, die in der betreffenden Stadt die öffentlichen Jugendbibliotheken betreut. Selbstverständlich sollen auch hier die Kinder und Jugendlichen zur Mitverwaltung der Bibliothek herangezogen werden. Die Bastelwerkstätten und der Gemeinschaftsbau zusammen bilden gleichsam ein Quartier- oder Bezirks-Freizeit- und Jugendhaus.

3. Hartbelag für Straßen- und Ballspiele.

Eine Hartbelagfläche sowie Plattenwege und »Spielstraßen« gehören wie zu jedem Kleinkinderspielplatz so auch zum Spielplatz für alle Altersstufen. Hier lassen sich alle Spiele betreiben, die sich sonst auf der Straße abspielen wie Rollerfahren, Rollschuh- und Stelzenlaufen, Hüpf-, Murmel-, Kreis- und Ballspiele (Völkerball, Tischtennis, Boccia, Federball). In regenreichen Gebieten, in denen der Rasen ständig naß und unbenutzbar ist, sind Hartbelagflächen besonders wichtig. Im Winter kann der Hartbelag in ein Eisfeld zum Schlittschuhlaufen umgewandelt werden.

4. Spielfeld.

Auf dem Spielfeld werden die verschiedensten Ballspiele wie Fußball, Handball, Korbball und alle übrigen Rasen- und Tummelspiele ausgeübt. Es soll kein nach olympischen Maßen und Regeln dimensioniertes großes Fußballfeld sein zur Austragung richtiger Fußballkämpfe, sondern eine Wiese mit Bäumen und Büschen, so daß kleine Spielfelder entstehen, auf denen verschiedene Gruppen gleichzeitig Sport treiben können.

5. Kleinkinderspielplatz.

Die größeren Kinder müssen ihre kleinen Geschwister auf den Spielplatz mitnehmen können. Daher muß ein besonderes Spielareal, ein richtiger Kleinkinderspielplatz vorhanden sein, damit die Kleinen ihrem Alter entsprechend spielen können und nicht die Großen beim Bauen oder bei ihrem musischen und sportlichen Spiel stören. Dieses getrennte Mitspielen läßt die Kleinen schrittweise in das schöpferische Spiel der Größeren hineinwachsen. So ergibt sich im entsprechenden Alter

ein ungezwungenes und ideales Hinüberwechseln von den Kleinkinder- zu den Buben- und Mädchenspielen. Gestaltung und Ausrüstung des Kleinkinderspielplatzes sind mit den im Abschnitt A beschriebenen Grundsätzen und Elementen identisch.

Im Gegensatz zum typischen Kleinkinderspielplatz, für den wir eher improvisierte Phantasiefahrzeuge, etwa ein Flugzeug aus Baumstämmen, empfehlen, gehört auf den Spielplatz für alle Altersstufen ein richtiges Auto, ein richtiges Flugzeug oder ein richtiger Tramwagen. Die größeren Kinder, vor allem die Buben, sind vor allem Technischem fasziniert; sie sollen deshalb ein solches Fahrzeug näher erforschen und daran herummanipulieren können. Gewiß, diese Fahrzeuge werden vielleicht demoliert oder zerstört. Aber ist dieses Zerstören wirklich immer ein Zerstören, ist es nicht meist ein Eindringenwollen in das Innere, ein Erforschen des Mechanismus, ein genaues Kennenlernenwollen des Ganzen, so wie wir früher eine Uhr, ein Fahrrad oder das Radio in ihre Bestandteile zerlegt haben? Zudem kann dieser Trieb zum Auseinandernehmen auf dem nahen Bauspielplatz leicht in eine aufbauende konstruktive Tätigkeit überführt werden. Unsere Erfahrungen mit solchen Fahrzeugen haben gezeigt, daß mutwillige Zerstörungen und Mißbräuche in der allermeisten Fällen nachts geschahen und auf das Konto von Erwachsenen oder Halberwachsenen gehen, ein soziales und psychologisches Problem, das wohl nie ganz gelöst werden kann. Mißbräuche dürfen uns aber nicht dazu verleiten, die Spielplätze so brav und langweilig wie möglich zu gestalten, nur damit nie etwas Unangenehmes geschieht. Jede Erziehungsaufgabe – und dazu gehören auch die Spielplätze – muß Positives und Negatives in Kauf nehmen und sich damit auseinandersetzen.

Die ausgedienten Fahrzeuge dienen auch als »Brücken«-Geräte. Ähnlich wie gewisse spannende Bücher als sogenannte Brückenliteratur die Jugendlichen vom Schund weg zum guten Buch führen, genau so dienen die aufgestellten Vehikel dazu, die heute vorwiegend technisch interessierte Jugend von der Straße weg zu schöpferischen Spielen hinzulenken.

Gestaltung und Organisation.

Wir sind uns bewußt, daß der oben geschilderte Spielplatz für alle Altersstufen in seiner Vielgestaltigkeit eine Idealform darstellt. Wir glauben aber, daß man bei den Spielplätzen für die Größeren in Zukunft immer mehr von den einstigen Tummelplätzen abkommen muß, auf denen nur Bewegungsspiele möglich sind. Es steht uns Erwachsenen nicht an, uns über die Passivität, die Interesselosigkeit, die Vergnügungssucht, den Hang zum Schausport und zum Spielsalon, das Rowdytum so mancher junger Leute zu beklagen, solange für die größeren Kinder und Jugendlichen nicht genügend Plätze vorhanden sind, auf denen sie schöpferisch spielen und ihre Freizeit aktiv gestalten können. Wie beim Kleinkinderspielplatz so ist es auch beim Spielplatz für alle Altersstufen Sache des Gestalters, durch eine geschickte Anordnung der verschiedenen Teile eine Einheit zu schaffen, damit die verschiedenen Spiele und Beschäftigungen ineinander überfließen, ohne sich gegenseitig zu stören. – Der Spielplatz für alle Altersstufen

braucht ein Gelände von mindestens 10000 qm, wobei ein modelliertes Terrain mit Hügeln, Büschen und Bäumen interessanter ist als ein völlig ebenes Areal.

Ein solcher Spielplatz ist von den Behörden (Bauamt, Gartenbauamt, Stadtgärtnerei usw.) in enger Zusammenarbeit mit privaten Körperschaften zu planen, einzurichten und zu betreuen. Die Behörde (Stadt, Gemeinde) stellt das notwendige Gelände zur Verfügung, sorgt für die entsprechenden baulichen Arbeiten wie Planierung, Einfriedung, sanitäre Anlagen, erstellt die Bauten (Bastelwerkstätten und Gemeinschaftsräume) und gewährt wenn möglich der privaten Körperschaft einen jährlichen finanziellen Beitrag zum Spielplatzbetrieb (für die Besoldung des Spielplatzleiters usw.).

Der private Träger, der »Kreis der Spielplatzfreunde«, die Spielplatzkommission oder eine ähnliche Körperschaft, bestehend aus den am betreffenden Spielplatz interessierten Persönlichkeiten und Institutionen (Vertreter von Behörden, Quartiervereinen, Jugendgruppen, ferner Anwohner, Eltern, Lehrer, Kindergärtnerinnen) übernimmt die Planung und Betreuung des Spielplatzes, bemüht sich bei ortsansässigen Firmen um Naturalspenden wie Werkzeug, Sand, Baumaterial, sowie Geldspenden zur Anschaffung von Spielgeräten und unterstützt den Spielplatzleiter, der ihr unterstellt ist.

Ein solcher Spielplatz braucht, besonders für den Bau- und Werkplatz und für die Bastelwerkstätten, unter allen Umständen einen Spielplatzleiter oder eine Spielplatzleiterin. Der Spielplatzleiter muß eine pädagogisch begabte Persönlichkeit sein und nicht einfach ein Aufseher. Er muß die Kinder anzuregen verstehen, ohne sie zu sehr zu bemuttern. Er darf nicht zu viele Spiele organisieren und die Kinder unterhalten wollen, sondern muß in ihnen, ohne daß sie es spüren, die eigene schöpferische Spielaktivität wecken.

Als Spielplatzleiter kommen in Frage: Lehramtskandidaten, Seminaristen, Seminaristinnen, Kindergärtnerinnen, Jugendleiter, Schüler und Schülerinnen von sozialen Schulen und Kunstgewerbeschulen, Handwerker, die Freude an der Jugend haben. Letzten Endes ist jedoch nicht eine bestimmte Fachausbildung, sondern die menschliche Eignung entscheidend. Ein Spielplatzleiter allein genügt auf die Dauer meistens nicht. Er muß ergänzt werden durch Praktikantinnen und Praktikanten. Hier ergeben sich wertvolle neue Praktikumsmöglichkeiten für angehende und ausgebildete Kindergärtnerinnen, Hortnerinnen, für Schülerinnen und Schüler von Sozialschulen und Lehrerseminaren und so weiter.

Aber auch die Eltern und vor allem die Kinder selbst sind vom Spielplatzleiter soweit wie irgend möglich am Spielplatzleben aktiv zu interessieren und zur Mitarbeit heranzuziehen. So stellen sich zum Beispiel auf den Zürcher Robinson-Spielplätzen immer wieder Väter und Mütter freiwillig zur Verfügung, um bestimmte Kindergruppen zu betreuen, mit ihnen zu basteln, zu modellieren, zu singen usw.

Um den Eltern, vor allem den Müttern, den Besuch des Spielplatzes möglichst anziehend zu machen, sind Liegestühle, die beim Leiter kostenlos entliehen und irgendwo auf dem Platz aufgestellt werden können, sehr willkommen. Überhaupt sollte jeder Spielplatz genügend bequeme Sitzgelegenheiten für die Erwachsenen bieten.

Auch die Kinder und Jugendlichen sollen auf ihrem Platz ihr Spielreich weitgehend selbst auf- und ausbauen. Der Spielplatz für alle Altersstufen wird deshalb nie ganz fertig sein, und er wird jedes Jahr anders aussehen. Bestimmte Teile, vor allem der Bau- und Werkplatz, sind für unsere Erwachsenenaugen nicht besonders schön – aber ist unser ästhetisches Empfinden unbedingt der rechte Maßstab für die Beurteilung eines Spielplatzes?

Im übrigen soll der Spielplatz den Kindern und Jugendlichen nicht nur Spielmöglichkeiten bieten, sondern mithelfen, die jungen Menschen »im Spiel« zu einer Gemeinschaft und zu gegenseitigem Verständnis zu erziehen. So bilden zum Beispiel die Kinder jedes schweizerischen »Robinson«-Spielplatzes ein eigenes Parlament, den »Robinsonrat«, gleichsam der Gemeinde- und Stadtrat des Spielplatzes. Der Robinsonrat hält regelmäßig Parlamentssitzungen ab, bei denen mit Assistenz des Spielplatzleiters alle wichtigen Fragen des Spielplatzlebens wie Materialbeschaffung, Öffnungszeiten, Ordnung, Gemeinschaftsaufgaben, Streitigkeiten in demokratischer Diskussion beraten werden. Es ist auch weitgehend Sache der Kinder, für den Nachschub von Baumaterial besorgt zu sein, indem sie auf anständige Art bei Baufirmen vorsprechen und sich für die Spenden mit Zeichnungen, Theateraufführungen usw. bedanken. So ist jeder dieser Spielplätze eine »Demokratie im Kleinen«, in der die Kinder spielerisch zu aktiven, verantwortungsbewußten Staatsbürgern heranwachsen.

Der Robinson-Spielplatz.

In einer ganzen Reihe von Ländern zeigen sich bereits erfreuliche Lösungen des Spielplatzes für alle Altersstufen. Da ist der Bauspielplatz, der »Skrammellegeplads« in Kopenhagen (siehe Seite 110–113), der Indianerspielplatz in Mannheim (siehe Seite 116–119) und andere gute deutsche Plätze, die amerikanischen Adventure Playgrounds (siehe Seite 96–99), und da sind die schweizerischen Robinson-Spielplätze. Der Robinson-Spielplatz in Zürich-Wipkingen (siehe Seite 130–139) ist das erste und heute noch typische Beispiel dafür.

Die Robinson-Spielplätze sind als Idee aus dem dänischen »Skrammellegeplads« und den »Trümmerspielplätzen« der Nachkriegszeit herausgewachsen.

Diese Trümmerspielplätze erlebte ich 1946 während meiner Kinderhilfsaufgabe im Ruhrgebiet. Noch gut erinnere ich an die quälenden Fragen, als ich zum erstenmal durch die Ruinenstädte pilgerte: Hat in den Trümmern, Kellerwohnungen und Erdlöchern das Leben der Menschen noch einen Sinn?

Kinder gaben mir Antwort: jene »Trümmerkinder«, die barfuß und in zerlumpten Kleidern, aber vergnügt, auf den für Erwachsenenaugen und -herzen so trostlosen Schutthügeln herumkletterten und voller Seligkeit mit Trümmersteinen spielten: »Gerümpelspielplätze« im wahrsten Sinn des Wortes. Gewiß, wir wollen über der Romantik nicht die Kehrseite solcher »Gerümpelspielplätze« verschweigen: Schmutz und Unrat, Verletzungs- und Krankheitsgefahr. Auch die materielle und seelische Not dieser Nachkriegsjugend wollen wir nicht

bagatellisieren. Eines aber hatten diese Kinder, wenn auch unbeabsichtigt und aus tragischen Gründen: Spielplätze voller Wagnisse und Abenteuer.

Solche Trümmerspielplätze hatte der dänische Gartenarchitekt C. Th. Sörensen 1943 in Kopenhagen künstlich angelegt, nachdem er bei seinen Gängen durch die Stadt immer wieder beobachtet hatte, wie das Hantieren mit Brettern und Altmaterial auf den Baustellen die Kinder mehr fesselte als die fertigen Geräte seiner schönen Spielplätze. Auf Grund dieser Erfahrung setzte er sich in Kopenhagen für die Schaffung eines ersten »Skrammellegeplads« ein (siehe Seite 110–113).

Dieser erste dänische Bauspielplatz wurde später in verschiedenen Ländern in der Form von Bauspielplätzen und Adventure Playgrounds usw. nachgeahmt. Auch beim Robinson-Spielplatz hat der »Skrammellegeplads« Pate gestanden, allerdings bringt die schweizerische Lösung eine entscheidende Weiterentwicklung und Ausweitung. Nach unserer Auffassung ist nämlich der Bauspielplatz für sich allein ebenso einseitig wie ein Sportfeld. Er ermöglicht zwar all die wertvollen Bau- und Konstruktionsspiele, vernachlässigt aber das ganze musische Freizeitschaffen (Theaterspielen, Musizieren, Basteln) sowie die im Jugendalter so notwendigen körperlichen und sportlichen Wett- und Gruppenspiele.

Der Robinson-Spielplatz, benannt nach dem Bubenhelden Robinson Crusoe, umfaßt deshalb außer dem Bauplatz alle übrigen Elemente eines Spielplatzes für alle Altersstufen. Der Robinson-Spielplatz ist nicht – wie das leider oft in Publikationen fälschlicherweise behauptet wird – einfach ein Bauspielplatz oder eine Ansammlung alter Fahrzeuge. Er ist ein kombinierter Spielplatz, der den Kindern und Jugendlichen aller Altersstufen die vielseitigsten schöpferischen Spiele und Beschäftigungen ermöglicht.

Ein paar Sätze aus einer Nummer des »Robinson-Blattes«, der Spielplatzzeitung eines Zürcher Platzes, die von den Kindern weitgehend selbst redigiert wird, können einen kleinen Einblick in das Wesen der schweizerischen Robinsonplätze geben: »In Zürich-Wipkingen gibt es wieder etwas, was kaum in anderen Städten zu finden ist: ein Quartierzentrum, ein Gemeinschaftszentrum, ähnlich der alten Dorflinde, die heute leider auch in ländlichen Gegenden nur mehr in der Erinnerung besteht. Wir denken dabei an eine Reihe unscheinbarer Begebenheiten, wie das Eiertütschen am Osterfest, die Lagerfeuer und die Sommerquartierfeste, an denen Eltern und Kinder mitgearbeitet und mitgespielt haben. Auch die ›Robinson-Band‹ der größeren Burschen wollen wir erwähnen, die hie und da zum Tanz aufspielte wie vor langer, langer Zeit unter der Dorflinde. Ebensolche Berühmtheit verdient der Kinderzoo, der von den Kindern selbst gebaut und dessen Kleintiere von ihnen betreut und gepflegt werden.

An jedem schönen Nachmittag sitzen zahlreiche Mütter in Liegestühlen strickend und flickend unter den Bäumen. Wie manche Mutter hat dabei erst erfahren, was das Spiel ihres Kindes ist und wie mancher Vater hat hier zum erstenmal seinem Buben beim Basteln und Werken helfen können.

So ist der Robinson-Spielplatz nicht einfach eine neue Möglichkeit, wo die Kinder von ihren Eltern ›abgestellt‹ werden, er ist auch kein ›Spielsalon im Freien‹, wo man sich passiv unter-

halten läßt. Der Robinson-Spielplatz ist ein eigentliches Freizeitzentrum des Quartiers, das alle Eltern, Großeltern und die Kinder aus der kalten Anonymität der Großstadt heraushebt und wieder zu Nachbarn macht.«

C. Das Spiel- und Gemeinschaftszentrum für jung und alt (Freizeitanlage).

Es geht heute nicht mehr darum, irgendwo in einem Stadtquartier, in einem Dorf zufällig einen Kleinkinderspielplatz, dort vielleicht einen Spielplatz für größere Kinder und an einer anderen Ecke eine Freizeitwerkstatt für Schulentlassene einzurichten. Und schließlich eröffnet man für die Alten und Pensionierten wieder woanders noch eine weitere spezielle Bastelwerkstatt. Die organisatorische und personelle Spezialisierung der verschiedenen Institutionen, die sich in einer Stadt für die Freizeitgestaltung einsetzen, führt leicht zu einer räumlichen Aufsplitterung und hilft so – unbeabsichtigt – mit, die Familien auch noch in der Freizeit auseinanderzureißen, statt sie zusammenzuführen.

Es ist deshalb heute eine dringliche Aufgabe, in jeder Stadt, in jedem Stadtquartier und in jedem Dorf alle wertvollen Freizeitbestrebungen unter dem Gesichtspunkt der Familie und der Gemeinschaft neu zu überprüfen und zu koordinieren. Gewiß, unsere Jüngsten brauchen wegen der verkehrsgefährlichen Straßen Spielplätze in Wohnungsnähe. Selbstverständlich müssen für die größeren Kinder Spielplätze für alle Altersstufen in den Quartieren errichtet werden, aber auch die Freizeitprobleme der Erwachsenen verlangen nach neuen Lösungen. Das rapide Arbeitstempo, die Alltagshetze, die Mechanisierung und Einseitigkeit des Arbeitsvorganges, die Verkürzung der Arbeitszeit und die Zunahme der Freizeit lassen die Freizeitgestaltung, die Spiel- und Erholungsfrage für die Erwachsenen in einem ganz neuen Licht erscheinen. Der Stadtmensch bedarf zu seiner seelischen Gesunderhaltung eines sinnvollen Ausgleichs. Die Alten und Pensionierten wollen mit ihren Mußestunden etwas Wertvolles anfangen.

Wir glauben deshalb, daß die Baubehörden unserer Städte und Dörfer in naher Zukunft sehr nachdrücklich darauf drängen sollten, daß die schon seit Jahrzehnten von modernen Stadtplanern proklamierte Humanisierung des Städtebaues greifbare Wirklichkeit wird. Sie werden nicht nur Kinderspielplätze schaffen müssen, sondern auch Spiel- und Erholungszentren, in denen Eltern und Kinder, Familien und ältere Leute ihre Freizeitstunden verbringen können, in denen aus der Masse anonymer gehetzter Stadtmenschen wieder eine Gemeinschaft der Muße, der Beschaulichkeit und des Spiels werden. Wertvolle Lösungen solcher Familien- und Volksparkanlagen kennen wir z. B. aus den USA (siehe Seite 129), wobei dort unseres Erachtens allerdings zu sehr die Bewegungsspiele und der Sport über die Möglichkeit zu schöpferischer, handwerklicher oder musischer Freizeitgestaltung dominieren.

In der Schweiz wurde in den letzten Jahren versucht, verschiedene Grünanlagen zu umfassenden Erholungs- und Spielzentren für die Bevölkerung eines Stadtquartiers auszugestalten. Ein solches Gemeinschaftszentrum wie das in Zürich-Bucheggg (siehe S. 146–149) besteht aus folgenden Teilen:

1. Eine oder mehrere Liegewiesen mit Spazierwegen, Ruhebänken, Liegestühlen, Spieltischen für Familien und ältere Leute.
2. Eine oder mehrere Spielwiesen für Ball- und Rasenspiele von jung und alt.
3. Ein oder mehrere Kleinkinderspielplätze für die Jüngsten.
4. Ein Spielplatz für alle Altersstufen (Robinson-Spielplatz) mit festen Gemeinschaftsbauten.

Die beiden Gemeinschaftsbauten bilden gleichsam ein Quartier- und Bezirksfreizeithaus mit Werkstätten, Jugend- und Erwachsenenbibliothek, sowie Spiel- und Klubräumen. Diese Räume werden an schulfreien Nachmittagen und in den Ferien von den Schulkindern zum Basteln und Werken, zum Theaterspielen, Lesen, Singen, Musizieren und Spielen benützt. An den Abenden stehen die gleichen Einrichtungen den Schulentlassenen als Jugendhaus offen. Außerdem können die Väter und Mütter hier zu Erziehungs- und Bastelkursen der Elternschule zusammenkommen. In der Bibliothek und Lesestube finden die jungen Leseratten alles Notwendige zum Schmökern, und auch den älteren Leuten bieten sich vielfältige Gelegenheiten zur Gestaltung ihrer Mußestunden.

Die Gemeinschaftszentren ermöglichen vor allem eine Vertiefung des Verhältnisses zwischen Eltern und Kind. Man sagt oft, die in manchen Fällen zwischen Eltern und Kind eingetretene Entfremdung sei eine Folge unserer raschlebigen, tempogeladenen Zeit: die Eltern kommen gar nicht mehr dazu, sich dem Kind zu widmen. Das mag stimmen. Zum Teil aber kann diese Entfremdungserscheinung auch darauf zurückgeführt werden, daß es den Eltern heute vielfach an Gelegenheit fehlt, sich mit ihren Kindern anderswo als in der Wohnung, in ihren vier Wänden, zu beschäftigen. Im gemeinsamen Spiel eröffnen sich den Eltern neue Möglichkeiten des Zusammenlebens mit dem Kind und der Einwirkung auf seine seelische und körperliche Entwicklung.

Die segensreiche Wirkung des Gemeinschaftszentrums beschränkt sich aber nicht nur auf Eltern und Kinder, sondern auch auf die Großeltern, die Pensionierten, die betagten Leute im allgemeinen, die ja über die meiste Freizeit verfügen. Die Gemeinschaftszentren schaffen eine geradezu ideale Voraussetzung zur Wiederbelebung der natürlichen Beziehungen zwischen alt und jung. Die Möglichkeit eines völlig freien und ungezwungenen Zusammenseins, die Gelegenheit, mit älteren und jüngeren Leuten zusammenzutreffen, sie zu beobachten, mit ihnen zu sprechen und sich ganz nach Belieben zu beschäftigen, können ihre Wirkung auf die älteren Leute unmöglich verfehlen. Die Großeltern können nach Herzenslust mit ihren Kindern und Enkeln zusammen sein, sei es als Mitspieler, Erzähler oder Zuschauer. Pensionierte finden die größte Freude daran, mit Lehrlingen um die Wette zu basteln. Auch können gelegentlich Ausspracheabende zwischen älteren und jüngeren Gästen des Zentrums durchgeführt werden, um so das gegenseitige Verständnis zu fördern.

Die Gemeinschaftszentren mit den verschiedenen Betätigungsmöglichkeiten verhindern auch die ungesunden Einseitigkeiten. Der junge Fußballfanatiker darf sich zwar auf der Spielwiese nach Herzenslust seinem geliebten Sport widmen, solange er will. Auf dem Platz nebenan aber entdeckt er viel-

leicht seine Kameraden beim Bauen und Basteln und läßt sich bald einmal gewinnen, in einer Bauequipe mitzumachen. Oder ein kleiner Lesewurm sieht sein Schwesterchen mit anderen auf der selbstgezimmerten Bühne Theater spielen und bekommt Lust, das Gelesene auf den Brettern darzustellen. Und ein verbissener Bastler hat bisher noch gar nie richtig gemerkt, daß es auf der Welt auch Bücher gibt, und da entdeckt er im Gemeinschaftszentrum eine Bibliothek und es öffnet sich ihm die wundervolle Welt des Buches.

So führt das Gemeinschaftszentrum mit seinen Gemeinschaftsbauten, mit seinen verschiedenartigen Spiel-, Bastel- und Tummelmöglichkeiten für alle Altersstufen, dem Freilichttheater, der Liegewiese, den Ruhebänken und Spazierwegen die moderne Familie, die durch Beruf und Schule tagsüber auseinandergerissen wird, in den Freizeitstunden zusammen zu gemeinsamem Tun und Erleben. Der Nervosität des Stadtalltags, der Aufsplitterung des Familienlebens, den Verlockungen der Vergnügungsindustrie und der passiven Zeitvergeudung wird hier eine schöpferische Erlebniswelt entgegengestellt zur Festigung der Familienbande und zur Stärkung der Gemüts- und Seelenkräfte des Stadtmenschen.

IV. »Spielplatz-Charta«

1. Spielplatzplanung – zehn städtebauliche Wünsche.

A. Kleinkinderspielplätze:

1. Für das Spiel des Kleinkindes ist ein möglichst großes Netz von Wohnungs-, Haus-, Hof-, Siedlungs- und Kindergartenspielplätzen anzustreben.
2. Die Anlage solcher Spielplätze ist von Behörden (Baubehörden, Schulbehörden, Gartenbauämtern) und Privaten (Baugenossenschaften und privaten Bauherren) in die Hand zu nehmen, wobei diese Bestrebungen finanziell durch staatliche Subventionen zu fördern sind.
3. Beim privaten und genossenschaftlichen Wohnungsbau ist durch entsprechende Gesetze, Verordnungen, Subventionsbedingungen oder freiwillige Vereinbarungen die Schaffung einer möglichst großen Zahl von Haus-, Hof- und Siedlungsspielplätzen für die kleinen Kinder anzustreben. Vor allem sollte keine Siedlung für Familien mehr geplant und gebaut werden ohne Spielplätze.
4. In den Altquartieren können durch Auskernung und Zusammenlegung von Parzellen Hofspielplätze gewonnen werden.

B. Spielplätze für alle Altersstufen:

5. Für das Spiel und die Freizeitgestaltung der Kinder und Jugendlichen aller Altersstufen sind Schulspielplätze in den Sportanlagen und Freibädern, bei den Jugend- und Freizeithäusern zu schaffen.
6. Beim Bau von Schulhäusern, Kindergärten, Gartenbädern, Sportplätzen, Parkanlagen ist im Raumprogramm von allem Anfang an die Verwendung der Freiflächen als »Mehrzweckanlagen« vorzusehen, oder es sind dem betreffenden Bauprogramm spezielle Spielplätze anzugliedern. Die hierzu notwendigen Spielgeräte und Einrichtungen gehören genauso zum Raumprogramm wie Schulzimmer oder Turngeräte.

C. Spiel- und Gemeinschaftszentren für jung und alt:

7. Für das Spiel und die schöpferische Muße von jung und alt (der Kinder, Familien und älteren Leute) sind die öffentlichen Grünflächen und Parkanlagen so auszugestalten, daß sie zu Spiel-, Erholungs- und Gemeinschaftszentren für die ganze Bevölkerung werden.
8. Die zuständigen Behörden und Parlamente haben rechtzeitig und auf weite Sicht, in jedem Dorf, in jeder Stadt, in jedem Stadtquartier, das notwendige Land als Grünzone zu sichern und von der Überbauung freizuhalten. Ferner sind entsprechende Gesetze oder Verordnungen zum Schutz der Grünzonen zu erlassen.
9. Für die Grünzonen ist ein Nutzungsplan aufzustellen, der nicht nur Schulbauten, Kindergärten, Sportplätze, Bäder umfaßt, sondern vor allem auch Spielpätze und Gemeinschaftszentren in die Gesamtplanung mit einbezieht. Geschieht dies nicht rechtzeitig, so ist eines Tages alles Grünzonenland benutzt und in der Nähe der Wohnhäuser kein freies Land mehr für Spiel und Erholung zu finden.
10. Erst wenn die Stadtplaner, Städtebauer und Baubehörden diesen »Generalplan für das Spiel« ebenso ernsthaft zu verwirklichen suchen wie die aktuellen Generalpläne für den Verkehr, dann wird der Städtebau die so dringend notwendige Humanisierung erreicht haben zum Wohle der Jugend und der ganzen Bevölkerung.

2. Spielplatzgestaltung – zehn spielpädagogische Wünsche.

1. Jeder Spielplatz muß von seiner Funktion, vom Spiel her eingerichtet und gestaltet sein.
2. Architekt, Gartenarchitekt und Pädagoge müssen zusammenarbeiten, um gute Spielplatzlösungen zu schaffen.
3. Der Spielplatz darf nicht der passiven Unterhaltung dienen. Er muß das aktive, selbsttätige und schöpferische Spiel fördern.
4. Wertvoller als mechanische Spielgeräte sind unfertige Spielelemente und Spielmaterialien.
5. Gestaltung und Einrichtung des Spielplatzes muß sich nach den typischen Spielen der betreffenden Altersstufen richten, für die er bestimmt ist.
6. Der Spielplatz darf nicht einseitig sein, er muß vielfältige Spielmöglichkeiten bieten.
7. Bei der Gestaltung ist auf die Funktionen und den Bewegungsablauf der verschiedenen Spiele zu achten.
8. Vergessen wir nicht die verträumten Spiele, die Spiele der Hingabe.
9. Der Architekt, der Gartenarchitekt soll bei der Gestaltung des Platzes selbst ein wenig »spielen«.
10. Für den Bau, die Gestaltung und die Betreuung des Spielplatzes sind, wo immer es geht, die daran interessierten Bevölkerungskreise (vor allem die Eltern und Anwohner) zur Mitarbeit heranzuziehen.

Play – Leisure-Time Activities – Recreation as Factors in Town-Planning

by Alfred Trachsel, Zürich

Spiel – Freizeitgestaltung – Erholung als Faktoren der Stadtplanung

von Alfred Trachsel, Zürich

For the healthy development of young people "play" is as important as food, shelter and clothing. Possibilities for play, even of an elementary nature, should be available near every living quarter. They are as essential as streets, car parks, garages, swimming pools and sports grounds.

»Das Spiel« ist für die gesunde Entwicklung der Jugend so nötig wie Nahrung, Wohnung und Kleidung. Elementare Spielmöglichkeiten sollten in jedem Wohnquartier in genügender Anzahl vorhanden sein, sie sind so wichtig wie Straßen, Parkplätze und Garagen, Schwimmbäder und Sportanlagen.

"Leisure-time activities" will gain more and more importance as working hours are shortened and the average expectancy of life is prolonged. Being spectators at sporting events, and mere entertainments, are a dubious and lazy substitute for leisure-time activities. In view of the ever increasing entertainments industry, it is necessary today to maintain and encourage the sensible use of leisure.

»Die Freizeitgestaltung« wird mit der Verkürzung der Arbeitszeit und der größeren Lebenserwartung immer mehr an Bedeutung gewinnen. Schausport und bloße Unterhaltung sind ein zweifelhafter, bequemer Ersatz. Es gilt heute, angesichts einer immer weiter um sich greifenden Unterhaltungsindustrie, die sinnvolle Freizeitgestaltung nach Kräften zu erhalten und zu fördern.

"Recreation and Relaxation", by way of contrast to concentrated work, are indispensable for the health of the population. Extensive footpaths linking up green spaces, parks, lawns and playgrounds have to be as carefully allowed for in the planning stage as road improvements for increased traffic.

»Erholung und Entspannung« sind als Ergänzung zur automatisierten, konzentrierten Arbeit für die Gesundheit der Bevölkerung unerläßlich. Ausgedehnte, zusammenhängende Fußgängerwege in Grünzügen mit Parkanlagen, Liege- und Spielflächen müssen bei der Planung ebenso sorgfältig berücksichtigt werden wie der Ausbau der Verkehrswege.

A. The Town as a Growing Organism

Creating playgrounds, recreation centres and green areas for recreation, with quiet places and footpaths linking various districts, away from the roar of traffic, is a task with which the town-planner is confronted in two quite different ways. On one hand is the operational problem of clearing and providing space within the organically developed town, and on the other hand he is facing the concept of new towns or districts.

An essential part of all town-planning endeavours is directed towards creating pleasant living conditions. As a town grows it should be sub-divided into individual communities of manageable size: this is one of the primary conditions of cultural life in urban areas and is also a successful remedy against mass uniformity.

While buildings and their interiors can be made to suit better the demands of the present time, out-of-date building bye-laws unfortunately often form an insufficient basis for planning as regards the siting and relationship of buildings to each other, to their surroundings and to streets. The great demand for building sites, which are becoming increasingly rare, encourages a speculative approach to landed property and also the tendency to utilise every available space from the angle of economic exploitation. Towns and cities which were unable to secure in time sufficient green spaces and zones are today, in view of the universal emphasis on technical improvements and comforts, in a very difficult position as regards either the provision of necessary open spaces, or the figures and facts with which to support their claims. It may be a serious handicap that purely "technical aspects" of town planning can be measured and show a relatively quick result; they can therefore be put forward with more convincing argument than "human considerations" which are more difficult to express in figures, and which only show results after years and generations.

The demands which a municipal authority has to face for road improvements, parking spaces, sports grounds and other needs of individual population groups are usually so strong that the desire for playgrounds, recreation centres and traffic-free footpaths can only assert itself with difficulty. In many instances, however, one can reasonably defend the point of view that when allocating available open spaces those projects which serve the entire population and not merely the special requirements of certain groups and sections, should be given preference. Schools, kindergartens, open-air swimming pools and sports grounds should be examined systematically to discover whether they could also be used for play and leisure activities. Existing buildings and grounds should be modified and new ones planned with such functions in view from the very beginning.

1. Playground problems with old property.

Play-spaces in courtyards

Play-spaces can be provided by clearing and throwing together derelict backyards. They will often be the only place where children from the narrow tall blocks of flats, built at the turn of the century, can play in the open air now that the streets have become too dangerous. Also the clearance of backyards is frequently the only possible way of providing old quarters with green areas and thus improving their residential value. For instance, Copenhagen, by means of bye-law which can be described as exemplary, has found some of the best solutions for play-spaces in courtyards. The sketch reproduced below shows a possible way of tackling a backyard clearance.

Play-space in a courtyard
1 Play space for small children provided with sand, water and facilities for crawling and climbing
2 Open space for romping games and play equipment
3 Combined garages and stores
🌳 Trees

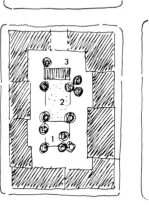

Play streets

Often, backyards cannot be cleared. Then the only alternative is to convert blind alleys and unimportant side streets into pedestrian precincts and play streets. The opponents of play streets maintain that the street should not be a place where play is sometimes allowed and sometimes not. If, however, there is no other solution to a particular problem than to convert a roadway into a play street, then it should be clearly differentiated from an ordinary street by planting trees and erecting play equipment such as partitions for ball games, niches for small children and seats for grown-ups. There are good examples of play streets in Copenhagen.

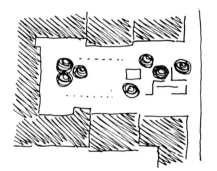

Play-spaces on roof-tops

On the roofs of a great many tall buildings play spaces for small children can be installed if they are provided with appropriate protective devices, as the illustrated example from New York shows. In contrast to the often dark and narrow backyards and streets, there is abundant fresh air and sunshine at roof level. Large buildings provide

favourable conditions for roof-top play-spaces; an excellent example of what can be achieved is demonstrated by Le Corbusier on the roof of the Unité d'Habitation at Marseilles (see illustration below).

A well designed playground for small children should stimulate a variety of games and must be in every way in scale with the child. Not only should there be sand but water too; and it is not enough to provide facilities for crawling and climbing but there must be ample space for team games and play niches for more individual games.

A. Die gewachsene Stadt

Die Aufgabe, Kinderspielplätze, Spiel- und Erholungsflächen, Gemeinschaftszentren, Ruheplätze und quartierverbindende Fußgängerwege durch Grünflächen abseits vom rollenden Verkehr zu schaffen, stellt sich dem Städteplaner auf zwei verschiedene Arten: einmal im Bereich der gewachsenen Städte als Ausbau- und Sanierungsproblem und zum anderen bei der Konzeption neuer Städte oder Stadtteile.

Ein wesentlicher Teil aller städtebaulichen Bemühungen gilt der Schaffung von guten Wohnverhältnissen. Die wachsenden Städte sollen in einzelne übersehbare Wohngemeinschaften gegliedert werden: eine der wesentlichen Voraussetzungen für das kulturelle Leben der Stadtgemeinschaften und wirksames Mittel gegen Vermassungserscheinungen.

Während die Wohnbauten selbst und ihre Einrichtungen den Erfordernissen der Zeit besser angepaßt werden können, sind veraltete baurechtliche Verhältnisse leider oft eine ungenügende Planungsgrundlage für die Beziehung der Bauten untereinander, zu ihrer Umgebung und zu den Straßen. Die große Nachfrage nach dem knapper werdenden Baugrund fördert die Bodenspekulation und die Tendenz, möglichst jede noch verfügbare Landreserve nach wirtschaftlichen Gesichtspunkten zu nutzen. Städte, die nicht rechtzeitig reichliche Grünflächen und -zonen sichern konnten, werden heute, angesichts der allgemeinen Überbewertung des technischen Komforts, aus finanziellen und psychologischen Gründen sehr schwer die nötigen Freiflächen für ihre zukünftige Entwicklung bereitstellen können. Erschwerend mag dabei der Umstand ins Gewicht fallen, daß die »technischen Belange« des Städtebaues meßbar sind, sich relativ rasch auswirken und damit besser begründet werden können als die »menschlichen Aspekte«, die uns hier beschäftigen. Sie sind schwerer in Zahlen zu erfassen und wirken sich erst nach Jahren und Generationen aus.

Die Ansprüche, die an die Stadtverwaltungen für Straßenbauten, Parkplätze, Sportanlagen und andere Sonderbedürfnisse einzelner Bevölkerungsgruppen gestellt werden, sind meist derart groß, daß die Forderung nach Spielplätzen, Gemeinschaftszentren und verkehrsfreien Fußgängerverbindungen sich nur mühsam durchsetzen kann. In vielen Fällen läßt sich jedoch der Standpunkt wohl begründen, daß bei der Nutzung noch vorhandener Flächen denjenigen Anlagen, die der gesamten Bevölkerung dienen, der Vorzug zu geben sei gegenüber Projekten für irgendwelche Spezialbedürfnisse und Interessengruppen. Schulen, Kindergärten, Freibäder und Sporteinrichtungen sollten systematisch auf die Möglichkeit geprüft werden, ob sie sich nicht zugleich auch für Spiel und Freizeitgestaltung verwenden lassen. Bestehende Anlagen müssen angepaßt und neue Bauten von Anfang an zweckmäßig geplant werden.

1. Spielplatzprobleme in Altquartieren.

Hofspielplätze.
Durch Sanierung und Ausräumung geschlossener, älterer Hinterhöfe können Hofspielplätze gewonnen werden. Solche Spielplätze bedeuten für die Kinder der engen, um die Jahrhundertwende entstandenen Wohnquartiere oft die einzige Spielmöglichkeit im Freien, nachdem die Straßen um den Wohnblock herum lebensgefährlich geworden sind. Darüber hinaus ist die Sanierung der Hinterhöfe häufig

die einzige realisierbare Möglichkeit, solche Altstadtquartiere zu durchgrünen und ihren Wohnwert zu verbessern. So hat beispielsweise die Stadt Kopenhagen durch vorbildliche gesetzliche Vorschriften überzeugende Lösungen für Hofspielplätze gefunden. Die untenstehende Skizze deutet die Möglichkeit einer Hinterhofsanierung an.

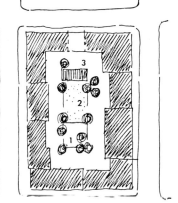

Hofspielplatz.
1 Kleinkinderspielplatz mit Sand, Wasser, Kriech- und Klettermöglichkeiten
2 Freie Spielfläche für Tummelspiele und Spielgeräte
3 Zusammengefaßte Garagen und Einstellräume
🌑 Bäume

Spielstraßen.
Oft können nicht einmal mehr die Hinterhöfe saniert werden, dann bleibt als einzige Möglichkeit die Umwandlung von Sackgassen und unbedeutenden Querstraßen in Fußgängerflächen und Spielstraßen. Die Gegner der Spielstraßen sagen mit Recht, die Straße sei kein Spielplatz, auf dem einmal das Spielen verboten und das andere Mal erlaubt sein könne. Wenn jedoch keine andere Lösung als der Ausbau einer Spielstraße möglich ist, dann sollte die Anlage so gestaltet werden, daß sie sich deutlich von den Verkehrsstraßen unterscheidet. Es sollten Bäume eingepflanzt und Spielgeräte (Ballwände, Kleinkinderecken und Sitzgelegenheiten für Erwachsene) aufgestellt werden. Auch für Spielstraßen finden sich in Kopenhagen gute Beispiele.

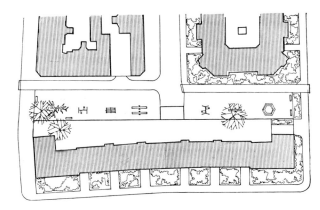

Dachspielplätze.
Auch auf den Dächern des städtischen Häusermeeres lassen sich Kleinkinderspielplätze einrichten, wenn sie mit entsprechenden Schutzvorrichtungen versehen werden. Im Gegensatz zu den oft dunklen und engen Hinterhöfen und Straßen gibt es hier Luft und Sonne genug.

Großbauten bieten für Dachspielplätze sehr günstige Voraussetzungen. Was sich daraus machen läßt, beweist beispielsweise die unten abgebildete Anlage auf dem Dach der Marseiller Unité d'Habitation von Le Corbusier.

Ein guter Kleinkinderspielplatz soll zu vielfältigem Spiel anregen und den Kindermaßstab berücksichtigen. Zum Sand gehört auch Wasser, neben Kriech- und Klettermöglichkeiten sind größere Flächen für gemeinsame Spiele und Spielnischen für individuelles Spielen nötig.

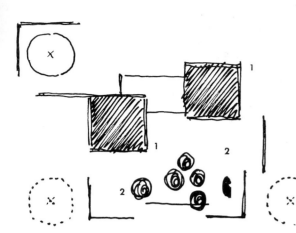

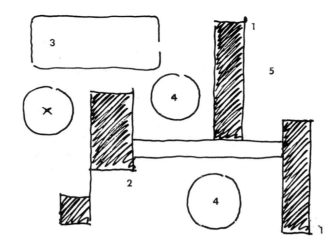

Kindergarten playgrounds
1 Kindergarten buildings.
2 Outdoor play-spaces. Hard surface with recesses for seats, sandpit and partitions as visual barriers with openings for playing hide-and-seek, and facilities for sketching and for ball games.
x = Playground with equipment so arranged that children at play do not disturb kindergarten activity. The playground thereby has the double function of serving the kindergarten and the unsupervised play of children who live in the neighbourhood.

Walls provide opportunities for climbing, for playing hide-and-seek, for ball games and for theatricals. These subdivide the grounds into individual play areas. The kindergarten playground at Chandigarh by Pierre Jeanneret is a typical example (see illustration below).

Playgrounds within the boundaries of schools
1 Class-room. 2 Gymnasium. 3 Space for play and gymnastics. 4 Courtyards for breaks, as far as possible sub-divided into small areas. 5 School garden. x = Playground of a size suitable for a whole housing estate, positioned where teaching will be least disturbed. In this way the remaining school grounds are kept free of playing children.

Playgrounds in green areas and public parks
It is recommended that playgrounds be incorporated with green areas where there are housing estates without play facilities. The main principle is that such play-spaces should be sited as far away as possible from busy streets. The illustration shows such a strip of green area in Zürich incorporating footpaths, play-spaces, a hill for sledging in winter and a playground.

Open-air swimming pools
Swimming pools should be planned from the outset in conjunction with well equipped playgrounds so that the children at play are kept away from areas where people relax in the sun and also from dangerous spots near the pools. Water is the main attraction of such playgrounds and affords a number of opportunities for designs incorporating such features as primitive huts on poles, small boats, streams (see next page above).

Sports grounds
It has long been recognised that it is desirable to provide counter-attractions to sporting events designed purely for spectators, with their mass entertainment and tendency to produce champion record-breaking athletes. Something must be done to protect the city dweller from being forced into the rôle of a passive onlooker, and to enable everyone to take physical exercises, which is now more than ever necessary as an antidote to the all-absorbing daily routine. Our highly specialised sports grounds are not designed for free and unorganised play and are therefore almost everwhere debarred from such use. Designers of sports grounds should for that reason encourage the provision of accessible lawns near residential districts, where free games are not prohibited. Such lawns could be either single plots or parts of larger sports grounds. The playground for small children should be included here too, so that they can play by themselves in a sheltered position while the parents with the older children can enjoy competitive games on improvised grounds.

2. Weitere Möglichkeiten für den Bau von Spielplätzen.

Kindergartenspielplätze (siehe Lageplan linke Seite außen).
1 Kindergartengebäude.
2 Spielflächen für den Kindergartenbetrieb im Freien. Hartbelag mit Sitznischen, Sandkasten, Wänden als Schutz gegen Einsicht, mit Durchbrüchen zum Versteck- und Puppenspiel, Flächen zum Ballspielen und Zeichnen.
x = Kinderspielplatz mit Geräten, so angeordnet, daß die spielenden Kinder den Kindergartenbetrieb nicht stören. So dient der Spielplatz während der Spielstunden zugleich dem Kindergarten selbst und außerdem dem freien Spielbetrieb der in der Nachbarschaft wohnenden Kinder.
Mauern schaffen Gelegenheiten für Verstecken und Ballspiele, zum Klettern und Theaterspielen; sie gliedern den Spielplatz in individuelle Spielräume. Beispiel: die Spielwände eines geplanten Kleinkinderspielplatzes. Entwurf A. Trachsel (Bild unten).

Spielplätze in Schulhausanlagen (siehe Lageplan links Mitte).
Klassenräume (1), Turnhalle (2), Spiel- und Turnplatz (3), Pausenhöfe, möglichst in kleinere Flächen aufgeteilt (4), Schulgarten (5).
Kinderspielplatz (x) von der Größe eines Siedlungsspielplatzes, an einer Stelle, an der er den Unterricht möglichst wenig stört. Auf diese Weise wird die übrige Schulhausanlage von spielenden Kindern entlastet.

Spielplätze in Grünzügen und Anlagen.
In Grünanlagen Kinderspielplätze einzubauen, empfiehlt sich dann, wenn die Siedlungen in der Nähe ohne Spielplatzmöglichkeiten sind. Grundbedingung ist, daß die Spielplätze möglichst weitab von verkehrsreichen Straßen errichtet werden. Die Abbildung unten zeigt einen solchen Grünzug in Stuttgart mit Fußgängerwegen, Schlittenhügel und Spielplatz. Planung Gartenbauamt der Stadt Stuttgart.

Spielplätze in Freibädern.
Freibadanlagen sollten von Anfang an mit gut ausgerüsteten Spielplätzen geplant werden, damit die spielenden Kinder die gefährlicheren Teile der Bäder und die Liegeflächen weniger belasten. Wasser ergibt – wie das oben abgebildete Projekt zeigt (siehe auch Seite 89) – als Thema für diese Anlagen vielfältige Entwurfsmöglichkeiten für die Errichtung von Pfahlbauten, Schiffchenbächen, Inseln und so weiter.

Sportanlagen.
Verantwortungsbewußte Sportkreise haben längst erkannt, wie notwendig es ist, dem reinen Schausport mit seinen Massenveranstaltungen und seiner Züchtung von Spitzenleistungen etwas entgegenzusetzen, das den Stadtmenschen nicht in die Rolle des passiven Zuschauers drängt, sondern jedem das körperliche Training ermöglicht, das er in der perfektionierten Welt seines Alltags heute mehr denn je braucht. Für den freien, ungebundenen Spielbetrieb sind unsere spezialisierten, hochgezüchteten Sportanlagen nicht eingerichtet und deshalb meist verschlossen. Die Sportplaner sollen darum die Schaffung von frei benutzbaren Spiel- und Tummelwiesen in der Nähe der Wohngebiete fördern, sei es als selbständige Anlagen oder als Teile von größeren Sportarealen. Der Kleinkinderspielplatz darf auch hier nicht fehlen, damit die Kleinen geschützt für sich spielen können, während die Eltern mit den größeren Kindern auf improvisierten Spielfeldern ihre Wettkämpfe austragen.

3. Recreation grounds and play-spaces in housing estates.

When planning entire housing estates, play-spaces for children with appropriate recreation grounds and paths for walking should be considered from the beginning as being equally essential parts of the over-all concept as access roads, garages, car parks or shops. This stipulation ought to be enforced at a stage before planning permissions is granted, especially in the case of projects which are subsidised by the state or local authorities. Otherwise after the completion of building operations there are usually no more suitable spaces available. The cost of providing play-spaces for children is, in comparison with the total expenditure, negligible, and will on apportionment to the individual houses of flats only increase the rent by approximately one per cent. Every family will willingly incur this extra expense for the safety of children.
The two following examples show housing estates in which from the master-plan stage allowance was made for play-spaces and recreation grounds with inter-connecting footpaths.

3. Erholungsflächen und Spielplätze in Wohnsiedlungen.

Bei der Planung von ganzen Siedlungen sollten Kinderspielplätze mit den entsprechenden Erholungsflächen und Spazierwegen von Anfang an ebenso als Bestandteile der Gesamtkonzeption betrachtet werden wie Zufahrtsstraßen, Garagen, Parkplätze und Ladenbauten. Diese Forderung müßte schon bei der Erteilung von Baubewilligungen, besonders bei staatlich unterstützten Bauvorhaben, beachtet werden, denn nach der Erstellung der Bauten lassen sich meist keine geeigneten Plätze mehr finden. Die Erstellungskosten von Kinderspielplätzen sind im Verhältnis zu den Gesamtaufwendungen denkbar gering und belasten die Mieten nur um etwa 1% zusätzlich, ein Betrag, den jede Familie gerne für die Sicherheit ihrer Kinder ausgeben wird.
Die beiden folgenden Beispiele zeigen Wohnsiedlungen, bei denen von Anfang an Spiel- und Erholungsflächen mit den zugehörigen Fußgängerverbindungen in der Gesamtplanung berücksichtigt wurden.

Heiligfeld-Letzigraben Housing Estate at Zürich (Architect: Building Department of the Zürich Municipal Administration)

Sketch 1
The general situation at the beginning presented many obstacles in the way of a conclusive architectural solution:
Many individual owners of property.
Difficulty of satisfying diverse interests.
Inadequate legal authority.
Lack of understanding of town-planning principles by the population as a whole.

- - - In the original plan a green area had been suggested serving the district as a public park.

Sketch 2
The usual ribbon development without any town planning or architectural conception resulted.
Because of the granting of planning permission for unconnected projects and of different development plans for the district, the green area was gradually encircled by buildings.

Sketch 3
Basic ideas for a town-planning scheme comprising 500 dwellings:
Green areas to be in organic relationship to houses and outdoor enclosures.
All flats should be well positioned in relation to the sun and away from the noise of traffic.
The interests of small traders should be met.
A restaurant, shops, workshops and garages should be incorporated.
For the benefit of pedestrians and children there should be footpaths linking recreation grounds, kindergartens and playgrounds.
Various types of outdoor enclosure should be provided.

Bebauung Heiligfeld-Letzigraben in Zürich (Hochbauamt der Stadt Zürich, Stadtbaumeister A. H. Steiner).

Schema 1
Ausgangslage. Widerstände gegen eine überzeugende bauliche Lösung:
Viele Grundeigentümer.
Schwer zu vereinigende Interessen.
Mangelnde gesetzliche Grundlagen.
Mangelndes Verständnis der Allgemeinheit für städtebauliche Fragen.

- - - Grünfläche als Quartierpark im Zonenplan vorgeschlagen.

Schema 2
Übliche Randbebauung ohne städtebaulich-architektonische Konzeption:
Notdürftige Regelung durch Kauf, Verhandlungen, Erteilung von Baurechten und durch Quartierpläne.
Grünfläche eingemauert.

Schema 3
Grundgedanken für eine gute städtebauliche Lösung (ca. 500 Wohnungen):
Grünfläche in organischer Beziehung zu Wohnungen und Gartenräumen.
Alle Wohnungen gut besonnt und abseits vom Verkehrslärm.
Wahrung der Interessen des Gewerbes. Restaurant, Läden, Werkstätten und Garagen zweckmäßig eingegliedert.
Wahrung der Bedürfnisse von Fußgängern und Kindern: Verbindungswege, Erholungsflächen, Kindergärten und Kinderspielplätze.
Differenzierte Kuben und Freiräume.

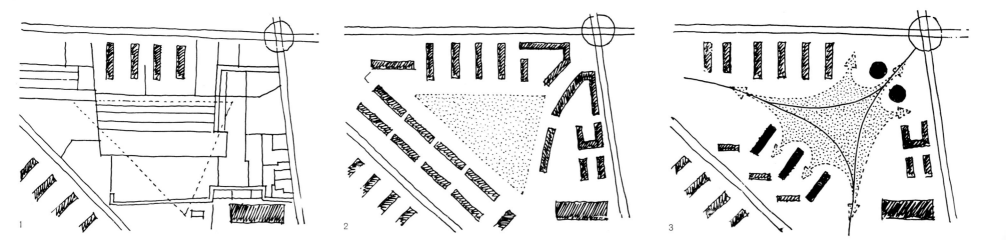

1   2   3

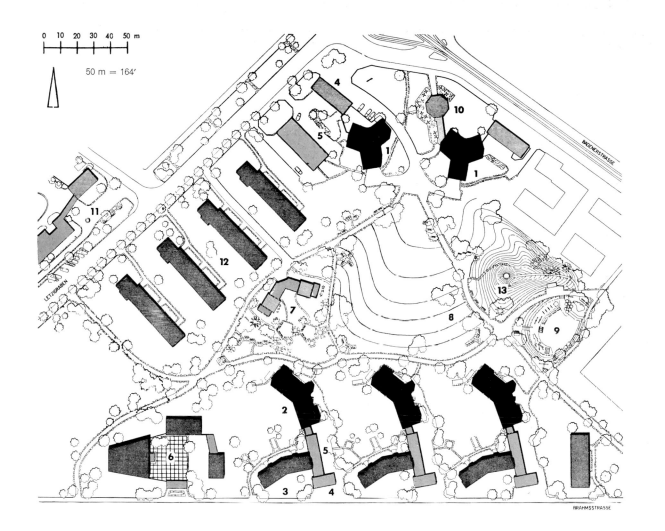

The Danish example illustrated below shows a neighbourhood with well-planned green areas. Green spaces have been allocated to all buildings. Footpaths link up the living quarters with the school and shops.

Fortunbyen housing estate (1950) near Copenhagen. An extensive suburb with direct train connection (1) and junction with speedway (2) to Copenhagen. Tall blocke (3) at the highest point of the site, medium-sized blocks for families (4) and detached one-family houses (5) at the southern, the lower part of the slope. Notice the separation of the building groups, by means of continuous green areas, into manageable administrative units. Shops and cinema (6), old peoples' houses (7), school buildings (8).

Das untenstehende dänische Beispiel zeigt eine größere Siedlung mit konsequenter Grünflächenplanung. Allen Bauten sind die nötigen Grünräume zugeordnet; zweckmäßige Fußgängerwege verbinden die einzelnen Siedlungsgruppen unter sich, mit der Schule und den Läden.

Siedlung Fortunbyen (1950) bei Kopenhagen. Größere Vorortsiedlung mit direkter Bahnverbindung (1) und Schnellstraßenanschluß (2) nach Kopenhagen. Differenzierte Bauweise: Hochbauten (3) an der höchsten Stelle des Terrains, mittlere Mehrfamilienhäuser (4) und Finfamilienhäuser (5) am südlichen Ende des nach Norden ansteigenden Hanges. Gliederung der großen Baumassen durch zusammenhängende Grünzüge in übersehbare einzelne, sich selbst verwaltende Siedlungsgruppen. Ladenbauten und Kino (6), Alterssiedlung (7), Schulbauten (8).

The result of studies in town planning. Built in 1953. There is a well balanced relationship between open spaces and buildings.

Heiligfeld-Letzigraben Housing Estate at Zürich
1 12-storey point block
2 8-storey block of flats with access balconies
3 4-storey block of flats
4 Shops
5 Workshops, garages
6 Proposed church
7 Kindergarten
8 Public park
9 Playground
10 Restaurant
11 Swimming pool
12 Existing 3-storey terrace houses
13 Hill for winter sports

Bebauung Heiligfeld-Letzigraben in Zürich. Ergebnis der städtebaulichen Studien und Verwirklichung im Jahre 1953. Die Freiflächen liegen in guter Beziehung zu den differenzierten Kuben der Bauten.

1 12-geschossiges Turmhaus
2 8-geschossiges Laubenganghaus
3 4-geschossiger Wohnblock
4 Läden
5 Werkstätten, Garagen
6 Projektierte Kirche
7 Kindergarten
8 Park
9 Kinderspielplatz
10 Restaurant
11 Schwimmbad
12 3-geschossiger Zeilenbau, alt
13 Schlittenhügel

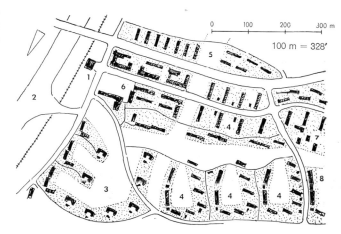

4. Playgrounds and Recreation Centres as scheduled items for Neighbourhood Planning.

The living quarters are more than mere dormitories. Real community life is meant to develop here. Besides technical necessities, requirements of a different nature must be taken into account, namely those which help to encourage the growth of a community in the social sphere.

4. Spielplätze und Gemeinschaftszentren als Faktoren der Quartierplanung.

Die Wohnquartiere sind mehr als bloße Schlafgelegenheiten für ein »Kollektiv«, hier sollen sich echte Gemeinschaften bilden können. Neben den technischen Notwendigkeiten müssen auch die menschlichen Bedürfnisse, welche das Gemeinschaftsleben fördern, angemessen berücksichtigt werden.

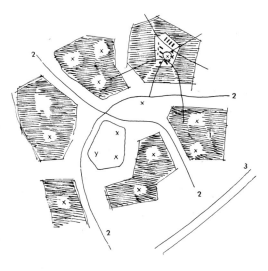

1 Living quarter
2 Footpaths
3 Main roads
x = There should be a closely woven network of play-spaces for small children near their homes:
Play-spaces in courtyards and play streets,
Playgrounds as part of kindergartens and schools,
Play-spaces in public parks, swimming pools and sports grounds.
y = Recreation centre.
A recreation centre in the locality should afford play facilities for young and old:
Playground with lawn for competitive sports and for unorganised games, hard surface for street games, open-air theatre, spare-time house with workshops, club-rooms and library, play-space for small children, open spaces for sun-bathing and recreation.

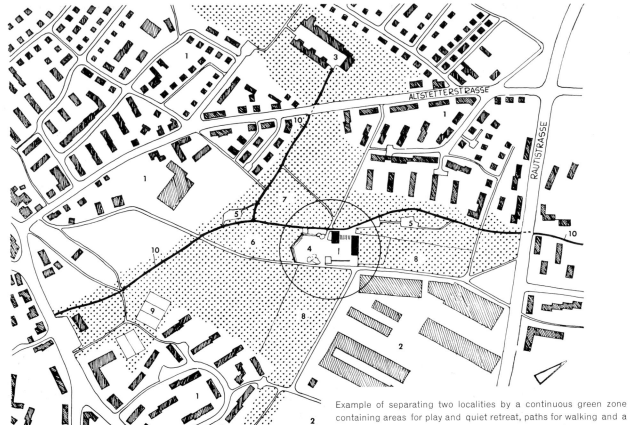

10 |50 |100

100 m = 328'

Legende zum links oben stehenden Plan:
1 Wohnquartier
2 Fußgängerverbindungen
3 Hauptverkehrsstraßen
x = Kleinkinderspielplätze als dichtes Netz im Bereich der Wohnungen: Hofspielplätze und Spielstraßen, Spielplätze der Kindergärten und Schulen, Spielplätze in Grünanlagen, Bädern und Sportanlagen.
y = Gemeinschaftszentrum im Bereich des Wohnquartiers, als Spielmöglichkeit für alle Altersstufen: Bauspielplatz, Sport- und Tummelwiese, Hartbelag für Straßenspiele, Freilichttheater, Quartier-Freizeithaus mit Werk-, Gemeinschafts und Klubräumen, Bibliothek. Kleinkinderspielplatz, Liege- und Erholungsflächen.

Example of separating two localities by a continuous green zone containing areas for play and quiet retreat, paths for walking and a well-equipped recreation centre. Family gardens form a screen around the adjoining industries (Bachwiesen green area at Zürich. Excuted in 1958).

Beispiel für die Trennung von zwei Wohnquartieren durch einen zusammenhängenden Grünzug mit Spiel- und Ruheflächen, Fußgängerwegen und einem gut ausgebauten Gemeinschaftszentrum. Die Familiengärten sind als Gürtel um das anliegende Industriegelände herumgeführt. (Grünzug Bachwiesen in Zürich. Ausführung 1958.)

1 Residential area / Wohnquartier
2 Industries / Industriegelände
3 School / Schule
4 Recreation centre with play-space for building activities, hard surface area, open-air theatre, hamlet of Wendy houses, leisure-time house with workshops, club-rooms and library
Gemeinschaftszentrum mit Bauspielplatz, Hartbelag, Freilichttheater, Spieldörfchen, Quartier-Freizeithaus mit Werk-, Gemeinschafts-, Klubräumen und Bibliothek
5 Playgrounds for small children / Kleinkinderspielplätze
6 Lawns for play and sports / Spiel- und Sportwiesen
7 Recreational areas for relaxation / Liege- und Erholungsflächen
8 Family gardens / Familiengärten
9 Tennis courts / Tennisplätze
10 Footpaths with seats in recesses / Fußgängerwege mit Sitzecken

Examples for planning green areas in residential districts.
Beispiele für Grünflächenplanung in Wohnquartieren.

Zürich-Wiedikon district.
In this housing estate large areas have been left free to be used for general amenities, thereby reducing the density.
Quartier Zürich-Wiedikon.
In der bestehenden Bebauung sind große zusammenhängende Flächen ausgespart worden; die Wohnquartiere werden damit aufgelockert.

1 Recreation centre connected to a school, swimming pool and sports grounds
  Gemeinschaftszentrum im Zusammenhang mit Schule, Bad und Sportanlagen
2 Playgrounds for children / Kinderspielplätze
3 School / Schule
4 Areas for organised games and sports / Turn- und Sportflächen
5 Outdoor swimming pool / Freibadanlage
6 Cemetery / Friedhof
7 Future hospital / Zukünftiges Stadtspital
8 Footpaths / Fußgängerwege
Scale / M 1:10000

Zürich-Seebach district
Before the development of the outskirts of Zürich was started, interconnected green belts were secured which divide the individual neighbourhoods.
Quartier Zürich-Seebach
Vor der Bebauung der Stadtrandgebiete wurden zusammenhängende Grünzüge gesichert, welche die Wohnsiedlungsgruppen trennen.

1 Recreation centre connected to an outdoor swimming pool and sports grounds
  Gemeinschaftszentrum in Zusammenhang mit Freibad- und Sportflächen
2 Playgrounds for children / Kinderspielplätze
3 School / Schule
4 Areas for organised games and sports / Turn- und Sportflächen
5 Outdoor swimming pool / Freibadanlage
6 Church / Kirche
/ Agricultural zone / Landwirtschaftszone
Scale / M 1:10000

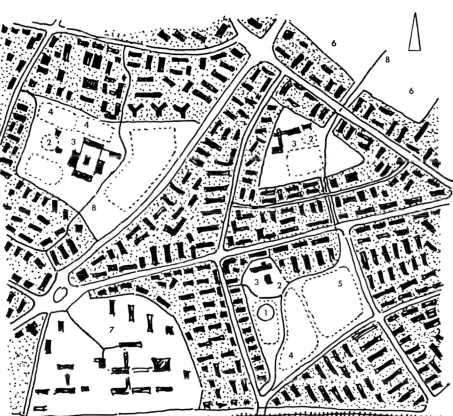

Recreation centres in residential areas of Zürich, Switzerland

Development plans for recreation centres with leisure-time houses and adjoining open spaces (Building Department of the city of Zürich, 1959).

The opportunities provided for the individual citizen, or whole families are of fundamental importance for the cultural life of a city. In this context, the question of where towns' people spend their leisure-time, will become increasingly acute. Reduction of working hours, automation, juvenile delinquency, problems of retirement, separation of families and of the generations, sporting events for masses of on-lookers, and other problems demand urgently a re-vitalising of the various leisure-time centres, especially as a counterweight for the ever-increasing entertainment industry.
Suitable buildings and grounds in residential areas for playing, leisure-time activity and recreation encourage the development and co-operation of local societies and clubs. But above all they serve the great majority of those people who do not want to belong to any club or organisation.
All leisure-time activity of an intellectual or creative nature, as well as sports, should be encouraged. If, in addition, these centres appeal to all age-groups of the population and if they are within easy reach of the living quarters, then one can be sure that they will exert a considerable influence on the formation of a community of really neighbourly people.

Gemeinschaftszentren in den Wohnquartieren von Zürich, Schweiz.

Übersicht über die Planung und Landreservierung für Gemeinschafts-zentren mit Freizeithäusern und zugehörigen Freiflächen (Hochbau-amt der Stadt Zürich, 1959).

Für das kulturelle Leben der Stadtbevölkerung sind die Entwicklungs-möglichkeiten des einzelnen, der Familien und Gemeinschaften von grundsätzlicher Bedeutung. In diesem Zusammenhang wird die Frage, wie und wo die Stadtbewohner ihre Freizeit verbringen, immer aktueller werden.
Arbeitszeitverkürzung, Automatisierung, Jugendverwahrlosung, Pen-sioniertenprobleme, Generationentrennung, Schausport und andere Erscheinungen verlangen dringend eine Stärkung und Aktivierung der vielfältigen Freizeiteinrichtungen, nicht zuletzt als Gegengewicht zur stets wachsenden kommerziellen Unterhaltungsindustrie.
Geeignete Anlagen für Spiel, Freizeitgestaltung und Erholung in den Wohnquartieren fördern Entwicklung und Zusammenarbeit der Frei-zeitorganisationen wesentlich und dienen darüber hinaus der weit größeren Zahl von Jugendlichen und Erwachsenen, welche keiner Organisation angehören oder angehören wollen.
Alle Tätigkeiten der Freizeitgestaltung auf geistigen, sportlichen und handwerklichen Gebieten sollen gefördert werden; wenn dazu noch alle Generationen mit einbezogen werden und die Anlagen in den Nachbarschaften der Wohnquartiere verankert sind, darf mit Be-stimmtheit eine gemeinschaftsfördernde Auswirkung von hohem Ausmaß erwartet werden.

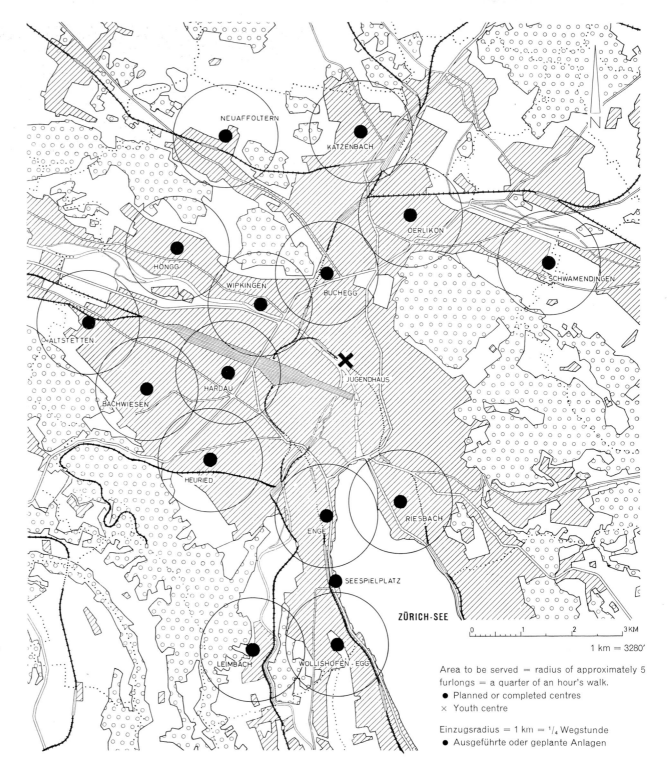

Area to be served = radius of approximately 5 furlongs = a quarter of an hour's walk.

● Planned or completed centres
× Youth centre

Einzugsradius = 1 km = ¼ Wegstunde
● Ausgeführte oder geplante Anlagen

36

B. The New Town

Residential, commercial and industrial zones are kept apart, as are footpaths and traffic roads. The inter-connected green areas which are adjusted to the topographical situation divide the various districts and provide sites for churches, school, swimming pools, buildings and grounds for sports, leisure-time activities and recreation.

B. Die neue Stadt

Wohn-, Geschäfts- und Industriezonen werden getrennt voneinander angeordnet, wie die Wege des motorisierten Verkehrs und der Fußgänger. Die zusammenhängenden, den topographischen Verhältnissen angepaßten Grünzüge gliedern die einzelnen Stadtteile und geben den Platz frei für Kirchen, Schulen, Bäder, Sportbauten und Anlagen für Spiel, Freizeitgestaltung und Erholung.

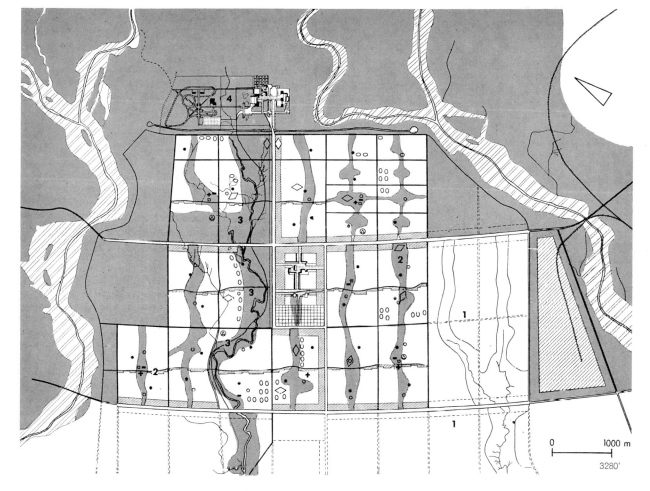

Ongar, England. The old village centre with church (1) surrounded by green areas is preserved. Public buildings like schools and recreation centres (2), footpaths and playgrounds for children form part of the green area (3). Shopping centre surrounding a pedestrian precinct (4), car park (5), main road (6).

Der alte Dorfkern von Ongar/England mit Kirche (1) wird von Grünflächen umgeben. Öffentliche Bauten (2) wie Schulen, Gemeinschaftszentren, Kinderspielplätze sind in die Grüngürtel mit Fußgängerwegen (3) eingeordnet. Geschäfts- und Einkaufszentrum um Fußgängerplatz (4), zugehöriger Parkplatz (5), Hauptstraße (6).

Chandigarh, the new capital of the Punjab, India, is being built to the designs of Le Corbusier. The first stage is intended to provide favourable living and working conditions for 150,000 people; the second stage, for double that number of people, is in process of being planned. The residential quarters are sub-divided into individual sectors of an area of approximately 2,700 feet by 4,000 feet, accommodating between 8,000 and 20,000 people. Vehicular traffic and pedestrians are provided with quite separate roads and paths; the streets (1) are of a geometrical pattern, the footpaths (2) lead through the residential quarters within green belts, where schools, recreation and sports grounds are appropriately arranged. The "valley of leisure" (3) is formed by a natural stream and links up the lower parts of the town with the upper ones. Footpaths alongside the stream, which has been enlarged by a weir, lead to the open-air theatre, cinema, rallying centres, platforms for dancing, playgrounds and other areas for leisure-time activities. Government buildings (4).

Chandigarh, die neue Hauptstadt des Punjab (Indien) wird gegenwärtig nach den Plänen des Architekten Le Corbusier gebaut. Der erste Bauabschnitt soll günstige Wohn- und Arbeitsbedingungen für 150000 Einwohner schaffen; der zweite Bauabschnitt für doppelt so viele Bewohner ist für die nahe Zukunft in Planung begriffen. Die Wohnquartiere sind in einzelne Sektoren von circa 800 × 1200 m Größe aufgeteilt für 8000–20000 Menschen. Die Wege der Fahrzeuge und Fußgänger werden vollständig getrennt geführt; die Straßen (1) streng geometrisch, die Fußgängerwege (2) mitten durch die Quartiere, in Grünflächen eingebettet, in die auch Schulhäuser, Sport- und Erholungsanlagen sinnvoll eingeordnet sind. Das »Tal der Freizeit« (3) führt einem natürlichen Flußlauf entlang und verbindet die untere Stadt mit der oberen. Fußgängerwege begleiten den aufgestauten Fluß und verbinden Freilufttheater, Kino, Tanz- und Versammlungsplätze, sowie Kinderspielplätze und sonstige Anlagen für die Freizeitgestaltung miteinander, Regierungsgebäude (4).

The Child and The City
by Aldo van Eyck, Amsterdam

Kind und Stadt
von Aldo van Eyck, Amsterdam

"expect poison from standing water"
(William Blake)

Here and everywhere else cities exercise both attraction and repulsion. Only if constructive enterprise were to offset, proportionally, the forces of decay and disintegration, would cities continue to reflect adequately and positively, our aspirations and our needs. But cities, like all other collective activities of mankind which are not properly regulated, continue to exist despite their failure to fulfil their purpose; and man himself remains but a subordinate cog in their accelerating motion, a spectator of it rather than a participant in it. That he should thus forsake his identity is tragic, but the loss is self-inflicted. The growing impersonality of the city is man's doing and his undoing. But a city which lacks all evidence of children's activities and especial rhythm of life is a hateful paradox: all the more so since the children themselves are never guilty of the basic negligence man inflicts on them.

Somehow the child with his free-ranging imagination survives in spite of being pushed towards the very fringe of public attention as an emotional, "unproductive" entity. He bravely discovers his identity despite overwhelming odds – in perpetual danger and only incidental sunshine. Man, in fact, makes far better provision in cities for cats and dogs.

The first four photographs show all too clearly what the city offers… and what it fails to offer; the boundless energy and grace of the human child – man in his early stages of development (it requires imaginative discerning eyes on the part of those photographers who pointed their lenses – to discover what is hidden or has hitherto been overlooked). What the city fails to offer is abundantly clear in the fifth photograph (page 40). This is why it has been chosen: as a symbol pointing towards at least a partial solution. All at once the child has become lord of the city: but his delight at being able to collect, from immobilised vehicles, this gift of snow from the skies is sadly short-lived.

What the child needs is something more permanent – if less abundant–than snow: something quite unlike snow, incidentally, but which the city can also absorb without losing what remains of its identity – something intended for the child and discovered by him as his own, though it is not entirely different from the incidental places, things and materials that serve totally different purposes; something which

Städte sind hier und überall – abstoßend und magnetisch. Wenn Zerfall und Konstruktivität wirklich als ambivalente Kräfte das städtische Geschehen bestimmten, so könnte man die Stadt als Spiegel, sogar als positiven Spiegel unserer Hoffnungen und Bedürfnisse betrachten. Doch mit Städten ist es wie mit allem, was der Mensch kollektiv ins Leben ruft und dennoch nicht zu ordnen weiß: sie verhalten sich immer nach eigenen Gesetzen, verleugnen ihren Sinn, indem der Mensch selber in ihrem Mechanismus zu etwas Nebensächlichem entartet: Zuschauer statt Teilnehmer.

Daß er seine Identität preisgegeben hat, ist tragisch – aber dieser Verlust kommt nicht von außen her. Die zunehmende Entpersönlichung »seiner« Städte hat er sich selber angetan. Eine Stadt aber ohne den besonderen Rhythmus des Kindes als wesentlichen Bestandteil des Gesamtrhythmus ist paradox. Das Nekropolhafte klebt ihr schon an.

Hand in Hand mit allem, was unverhüllte Imagination vergegenwärtigt, überlebt das Kind, an den Rand der zivilen Aufmerksamkeit hingedrängt; ein emotionales und »unproduktives« Quantum. Auf wunderbare Weise entdeckt es seine Identität, allen Widerständen zum Trotz, gefährdet und gefährdend, besudelt und besudelnd, in beständiger Gefahr und zufälligem Sonnenschein. Während es für Hunde genug Platz gibt.

Die ersten vier Abbildungen zeigen deutlich genug, was da ist – und was fehlt: die unbändige Energie und Anmut des »menschlichen« Kindes (es braucht scharfsichtige Augen, in diesem Fall diejenigen der Fotografen, die ihre Linsen darauf richten, um zu entdecken, was heute verborgen oder unbeachtet bleibt).

Und was fehlt, zeigt in wundervoller Fülle das fünfte Bild (Seite 40), das als Symbol einer Teillösung gewählt wurde. Das Kind ist auf einmal Herr der Stadt geworden. Aber die Freude, diesen Spaß des Himmels von gelähmten Fahrzeugen zu sammeln, ist von kurzer Dauer.

Was das Kind braucht, soll dauerhafter sein als Schnee – wenn auch weniger reichlich. Etwas – ganz anders als Schnee –, das die Stadt aufnehmen kann, ohne ihre letzte Identität zu verlieren, etwas, für das Kind bestimmt und von ihm als Eigenes entdeckt. Etwas, das sich übrigens von den zufälligen Plätzen, Dingen und Stoffen, die das Kind ohnehin seiner Imagination und Vitalität anpaßt, die aber ganz

the child adapts in its own way to its imaginative life; something elementary, which is placed where there is still room for it, to attract the child from darkness and danger into light and greater safety.

The child cannot discover the city unless the city rediscovers its children: the discovery must be reciprocal or it is no discovery at all. Since the end of the war I have had the opportunity of adapting a large number of sites to the needs of children by re-designing them. Of these, some 70 have been completed in the densely built-up quarters of Amsterdam and about an equal number in new housing districts, where the problem is less acute. The sites thus adapted were for the most part there, waiting (as many similar sites are waiting in every city of the world), forsaken, useless and dead: innumerable formless islands and plots left over by road engineers and demolition workers; often better suited for use by children than for development as ornamental public gardens.

The effect on the city at large of what has been done so far is fundamental because it influences more than just the children who play there. These playing children demonstrate the latent possibilities of urban renewal in general. With the aid of a little concrete, wood and aluminium there have come into existence social centres: places where children and parents meet, true extensions of the doorstep – for it is on the doorstep that the outside and inside worlds, the spheres of collective life and of individual life, intersect.

Here at any rate the child has moved to the centre.

Since the artist is essentially an ally of the child, the job has been particularly rewarding. But there is so much more to be done. Disorder and suffering need not remain the principal ingredients of city life. It is surely for the artist – whatever his medium – to introduce grace and beauty where they have vanished or gone into hiding. Local authorities should strive hard to lure him out of his ivory tower. If childhood is a journey, let us see to it that the child does not travel by night.

5

40

anderen Zwecken dienen, nicht zu sehr unterscheidet. Etwas Elementares, sinnvoll dorthin gestellt, wo es noch Raum gibt, und fähig, das Kind aus Dunkelheit und Gefahr in Licht und größere Sicherheit zu ziehen.

So entdeckt das Kind die Stadt wieder und die Stadt ihre Kinder. Dies ist eine wechselseitige Entdeckung oder überhaupt keine.

Seit dem Ende des Krieges hatte ich Gelegenheit, eine große Anzahl von Plätzen den Bedürfnissen des Kindes anzupassen. Etwa siebzig davon sind in den engbebauten alten Vierteln von Amsterdam ausgeführt worden und etwa die gleiche Anzahl in den neuen Außenbezirken, wo das Problem weniger akut ist. Die Grundstücke, die dafür verwendet wurden, waren großenteils schon vorhanden, nutzlos, leer und tot. (Ebenso viele gleichartige Grundstücke warten in jeder Stadt der Welt.) Unzählige formlose Inseln und Parzellen, vom Straßenbauingenieur und Abrißarbeiter übriggelassen, kleine staubige und spießige, von Papier übersäte Grünflächen. Orte, für das Kind immerhin besser geeignet als für eine öffentliche Bedürfnisanstalt.

Die Auswirkungen dessen, was bisher getan wurde, auf die Stadt im ganzen, reichen über die Kinder hinaus, die dort spielen. Sie zeigen die latenten Möglichkeiten, die in dem Prinzip der Neubelebung eines Stadtteils durch »Injektion« stecken. Mit einem bißchen Beton, Holz und ein paar Aluminiumrohren sind Konzentrationspunkte entstanden, wo Energie sich zusammenballt und ausdehnt. Wo Kinder und Eltern sich treffen. Anweisungen also zur größeren Gemeinschaftlichkeit. Es sind Fortsetzungen der Türschwelle. Denn gerade dort durchdringen sich Innen- und Außenwelt, kollektive und individuelle Sphäre. Hier gelangt das Kind wieder in den Mittelpunkt.

Da der Künstler seinem Wesen nach ein Verbündeter des Kindes ist, war es eine besonders stimulierende Tätigkeit. Doch es bleibt noch so viel zu tun. Unordnung und Leid brauchen keine Hauptbestandteile im städtischen Leben zu sein. Es ist Sache des Künstlers, was immer auch seine Mittel sind, Anmut zu erregen, wo Anmut verschwunden ist oder sich verborgen hält.

Behörden, lockt ihn aus seiner Abseitigkeit!

Wenn Kindsein eine Reise ist, laßt uns dafür sorgen, daß das Kind nicht bei Nacht fährt.

6

Temporary playground on a building plot, Dijkstraat, Amsterdam, Holland

Designed by Aldo van Eyck, Amsterdam, in collaboration with the Department of Public Works, Amsterdam

Provisorischer Spielplatz auf einem Baugrundstück, Dijkstraat, Amsterdam, Holland

Planung: Aldo van Eyck, Amsterdam, in Zusammenarbeit mit »Dienst der Publieke Werken«, Amsterdam

Several playgrounds of this particular type have been made in the ancient part of the city. During World War II a great many houses were pulled down for fuel after their deported owners, mostly Jews, had left them empty. These sites–building sites in actual fact–were purchased by the municipality for playground purposes. Although not very suitable they nevertheless afforded at least some play-space for children who would otherwise have been forced to make the best of traffic-ridden streets. Some were only temporary, awaiting the general restoration of the district. As to the arrangement of the example reproduced on page 43, the sandpit is triangular and close to the wall facing south in order to avoid cutting the playground into two and losing the little sunshine there is. Furthermore, in order to keep children from suddenly darting across the street from behind walls a narrow "entrance" was formed between two climbing bars. The diagonal arrangement of the various play elements as well as the diagonal paving in two materials – concrete tiles 12×12 inches and dark bricks – help to break up the space which is narrow and vertical in character.

Einige Spielplätze dieses Typs wurden im alten Teil der Stadt angelegt. Während des zweiten Weltkrieges wurden sehr viele Häuser, die von ihren Bewohnern, meistens deportierten Juden, verlassen worden waren, abgerissen, um Heizmaterial zu gewinnen. Diese Baugrundstücke, die von der Stadt zunächst für Spielplätze aufgekauft wurden, sind zwar nicht in jeder Hinsicht geeignet, geben aber doch wenigstens etwas Raum zum Spielen und ziehen die Kinder von den verkehrsreichen Straßen ab. Einige wurden bis zur endgültigen Sanierung des Stadtviertels nur vorübergehend angelegt. Das Beispiel auf Seite 43 weist einen dreieckigen Sandkasten auf, der an die südliche Stirnwand gerückt ist, um eine Zweiteilung des Platzes zu vermeiden und den wenigen Sonnenschein so viel wie möglich auszunutzen. Damit die Kinder nicht plötzlich auf die Straße hinausrennen, bilden zwei Klettergerüste einen engen Eingang. Die diagonale Anordnung der verschiedenen Spielelemente ebenso wie die diagonale Pflasterung in zwei Materialien – Betonplatten 30×30 cm und dunkle Ziegelsteine – suchen gegen die sonst allzu stark ausgeprägte Tiefe und Vertikalität des Raumes anzugehen.

Play-space on a traffic island, Bonaireplein, Amsterdam, Holland

Designed by Aldo van Eyck, Amsterdam, in collaboration with the Department of Public Works, Amsterdam

Spielplatz auf einer Straßeninsel, Bonaireplein, Amsterdam, Holland

Planung: Aldo van Eyck, Amsterdam, in Zusammenarbeit mit »Dienst der Publieke Werken«, Amsterdam

Originally covered with greenery, this road island was adapted by means of only two elements: a series of five climbing arches forming a pentagon, with a single sandpit in the middle. The arches are sited in such a way as to balance equally the degree of openness and enclosure of the space within. The pedestrian passing from one street to the other crosses the playground naturally along the sides of the pentagon. A large number of sewers, ducts and cables dictated the placing of the trees.

Diese ursprünglich mit Grünanlagen bedeckte Straßeninsel wurde mit nur zwei Spielelementen als Spielplatz eingerichtet: mit fünf Spielstangen, die ein Fünfeck bilden, und einem runden Sandkasten in der Mitte. Die Spielstangen öffnen und schließen den inneren Raum zugleich. Der Fußgänger, der von einer Straße zur anderen wechselt, überquert den Spielplatz natürlicherweise entlang der stumpfen Winkel des Fünfecks. Die Baumbepflanzung hatte sich nach einer großen Zahl unterirdischer Rohrleitungen zu richten.

Play-space on a traffic island, Saffierstraat, Amsterdam, Holland

Designed by Aldo van Eyck, Amsterdam, in collaboration with the Department of Public Works, Amsterdam

Spielplatz auf einer Straßeninsel, Saffierstraat, Amsterdam, Holland

Planung: Aldo van Eyck, Amsterdam, in Zusammenarbeit mit »Dienst der Publieke Werken«, Amsterdam

Although at first sight the particular island seemed unsuitable owing to its extreme narrowness and length, the successful design brought out latent possibilities. The length was "punctuated" by two contrasting paving materials as used in the other examples reproduced here. The white planes clearly mark off the narrow strip from the brick roadway on either side while at the same time the diagonal direction of the paving tends to increase the breadth visually. The small triangular sandpits cater for small groups of children. The rotating turnstile – the only mobile item used in van Eyck's playgrounds anywhere – was purposely placed at the pivotal end where the road turns away at right angles.

Obwohl gerade diese Verkehrsinsel auf den ersten Blick wegen ihrer außerordentlichen Enge und Ausdehnung ungeeignet schien, zeigte die gefundene Lösung unerwartete Möglichkeiten. Die Länge wurde sozusagen »rhythmisiert« durch die gleichen kontrastierenden Pflastermaterialien, die in den anderen hier wiedergegebenen Beispielen verwendet wurden. Die weißen Flächen setzen den schmalen Streifen auf jeder Seite deutlich von der mit Ziegeln gepflasterten Straße ab, während gleichzeitig die diagonale Richtung des Pflasters die Breite optisch zu vergrößern sucht. Jeder der kleinen dreieckigen Sandkästen nimmt eine kleine Gruppe von Kindern auf. Das Drehkreuz – der einzige bewegliche Gegenstand, der auf den Spielplätzen van Eycks überhaupt verwendet wird – wurde mit Absicht an dem Angelpunkt aufgestellt, an dem die Straße rechtwinklig abbiegt.

1

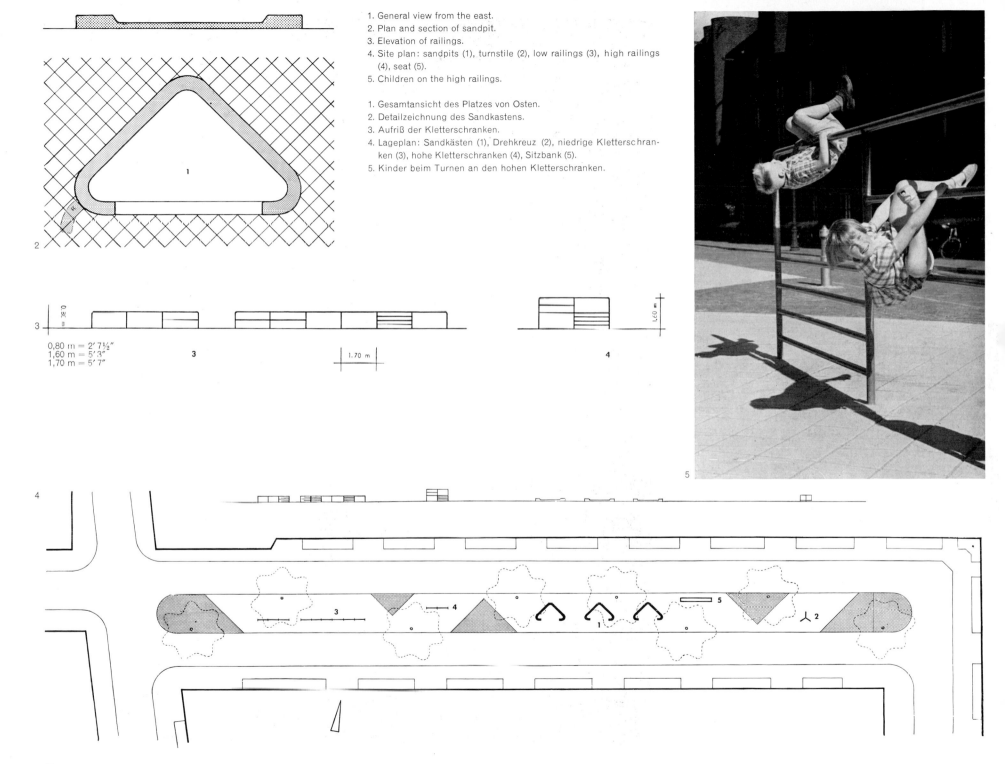

1. General view from the east.
2. Plan and section of sandpit.
3. Elevation of railings.
4. Site plan: sandpits (1), turnstile (2), low railings (3), high railings (4), seat (5).
5. Children on the high railings.

1. Gesamtansicht des Platzes von Osten.
2. Detailzeichnung des Sandkastens.
3. Aufriß der Kletterschranken.
4. Lageplan: Sandkästen (1), Drehkreuz (2), niedrige Kletterschranken (3), hohe Kletterschranken (4), Sitzbank (5).
5. Kinder beim Turnen an den hohen Kletterschranken.

0,80 m = 2' 7½"
1,60 m = 5' 3"
1,70 m = 5' 7"

1.70 m

Play-space on a traffic island, Jacob Thijseplein, Amsterdam, Holland

Designed by Aldo van Eyck, Amsterdam, in collaboration with the Department of Public Works, Amsterdam

Spielplatz auf einer Straßeninsel, Jacob Thijseplein, Amsterdam, Holland

Planung: Aldo van Eyck, Amsterdam, in Zusammenarbeit mit »Dienst der Publieke Werken«, Amsterdam

The monotony of this huge triangle was relieved by means of large and small circles of brick paving, and by the grouping of the trees in large rectangular blocks. This was one of the first playgrounds to be completed; more recently equipment has been used less sparingly.
1. Site plan: sandpits (1), climbing arches (2), small horizontal bars (3), turnstile (4), fountain (5), seats (6).
2. General view of the square.

Die Monotonie dieses riesigen Dreiecks wurde durch größere und kleinere, mit Ziegeln gepflasterte Kreise gemildert, sowie durch die Gruppierung der Bäume in großen rechteckigen Blöcken. Dieser Spielplatz ist als einer der ersten ausgeführt worden; neuerdings werden die Spielelemente allgemein weniger sparsam verwendet.
1. Lageplan: Sandkasten (1), Kletterbögen (2), Spielstangen (3), Drehkreuz (4), Brunnen (5), Sitzbänke (6).
2. Gesamtansicht des Platzes.

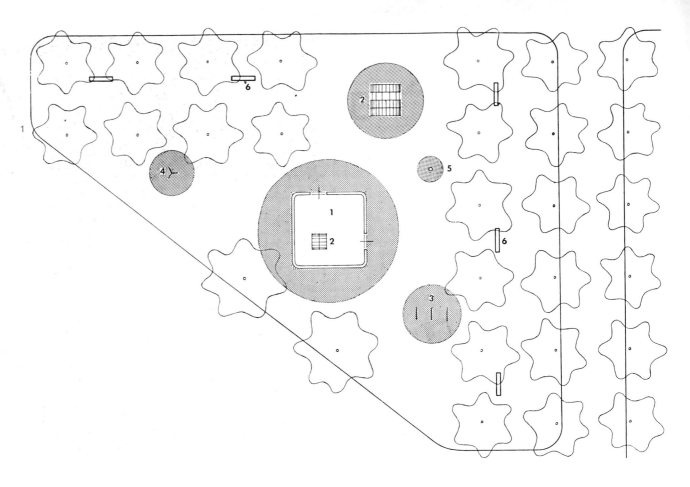

Play-space in a green strip, Zaanhug, Amsterdam, Holland

Designed by Aldo van Eyck, Amsterdam, in collaboration with the Department of Public Works, Amsterdam

Spielplatz in einem Grünstreifen, Zaanhug, Amsterdam, Holland

Planung: Aldo van Eyck, Amsterdam, in Zusammenarbeit mit »Dienst der Publieke Werken«, Amsterdam

Many of the neat urban patches of greenery have been sacrificed either partly, as here, or completely, as in the play-space shown on page 42. The existing brick pavement continues around and between four rectangles of white concrete, each furnished with simple equipment. The concrete bollards for jumping have proved successful and have been used many times since throughout the city, sometimes with bollards of varying height.

1. General view of the playground.
2. Plan of the entire green area, part of which was turned into a play-space for children of the neighbouring blocks of flats.
3. Playing on these concrete pads calls for courage and agility.
4. Site plan: sandpit (1), railings (2), turnstile (3), concrete pads for hopping games (4), seats (5).

Von den vielen »schmucken« Grünanlagen der Stadt sind manche – wie bei Projekt auf Seite 42 – vollständig oder auch – wie hier – teilweise »geopfert« worden. Die Ziegelpflasterung, die bereits vorhanden war, umgibt die vier weißen, mit Betonplatten verlegten Rechtecke und setzt sich zwischen ihnen fort. Jedes von ihnen ist mit einem wichtigen Spielelement ausgerüstet. Die zylindrischen Springsteine aus Beton erwiesen sich als erfolgreich und sind seitdem oft in der ganzen Stadt verwendet worden, manchmal mit den Zylindern in verschiedener Höhe.

1. Gesamtansicht des Spielplatzes.
2. Gesamtplan der städtischen Grünanlage mit dem Spielareal.
3. Das Spiel auf den Springsteinen erfordert Mut und Geschicklichkeit.
4. Lageplan: Sandkasten (1), Spielstangen (2), Drehkreuz (3), Springsteine aus Beton (4), Sitzbänke (5).

1

3

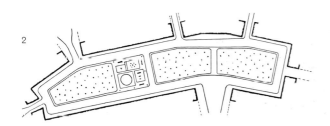

2

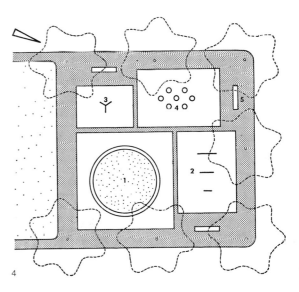

4

Play streets in Copenhagen, Denmark

Designed by the Municipal Planning Department of Copenhagen
(Max Siegumfeldt)

Spielstraßen, Kopenhagen, Dänemark

Planung: Stadtplanungsamt Kopenhagen (Max Siegumfeldt)

In densely populated districts one possibility of creating playgrounds
besides clearing backyards and throwing them into one, is the provision of play streets. Originally started as an experiment, Copenhagen in recent years has transformed a number of short streets into
play streets on account of the general traffic situation. As they are
predominantly used for street games there is no need to stress the
importance of equipment. Special care was given, however, to the
ends of the streets in order to prevent children from running into
traffic when playing certain action games. The provision of play
streets has been made legal by the Danish traffic law of 1955.

Neben der Hinterhofsanierung ist die Einrichtung von Spielstraßen
eine weitere Möglichkeit, in dichtbebauten Wohngebieten Spielraum
zu schaffen. Ursprünglich als Experiment begonnen, hat die Stadt
Kopenhagen in den vergangenen Jahren unter Berücksichtigung der
Verkehrssituation eine Reihe von kurzen Verbindungsstraßen zu
Spielstraßen erklärt. Da sie vorwiegend für Straßenspiele benutzt
werden, ist auf die Ausstattung mit Spielgeräten kein allzu großer
Wert gelegt. Besondere Sorgfalt wurde jedoch darauf verwandt, die
Straßenenden so zu gestalten, daß die Kinder bei Lauf- und Bewegungsspielen nicht in den Verkehr der angrenzenden Straßen hinein-
rennen. Die Anlage von Spielstraßen ist in das dänische Verkehrs-
gesetz von 1955 aufgenommen.

1

2

1. Plan with streets scheduled as play streets (shaded areas). In order
to guarantee an unhindered flow of traffic, ordinary streets alternate
with play streets.
2. Water at the kerbstone. At the edge of a play street children can
have their adventures by building dams and by floating objects, undisturbed by the traffic.
3. Street games 400 years ago. A detail from Pieter Brueghel's "Children's Games", from the Museum of the History of Art in Vienna.

1. Straßenplan mit vorgesehenen Spielstraßen (Rasterflächen). Um
einen flüssigen Verkehrsablauf zu gewährleisten, wechseln Fahr-
straßen und Spielstraßen in sinnvoller Folge ab.
2. Wasser im Rinnstein. Am Rande einer Kopenhagener Spielstraße
erleben die Kinder ungefährdet durch den Verkehr ihre Abenteuer
mit Dammbauten und Schiffen.
3. Straßenspiele vor 400 Jahren. Ausschnitt aus Pieter Brueghel »Kinderspiele«, Kunsthistorisches Museum Wien.

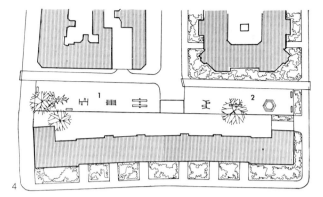

4. Plan of the Musholm Gade play street.
   1 Play-space for older children
   2 Play-space for small children
5. The play-space for small children at the Musholm Gade play street. The former street level was raised to that of the pavement in order to provide a plain surface for action games.

4. Plan der Spielstraße »Musholm Gade«.
   1 Spielfläche für größere Kinder
   2 Spielfläche für Kleinkinder
5. Blick in den Kleinkinderteil der Spielstraße »Musholm Gade«. Der Niveau-Unterschied zwischen Gehweg und Fahrbahn wurde beseitigt, um eine möglichst große, einheitliche und gefahrenarme Spielfläche zu schaffen.

Clearing backyards for use as playgrounds in the older parts of Copenhagen, Denmark

Designed by the Municipal Planning Department of Copenhagen (Max Siegumfeldt)

Hinterhofsanierung für Spielplatzanlagen in Altstadtgebieten von Kopenhagen, Dänemark

Planung: Stadtplanungsamt Kopenhagen (Max Siegumfeldt)

1

2

Copenhagen with its densely populated old quarters was faced with the problem of meeting the demand for children's play-spaces. The municipal administration in 1939 enacted a by-law requiring that play-spaces should be provided by combining and clearing backyards. In this way in recent years about 40 playgrounds were provided on a voluntary basis and a further fifty were obtained compulsorily. The financing and maintenance of the playgrounds are undertaken by the building owners. The municipal gardens department is responsible for planning and providing play equipment.

Kopenhagen mit seinen dichtbesiedelten alten Wohngebieten sah sich dem Problem gegenübergestellt, den Mindestanforderungen nach Spielflächen gerecht zu werden. 1939 erließ die Stadtverwaltung ein Gesetz, das vorschreibt, durch Zusammenlegung und Sanierung von Hinterhöfen Spielplätze zu schaffen. So wurden in den letzten Jahren etwa 40 Hinterhofspielplätze freiwillig erstellt und 50 weitere gesetzlich erzwungen. Die Finanzierung und Erhaltung der Spielplätze ist Sache der Hauseigentümer. Planung und Beschaffung der Spielgeräte werden von der Stadtgärtnerei übernommen.

3

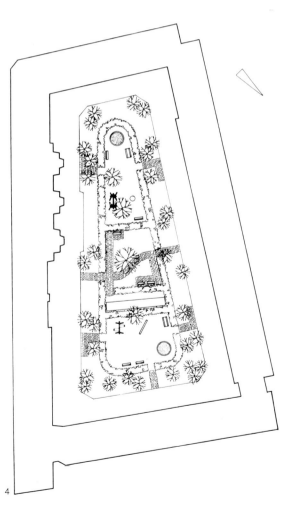

4

5

6

1+2. The cheerless atmosphere of a backyard was not fundamentally changed by the removal of fences and the provision of a play-space: yet this example shows that even in an apparently hopeless situation there are still possibilities of providing room for children to play.

3+4. Fences and ancillary buildings divided up the large space into five backyards (see illustrations 1+3). By appropriate grouping and planting, several play-spaces were created, separated only by trees or shrubs. Paved footpaths serve for street games. In some corners seats for grown-ups are provided.

5–7. In spite of unfavourable conditions a play-space and recreation ground of lively spatial composition were created through an unconventional lay-out of the paths, well contrived landscaping and articulation with the help of raised flowerbeds and shrubberies.

1+2. Durch Beseitigung der Zäune und Einrichtung eines Spielplatzes wurde die trostlose Atmosphäre eines Hinterhofes zwar nicht grundlegend geändert, doch zeigt dieses Beispiel, daß es auch in einer scheinbar hoffnungslosen Situation noch Möglichkeiten gibt, Spielraum für Kinder zu schaffen.

3+4. Zäune und Einbauten unterteilten diesen großen Hof (siehe Abbildungen 1+3) in fünf Hinterhöfe. Durch entsprechende Gliederung und Bepflanzung konnten mehrere nur durch Grünanlagen getrennte Spielplätze geschaffen werden. Gepflasterte Wege dienen gleichzeitig für Straßenspiele. In Sitzecken wurden Ruhebänke für Erwachsene aufgestellt.

5–7. Durch unkonventionelle Wegführung, durchdachte gärtnerische Gestaltung und ihre Gliederung mit erhöhten Blumen- und Buschreihen wurde unter ungünstigsten Voraussetzungen ein Spiel- und Erholungsplatz geschaffen, der ein lebendiges räumliches Gebilde darstellt.

7

Vest Pocket Park, Quincy Street, Bedford-Stuyvesant Area of Brooklyn, New York, U.S.A.

Designed by M. Paul Friedberg & Associates, New York

»Westentaschen«-Spielplatz, Quincy Street, im Bezirk Bedford-Stuyvesant, Brooklyn, New York, USA

Planung: M. Paul Friedberg & Associates, New York

This small park of only 5000 square feet, with playground, has special significance for this uninviting district of New York, despite its small size and simple facilities. In this densely built-up area with no back-yards, the children could only play in the street or on abandoned refuse-cluttered lots until some-one had the idea of converting a dilapidated site into a "Vest-Pocket Park". While most of these minia-ture playgrounds are designed without imagination and lie in derelict corners, Friedberg's solution was planned from the outset to fit its environment. His playground extends over two lots and is thus more open and accessible than the usual dead-end small park, and its creation was a neighbourhood affair. Apart from a few out-of-work landscape gardeners, who were brought in for the heavy tasks, the job was largely done by children of all ages, who regarded the park right from the start as their own property. The success of this realisa-tion has encouraged further renewal schemes, which provide a con-tinuous zone of small playgrounds for eight blocks of flats by combin-ing unbuilt-on lots.

Dieser kleine, nur etwa 450 qm umfassende Park mit Spielplatz hat trotz geringer Größe und einfacher Ausstattung für diese wenig ein-ladende Gegend New Yorks besondere Bedeutung. Bei der dichten Blockbebauung ohne Hinterhöfe konnten die Kinder nur auf der Straße oder auf verlassenen, abfallübersäten Grundstücken spielen, bis man auf die Idee kam, einige ehemalige Ruinengrundstücke in »Westentaschenparks« zu verwandeln. Während die meisten dieser Miniaturspielplätze phantasielos gestaltet sind und in toten Winkeln liegen, hat Friedberg seine Lösung von vornherein zur Umgebung in Beziehung gesetzt. Sein Platz erstreckt sich über zwei Grundstücke, ist damit offener und besser zugänglich als die üblichen sackgassen-artigen Kleinparks, und auch seine Gestaltung war eine nachbar-schaftliche Angelegenheit. Neben einigen arbeitslosen Landschafts-gärtnern, die für die schwereren Arbeiten herangezogen wurden, betätigten sich vor allem Kinder jeden Alters und machten so den Park von Anfang an zu ihrem Eigentum. Der Erfolg dieser Lösung hat nun zu weitergehenden Sanierungsplänen ermutigt, die für acht Häuserblocks durch Zusammenfassung unbebauter Grundstücke eine durchgehende Zone aus Kleinspielplätzen vorsehen.

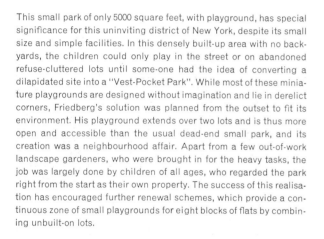

1–7. Except for the slide no manufactured play equipment was used. Two tree stumps serve as supports for the tree house and fire station. Used building timbers and metal piping make sand boxes, things for sitting-on and climbing, see-saws, a small amphitheatre and a stylized dragon.

1–7. Außer der Rutschbahn wurden keine vorgefertigten Spielgeräte verwendet. Zwei Baumstümpfe dienen als Stützen für Baumhaus und Feuerwehrstation. Aus gebrauchtem Bauholz und Eisenrohren entstanden Sandkästen, Sitz- und Klettergelegenheiten, Wippen, ein kleines Amphitheater und eine stilisierte Drachenfigur.

4

5

6

7

Vest Pocket Playground and Nature Study Center, Twenty-Ninth Street, Manhattan, New York, U.S.A.

Designed by M. Paul Friedberg & Associates, New York

»Westentaschen«-Platz für Spiel und Naturbeobachtung Twenty-Ninth Street, Manhattan, New York, USA

Planung: M. Paul Friedberg & Associates, New York

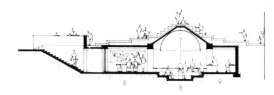

0 10 20 30m   10m = 32'10''

The vest pocket park at East 29th Street and Second Avenue serves not only as a playground for the neighbourhood children, but offers young people and their elders, who in a city like New York have few chances of direct contact with nature, creative leisure activities and an opportunity to take up a natural science. This scheme, part of a large programme, has been carried out as a prototype for further centres, each focusing on a different facet of natural science. Here the middle feature is a planetarium placed below the level of the ground, so that none of the play area of the constricted site is lost. Thus the dome of the planetarium is a pyramid for climbing. A laboratory, also below ground, has work tables for individual research. In the design of the planetarium and some of the equipment (see page 157) the architect collaborated with the Science Education Planning Committee.

Diese Parkanlage im Westentaschenformat Ecke 29th Street und Second Avenue dient nicht nur als Spielplatz für die Kinder der Nachbarschaft, sie soll auch Jugendliche und Erwachsene, die in einer Stadt wie New York wenig Gelegenheit zu direktem Kontakt mit der Natur haben, spielend zu einem schöpferischen Hobby hinführen und ihnen die Möglichkeit geben, selbst naturwissenschaftliche Studien zu treiben. Innerhalb eines größer angelegten Programms ist dieser Platz als Prototyp für weitere Zentren gebaut worden, die sich jeweils auf einen anderen Zweig der Naturwissenschaften konzentrieren könnten. Hier steht im Mittelpunkt ein Planetarium, das unter das Niveau des Spielareals verlegt wurde, damit bei der knappen Grundstücksgröße keine Spielfläche verlorengeht. Die Kuppel des Planetariums ist deshalb in eine Kletterpyramide eingebaut worden. In einem ebenfalls unterirdischen Laboratoriumsraum sind Arbeitstische für individuelle Versuche aufgestellt. Bei der Gestaltung des Planetariums und einiger Arbeitsgeräte (siehe auch Seite 157) arbeitete der Architekt mit dem Science Education Planning Committee zusammen.

.1 Section in East-West direction through play park at ground level (above), and planetarium basement (below). Key: sun-protection roof, to cover toilets and snackbar (1), paddle pool (2), climbing pyramid with slide (3), sanded play area and "mountain peaks" (4), climbing frame (5), work benches (6), planetarium dome (7), projector (8), storage cabinets and sink (9).
2. View from climbing frame over playground.
3–5. Detail views and plan of playground, its equipment comprising simple wooden structures. The nature study centre is in the charge of a fully qualified leader, with other science teachers (biologists, geologists, astronomers) at his disposal and students for part-time help.

1. Schnitt in Ost-West-Richtung durch die Spielanlagen auf Platzniveau (oben) und das Planetarium im Untergeschoß (unten). Legende: Sonnenschutzdach, zum Ausbau als Toilettenanlage und Snackbar vorgesehen (1), Planschbecken (2), Kletterpyramide mit Rutschen (3), Sandspielplatz und Pfahlgebirge (4), Klettergerüst (5), Arbeitstische (6), Planetariumskuppel (7), Projektor (8), Schränke und Wasserausguß (9).
2. Blick vom Klettergerüst über den Spielplatz.
3–5. Detailansichten und Grundriß des Spielplatzes, dessen Aufbauten aus einfachen Holzkonstruktionen bestehen. Das »Nature Study Center« wird von einem hauptamtlich tätigen Leiter betreut, dem weitere Naturwissenschaftler (Biologen, Geologen, Astronomen) als Assistenten und Studenten als Hilfskräfte zur Verfügung stehen.

3

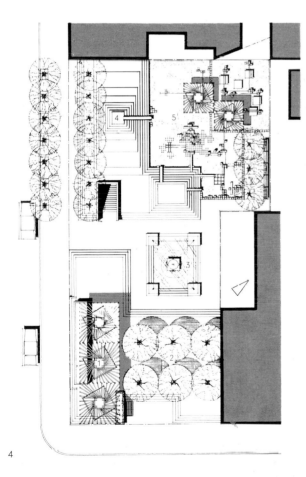

4

5

Traffic Island Playground, Deckerstrasse, Stuttgart, Germany

Designed by Stuttgart City Parks Department
(Director: Dr. Werner Kaufmann)

Spielplatz auf einer Straßeninsel, Deckerstraße, Stuttgart, Deutschland

Planung: Gartenbauamt der Stadt Stuttgart,
Gartenbaudirektor Dr. Werner Kaufmann

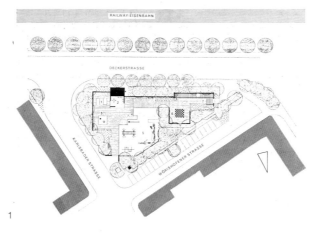

1

1. Site plan: table-tennis (1), skat (2), sandpit (3), roundabout (4), sanded playground, with tree trunks and logs for climbing, slides and swings (5), chess "board" (6), pergola (7).
2. East half of playground, from one of the buildings on the North side. In the background, the railway. In front, the sanded playground; to left of play shelter, the table-tennis corner and small children's sandpit. Walls of solid concrete with an impressed line pattern (left), or of purpose-made bricks to form an openwork screen.

1. Lageplan: Tischtennis (1), Skat (2), Sandkasten (3), Karussell (4), Sandplatz mit Kletterstämmen, Rutsche und Schaukeln (5), Schachplatz (6), Pergola (7).
2. Die östliche Platzhälfte, von einem der Häuser im Norden aus. Im Hintergrund die Bahnlinie. Vorn der Sandplatz, links vom Schutz- und Spielhaus die Tischtennisecke und der Kleinkinder-Sandkasten. Mauern aus massivem Beton mit eingedrückten Stabmustern (links) oder filigranartig durchbrochen aus Formsteinen.

On an island at a street triangle, bordered on the North and East sides by flats and to the South by railway property, a recreation and playground for all age groups has been created by skilfully exploiting the site. So that the playground can be reached safely, the Wörishofener Strasse has been blocked at the West end to through-traffic and converted into a cul-de-sac by a row of trees, while on the other sides walls and fences, lining the busy streets, protect and prevent children from heedlessly running on to the road. The centre includes a large sanded surface, equipped for climbing and games of movement, and surrounded by paved surfaces for street games. The path from the main entrance leads to a play and badweather shelter, built on to an existing tranformer station. On the East side of this is a small enclosure for table-tennis, and another sandpit for small children. Immediately to the West is a third zone, the older people's domain, with seats under a pergola, and an open-air chess "board" as its main attraction.

Auf der Insel in einem Straßendreieck, das im Norden und Osten von Wohnbauten und im Süden von einem Eisenbahngelände begrenzt ist, wurde durch geschicktes Ausnutzen des Grundstücks ein Spiel- und Erholungsareal für alle Altersstufen geschaffen. Damit die Anwohner gefahrlos auf den Spielplatz gelangen können, wurde die Wörishofener Straße auf der Westseite für den Durchgangsverkehr gesperrt und durch einen Baumriegel in eine Sackgasse verwandelt, während auf den übrigen Seiten entlang der stark befahrenen Straßen Mauern und Zäune den Platz abschirmen und verhindern, daß Kinder unbedacht auf die Straße rennen. Das Zentrum nimmt eine große Sandfläche mit Geräten für Kletter- und Bewegungsspiele ein, umgeben von gepflasterten Flächen für Straßenspiele. Der Zugangsweg vom Haupteingang aus führt auf ein Spiel- und Regenschutzgebäude, das an eine bestehende Transformatorenstation angebaut wurde. Östlich davon entstand eine kleinere Bucht, mit Tischtennisplatten und einem weiteren Sandkasten für Kleinkinder. Auf der Westseite schließt als dritte Zone der Bereich für ältere Leute an, mit Sitzplätzen unter einer Pergola und einem Schachspielfeld als Hauptanziehungspunkt.

2

3. Table-tennis corner with weather-resistant concrete tables.
4+5. To test agility, the balance bridge, its treads suspended independently on chains.
6. The chess "board", in the quieter area for adults, is made of stone slabs in two colours. The pieces are simple wooden figures. Seats of precast concrete parts.

3. Die Tischtennisecke mit wetterfesten Betontischen.
4+5. Für Geschicklichkeitsspiele die Balancierbrücke, deren Bohlen beweglich an Ketten aufgehängt sind.
6. Das Schachfeld in der ruhigeren Zone für Erwachsene besteht aus zweifarbigen Steinplatten. Gespielt wird mit einfachen Holzfiguren. Betonfertigteile als Sitzbänke.

Playgrounds attached to blocks of flats at Herlev Byvænge, Denmark

Designed by Erik and Agnete Mygind, Virum

Hausspielplätze, Herlev Byvænge, Dänemark

Planung: Erik und Agnete Mygind, Virum

1

1. Courtyard playground with Wendy house.
2. Part of the plan of Herlev Byvænge with various play-spaces.
   1 Sandpits
   2 Space for ball games
   3 Play equipment
   4 Hard surface

1. Spielhof mit Spielhäuschen.
2. Plan von Herlev Byvænge (Ausschnitt) mit verschiedenen Hausspielplätzen.
   1 Sandspielplätze
   2 Ballspielfläche
   3 Gerätespielplatz
   4 Hartbelag

In 1939 a by-law was enacted which makes compulsory the provision of appropriate playgrounds by the individual or corporate owner of new blocks of flats designed to accommodate more than eight families. Building and maintenance of the playground are the responsibility of the house owner, who is entitled to a playground levy of about one shilling on the monthly rent of a flat. The architects Eric and Agnete Mygind designed a number of playgrounds attached to blocks of flats at Herlev Byvænge, a suburb of Copenhagen, which in their generous scope considerably surpass the minimum conditions laid down by law. These playgrounds for small children have been placed among blocks of flats in such a way that they are protected from the traffic and in close proximity to the homes, and afford many possibilities for play with their varied equipment, sandpits, romping lawns and hard surfaces. The scattered distribution of the play-spaces facilitates the formation of small intimate groups rather than the large numbers of children which one finds at many large playgrounds.

In Kopenhagen können private und genossenschaftliche Hauseigentümer durch ein Baugesetz von 1939 verpflichtet werden, bei neu zu errichtenden Wohnhäusern, die für mehr als acht Familien bestimmt sind, angemessene Spielplätze anzulegen. Errichtung und Unterhaltung ist Aufgabe des Hausbesitzers, der eine Spielplatzumlage von etwa 1 DKr auf die Monatsmiete aufschlagen darf. Die Lösung, die die Architekten für eine Reihe von Hausspielplätzen in Herlev Byvænge, einer Vorstadt von Kopenhagen, fanden, dürfte in ihrer Großzügigkeit beträchtlich über die gesetzlichen Mindestforderungen hinausgehen. In ein Gelände mit weitläufiger Blockbebauung ist ein System von Kleinkinderspielplätzen eingestreut, das – geschützt gegen den fließenden Verkehr und in nächster Nähe der Wohnungen – vielseitigste Spielmöglichkeiten bietet. Die lockere Verteilung der Spielgelegenheiten ermöglicht die Bildung kleiner Spielgruppen anstelle des Massenbetriebs auf großen Spielarealen.

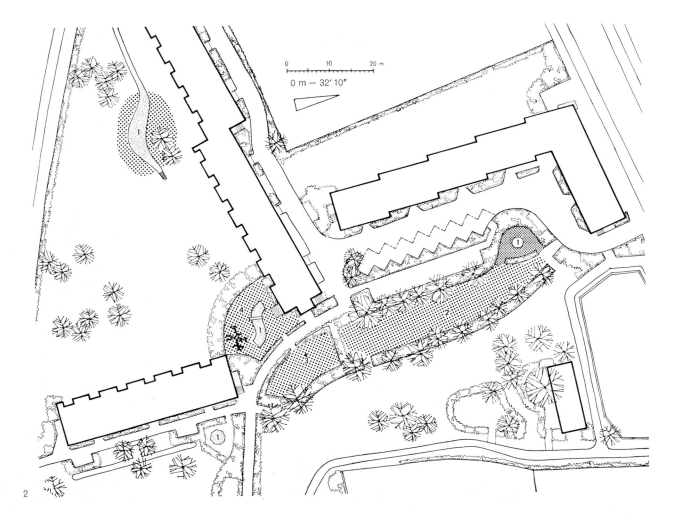

0   10   20 m

0 m = 32' 10"

2

3+4. The ground has simple equipment and offers various possibilities for play with the inexpensive shop made of rough boarding, the concrete tube, the stones for jumping games and the see-saw.
5. Courtyard playground in close proximity to the surrounding flats.

3+4. Der Platz ist mit einfachen Elementen ausgestattet und bietet bei geringem Kostenaufwand mit seinem Verkaufsstand aus rohen Brettern, der Betonröhre mit Hüpfsteinen und der Balkenschaukel vielfältige Spielmöglichkeiten.
5. Spielhof in enger Beziehung zu den umgebenden Wohnblocks.

Roof playground on a block of flats at Marsailles, France

Designed by Le Corbusier, Paris

Dachspielplatz eines Wohnblocks mit 337 Wohnungen, Marseille, Frankreich

Planung: Le Corbusier, Paris

The open roof terrace on the 17th floor of the Unité d'Habitation, which contains 337 flats, has been arranged as a playground for children with paddling pool, an outdoor stage, a sports area and gymnasium. It also incorporates both a kindergarten and a crèche. Through the functional integration of the whole, a real community centre has emerged in practice, which not only links together the children of the Unité but also the grownups in sports, play and on special occasions. Le Corbusier has achieved a masterpiece of modern architecture in the spatial plasticity of the articulation of the whole roof resulting from the use of most simple means, usually concrete with exposed shuttering marks.

Die offene Dachterrasse im siebzehnten Stockwerk des Wohnblocks der Unité d'Habitation wurde, gemeinsam mit Krippe und Kindergarten, als Kinderspielplatz mit Planschbecken, Freilichttheater, Sportfeld und Turnhalle eingerichtet. Durch die funktionelle Durchdringung der Gesamtanlage ist hier in der Praxis ein echtes Gemeinschaftszentrum entstanden, das nicht nur die Kinder des Wohnblocks, sondern auch die Erwachsenen bei Sport, Spiel und Fest vereint. In der räumlich-plastischen Gliederung der Gesamtanlage gelang Le Corbusier hier mit einfachsten Mitteln (meist schalungsrauh belassenem Beton) ein Meisterwerk moderner Architektur.

1. Crèche with paddling pool below. In the foreground is the ramp to the play space. On the right is the ventilation shaft. Stairs, ramps and walls provide possibilities for play such as scribbling on the concrete walls or hide-and-seek around the superstructure.
2. The extensive flat surface at the south side of the roof was articulated by the stage wall and the wind-break on the western side.
3. Site plan.
  1 Roof terrace with the stage wall, the ventilation shaft and a flower bed
  2 Gymnasium
  3 Terrace and solaria
  4 Lifts
  5 Play space with ventilation shaft and ramp leading to the ambulatorium
  6 Crèche and ambulatorium
  7 Play niches
  8 Paddling pool
  9 Play terrace with concrete climbing sculptures
4. Play-time at the north end of the terrace. The concrete climbing sculptures are in the background. On the right the niches for playing or eating snacks. The paddling pool in the foreground underneath the crèche.

1. Kinderkrippe mit darunterliegendem Planschbecken und Verkehrsrampe zum Spielplatz, rechts der Ventilationsschacht. Treppen, Rampen und Mauern lassen reiche Spielmöglichkeiten entstehen, die vom Bemalen der rohen Betonwände bis zum Versteckspiel reichen.
2. Die große Fläche am Südende der Terrasse wurde durch die Theaterwand und eine an der Westseite stehende Schutzwand großzügig gegliedert.
3. Lageplan.
  1 Dachterrasse mit Theaterwand, Blumenbeet und Ventilationsschacht
  2 Turnhalle
  3 Terrasse mit Solarien
  4 Aufzüge
  5 Spielfläche mit Ventilationsschacht und Aufgangsrampe zum Ambulatorium
  6 Kinderkrippe und Ambulatorium
  7 Spielnischen
  8 Planschbecken
  9 Spielterrasse mit Gebirge aus Beton
4. Spiel auf dem Nordende der Terrasse mit dem künstlichen Gebirge, den Nischen für Spiel und kleine Mahlzeiten und dem Planschbecken.

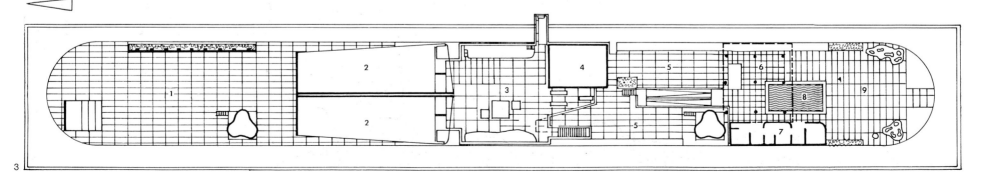

"Play-ways" of the Lohn-Lissen housing scheme, Karlsruhe-Durlach, Germany

General plan by Municipal Parks Department of Karlsruhe, Director Robert Mürb
Playgrounds designed by Wolfgang Fuchs, landscape architect, Pforzheim

Spielwege in der Siedlung Lohn-Lissen, Karlsruhe-Durlach, Deutschland

Gesamtplanung: Gartenbauamt der Stadt Karlsruhe, Gartenbaudirektor Robert Mürb
Planung der Spielplätze: Wolfgang Fuchs, Gartenarchitekt, Pforzheim

1. Part of site plan, showing Play-way 1, with the big playground at the end.
2. One of the yardlike extensions of the play-way.
3. The simple playthings are principally intended for small children playing near their houses.
4. Stepping-stones laid in paving can also be enjoyed on the way to school.

1. Lageplanausschnitt mit dem Spielweg 1, an dessen Ende der große Spielplatz liegt.
2. Eine der platzartigen Erweiterungen des Spielwegs.
3. Die einfachen Klettergeräte sind vor allem für Kleinkinder gedacht, die in Wohnungsnähe spielen.
4. Hüpfsteine im Pflasterbelag werden auch gerne im Vorbeigehen auf dem Schulweg benutzt.

2

As this housing scheme is accessible by service driveways from an outer ring road, the centre could be kept completely free from wheeled traffic. A solution therefore was found by laying out the footpaths between the housing blocks as "play-ways" and, by decentralizing the play areas, reducing the volume of noise. This layout, too, made it possible to keep an eye on the children from the windows of their homes, a further advantage being the combination of movement-play like roller-skating, tricycling and scootering with quieter games in sandpits, and with simpler playthings on separate small children's playgrounds. Places where mothers and older people can sit lie close to house doors also. The zigzag play-ways offer sanded surfaces, stepping stones and climbing objects (like tree trunks and concrete cylinders) on their inter-connecting yardlike extensions. The concrete walls carry wooden slat seats. One of the play-ways opens into a bigger playground, largely composed of tree trunks and concrete tubes, fixed flat or on end into the ground.

Da diese Wohnsiedlung mit Stichstraßen von einem äußeren Verkehrsring aus erschlossen wird, konnte das Zentrum völlig frei vom Fahrverkehr gehalten werden. So bot sich die Lösung an, die Fußgängerverbindungen zwischen den Hausblöcken als Spielwege anzulegen und durch eine Dezentralisation der Spielflächen die Lärmbelästigung zu verringern. Zugleich war dadurch eine leichte Beaufsichtigung der Kleinen vom Wohnungsfenster aus möglich. Als weiterer Vorteil erwies sich die Verbindung von Bewegungsspielen wie Rollschuhlaufen, Dreirad- oder Rollerfahren mit ruhigen Spielmöglichkeiten in Sandmulden und an einfachen Spielgeräten auf den einzelnen Kleinkinderspielplätzen. Auch die Sitzplätze für Mütter oder ältere Leute liegen in unmittelbarer Nähe der Haustür. Die abgewinkelten Spielwege bieten auf ihren aneinandergereihten platzartigen Erweiterungen Sandflächen, Hüpfsteine und Klettergeräte wie Baumstämme oder Betonröhren. Betonmauern tragen Holzroste als Sitzflächen. Einer der Spielwege mündet in einen größeren Spielplatz, der vorwiegend mit Holzstämmen und liegenden oder stehend eingegrabenen Betonröhren gestaltet ist.

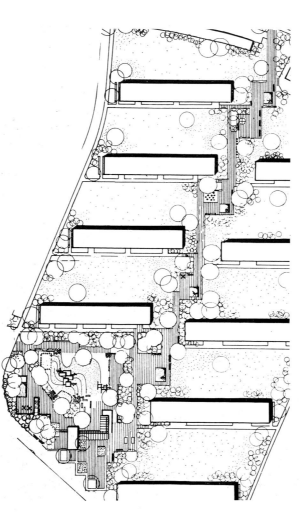

1

3

4

5. Shrubberies and trees shield the play-way's "yards" from one another.

6+7. A play-hillock of treetrunks and concrete cylinders attracts older children also to the big playground.

8. Concrete table-tennis "courts" and a swing (see page 175) complete the playground's facilities.

5. Buschgruppen und Bäume schirmen die einzelnen platzartigen Erweiterungen des Spielwegs gegeneinander ab.

6+7. Auf dem großen Spielplatz zieht ein Spielhügel aus Stämmen und Betonröhren auch die älteren Kinder an.

8. Tischtennisplatten aus Beton und ein Schwinggerät (siehe Seite 175) vervollständigen die Ausstattung des Spielplatzes.

5

6

7

8

"Sonnengarten" playground at the Zürich-Triemli housing estate, Switzerland

Designed by Alfred Trachsel, Zürich, in collaboration with the Pro Juventute Foundation, Zürich

Siedlungsspielplatz »Sonnengarten«, Zürich-Triemli, Schweiz

Planung: Architekt Alfred Trachsel, Zürich, in Zusammenarbeit mit der Stiftung Pro Juventute, Zürich

1. Site plan: Hard surface with pavilion (1), small paddling pool (2), slide situated on the slope (3), disused lorry (4), concrete drum in upright position (4 feet ⌀) (5), sand heap on extensive sand area (6), concrete ducts (2 feet ⌀ – 4 feet ⌀) (7–10), climbing tree (11), see-saw (12), climbing tower (13), aeroplane of tree trunks (14), concrete elements forming the bank of the slope (15).

2. The playground from the south-east. In the foreground is the sand area, with the hard surface and the pavilion behind. Quite simple elements such as concrete drums or angular castings and tree trunks – aeroplane in the foreground – form the play equipment which is adapted to the child's imagination by the way it is grouped and painted. The seats for mothers are placed so that the children can be kept under supervision without their play being disturbed.

1. Lageplan: Hartbelagfläche mit Pavillon (1), Planschbrunnen (2), Rutschbahn in der Böschung (3), Auto (4), stehendes Betonrohr ⌀ 130 cm (5), Sandhaufen in unbegrenzter Sandfläche (6), Betonröhren ⌀ 75–120 cm (7–10), Kletterbaum (11), Balkenschaukel (12), Kletterturm (13), Flugzeug aus Rundholz (14), Böschungskrone aus Betonelementen (15).

2. Blick von Südosten. Vorn die Sandfläche, dahinter der Hartbelag mit dem Spielpavillon. Ganz einfache Elemente wie Betonröhren, Betonsockel und Holzstämme (Flugzeug im Vordergrund) ergeben Spielgeräte, die in ihrer Gruppierung und Bemalung der Phantasie des Kindes angemessen sind. Die Bänke für die Mütter stehen am Rande des Spielplatzes, damit die Erwachsenen das Spiel zwar beaufsichtigen können, aber nicht stören.

This playground, which was constructed by a corporate building society as a voluntary effort, is one of the earliest solutions in Switzerland which are still worthy of being cited as exemplary. Its erection was the result of the initiative of the architect, who worked together with other members of the society without payment and without any organisational or financial help from the authorities. As the ground falls away towards the north, it was possible to form a terrace by cutting into the slope and incorporating it into the play area by placing a slide there. The provision of a lawn was unnecessary as there are large areas of grass south and west of the ground. The larger part of the playground is covered by a hard surface for street and action games, unobstructed by any equipment. An open pavilion with seats serves as a shelter for mothers and as a stage for performances. The triangular eastern corner of this playground is a sand area on which climbing and balancing objects as well as a see-saw are placed.

Dieser Platz, als Gemeinschaftswerk einer Baugenossenschaft entstanden, gehört zu den frühesten und heute noch vorbildlichen Lösungen der Schweiz. Seine Errichtung geht auf die Initiative des Architekten zurück, der ihn gemeinsam mit anderen Genossenschaftsmitgliedern in freiwilligen Arbeitsstunden ohne jede organisatorische oder finanzielle Hilfe der Behörden ausführte. Das nach Norden abfallende Gelände macht es möglich, den Platz terrassenartig an eine steile Böschung heranzuschieben und diese in den Spielbetrieb mit einzubeziehen (Rutschbahn in der Böschung). Nach Süden und Westen steigen große Spielwiesen an, so daß auf eine eigene Rasenfläche im Programm des Platzes verzichtet werden konnte. Der größere Teil der Spielplatzfläche erhielt einen Hartbelag für Straßen- und Bewegungsspiele, der frei von Geräten ist. Ein offener Pavillon mit Sitzbänken dient als Schattenplatz für die Mütter, als Wetterschutz bei Regen und als Bühne für Aufführungen. Das spitze Platzdreieck auf der Ostseite besteht aus einer Sandfläche, auf der verschiedene Kletter- und Bewegungsgeräte aufgestellt sind.

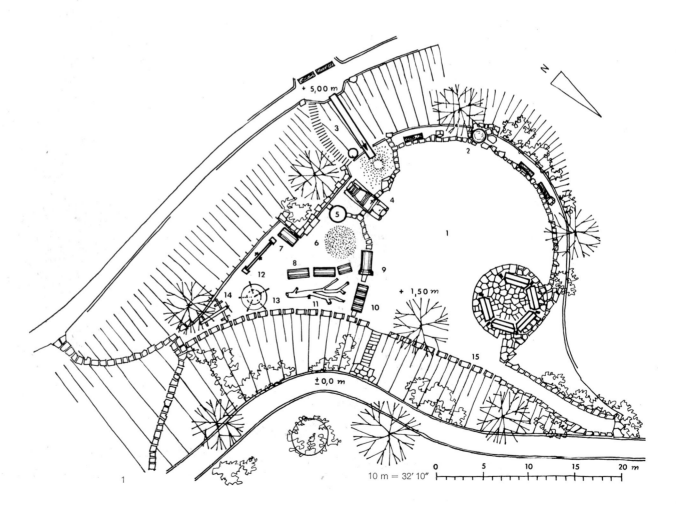

1

10 m = 32' 10"   0   5   10   15   20 m

3. Concrete ducts for crawling and climbing. In the foreground, a duct consisting of three elements painted to look like a caterpillar; behind it another painted as a dragon. In the child's imagination the three ducts form an entity. That is why the painting only makes sense when it stresses the unity of the objects. Small pictorial patterns may be well intended but they do not correspond to the imagery in the child's mind, as can be seen from the upright concrete drum in illustration No. 7.

4. This cart with a barrel was presented by a firm, as were the disused lorry and a large part of the other equipment. The cart is especially popular because the children can crawl into the barrel through a small opening.

5. At one end of the hard-surface area is a spring which is lined with stones and has been made into a small paddling pool from which the children carry water for their sand castles. The sculpture is by Uli Schoop.

3. Betonröhren zum Kriechen und Klettern. Vorne eine Raupe aus drei Röhren, dahinter eine als Drachen bemalte Röhre. Für die Phantasie des Kleinkindes ist die Röhre ein Ganzes. Die Bemalung hat also nur dann einen Sinn, wenn sie diesen Gesamteindruck unterstreicht. Aufgemalte Bildchen mögen zwar gut gemeint sein, entsprechen aber nicht der kindlichen Vorstellungswelt, wie die stehende Betonröhre auf Abbildung 7 zeigt.

4. Wie das ausgediente Lastauto und der große Teil der übrigen Spielgeräte wurde auch dieser Spritzenwagen von einer Firma gestiftet. Er ist vor allem deshalb beliebt, weil die Kinder durch eine kleine Öffnung ins Innere des Fasses kriechen können.

5. Am Rand der Hartbelagfläche ist eine Quelle in einen Brunnen gefaßt, aus dem die Kinder Wasser für ihre Sandspiele holen. Plastik von Uli Schoop.

6. Climbing tower of tubular steel with cone-shaped r
called "Altra-Turm". Concentric rings at convenien
climbing form the core, with poles for sliding down
7. The south-east corner of the playground. Instead of a restric
sandpit here the children have at their disposal an extensive area
of sand. On the left next to the climbing tower are two of the angular
concrete elements, which mark the border of the ground and at the
same time can be used for sitting and jumping or as tables.

6. Kletterturm aus Stahlrohr mit Schutzdach (sogenannter Altra-turm). Konzentrische Ringe mit senkrechten Streben zum Klettern, äußere Stützstangen zum Herunterrutschen.
7. Die Südost-Ecke des Spielplatzes. Statt eines engen Sandkastens steht hier den Kindern die ganze Fläche für Sandspiele zur Verfügung. Links neben dem Kletterturm zwei der Betonelemente (Wildbachschalen), die den Platz zur Talseite begrenzen und zum Hüpfen und Sitzen oder auch als Kuchentische zu verwenden sind.

Playground for small children at the "Heiligfeld" housing estate, Zürich-Heiligfeld, Switzerland

Designed by the Municipal Building Department of Zürich (Alfred Trachsel) in collaboration with the Pro Juventute Foundation, Zürich

Siedlungsspielplatz »Heiligfeld«, Zürich-Heiligfeld, Schweiz

Planung: Hochbauamt der Stadt Zürich (Alfred Trachsel) in Zusammenarbeit mit der Stiftung Pro Juventute, Zürich

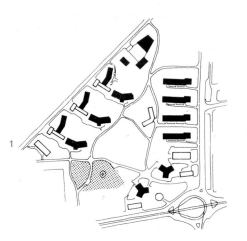

1. Location plan. Playground and green area surrounded by point blocks and terrace house.
2. Site plan.
   1 Hard surface
   2 Sandpit
   3 Paddling pool
   4 Belt of sand with climbing trees and swings
   5 Train of concrete ducts
   6 Tubular climbing arch
   7 Railway station of concrete ducts
   8 Aeroplane of tree trunks
   9 Wendy houses
   10 Slide
   11 Toilets
   12 Hill with pergola-like pavilion

1. Städtebauliche Gesamtsituation. Spielplatz und Grünzone im Kern der Hochhaus- und Reihenhausbebauung.
2. Lageplan.
   1 Hartbelag
   2 Sandfläche
   3 Planschbrunnen
   4 Weichbelaggürtel mit Klettergeräten und Schaukeln
   5 Eisenbahn aus Betonröhren
   6 Kletterbogen
   7 »Bahnhof« aus Betonröhren
   8 Balkenflugzeug
   9 Spielhäuschen
   10 Rutschbahn
   11 Toiletten
   12 Schlittenhügel mit Pavillon

In this new housing estate a large continuous green area for recreational purposes was secured by high density concentration in several point blocks. The eastern section of this space was made into a playground, and is placed in a sunken area sheltered by the surrounding buildings. The excavated soil has been used for making the hill adjacent to the playground. In the winter it is an ideal place for sledging. There is a pergola-like pavilion with seats at the top of the hill. The Heiligfeld playground is one of the outstanding examples of the functional placing of equipment which facilitates a sequence of increasingly exciting games. Use is made of the slope for a slide and an aeroplane of tree trunks. The belt of sand with the climbing tree and swings is separated from the hard surface in the centre of the ground by a "crawling-duct-train". At the north-eastern corner of the site, on slightly raised ground, are the sandpit and the paddling pool of eight concrete basins.

Durch die lockere Bebauung mit mehreren Hochhäusern konnte in dieser neuen Siedlung eine große, zusammenhängende Grünfläche als Erholungsgebiet gewonnen werden. Im östlichen Teil des Geländes wurde ein Kinderspielplatz angelegt, der, geschützt durch die umgebende Randbebauung, in eine Mulde eingebettet liegt. Der Aushub ist unmittelbar neben dem eigentlichen Spielplatz zu einem Hügel mit Aussichtspavillon aufgeschüttet, der im Winter eine ideale Schlittenbahn abgibt. Der Spielplatz Heiligfeld gehört zu den besten Beispielen für eine spielpädagogisch sinnvolle Aufteilung und Anordnung der Geräte, die eine überzeugend ablaufende Spieldramatik ermöglicht. Die Böschung wird durch Anlehnen einer Rutschbahn und durch das Aufstellen eines Balkenflugzeugs in das Spielgeschehen einbezogen. Der Weichbelaggürtel mit den Kletter- und Bewegungsgeräten ist durch eine Kriechröhreneisenbahn zwanglos gegen die Hartbelagfläche im Zentrum des Platzes abgegrenzt. Im Nordosten liegen, etwas erhöht und geschützt, Sandfläche und Planschbrunnen.

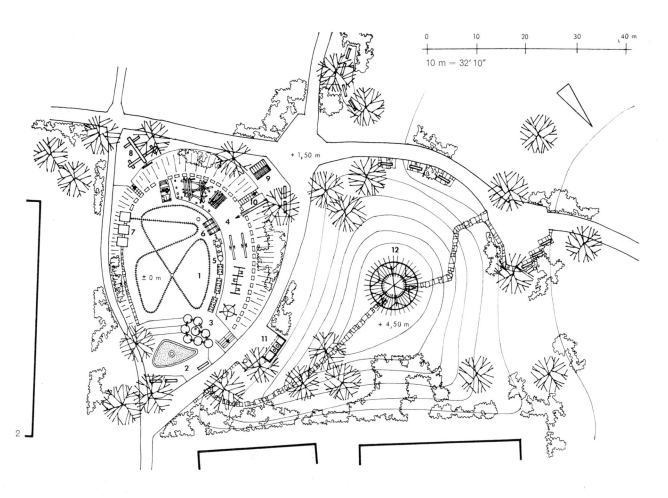

3. The hard surface with the "crawling-duct-train". The hill and point blocks are visible in the background.

4. The model. The railway tracks, which can also be seen in the site plan, have since been painted on the hard surface.

5. The playground from the south. In the centre is the hard-surface area for street games. On the left the belt of sand with equipment. In the background paddling pool and sandpit.

3. Blick über Hartbelag und Kriechröhreneisenbahn auf Schlittenhügel und begrenzende Hochhausbebauung.

4. Modellaufnahme. Die in Modell und Plan vorgesehenen »Eisenbahnschienen« sind inzwischen auf dem Hartbelag aufgemalt.

5. Blick auf den Platz von Süden. In der Mitte Hartbelag für Straßenspiele, links Weichbelaggürtel mit Geräten, im Hintergrund Planschbrunnen und Sandfläche.

3

4

5

6

7

8

9

6. The aeroplane made of tree trunks rests on the slope, thereby giving the children the illusion of being airborne above the ground.
7. The train consists of simple concrete elements. The track leads through the "tunnel", formed by the tubular climbing arch, and via crossings and curves to the station on the opposite side of the ground.
8. View of the "station", with the hill in the background, as seen from the south-east. From the pavilion, on the top of the hill, mothers can keep an eye on their children without disturbing their play.
9. Climbing tree for games requiring courage. In the background is the slide leading from the edge of the slope down to the sand.
10. The paddling pool consists of brightly coloured concrete basins of different height. From the central fountain-head the water runs into the highest basin and thence from one basin to another. The water level is 4 inches in each basin. Due to the constant flow of water the paddling pool does not get soiled so quickly as other pools do. Small children can play without danger in the various basins which correspond to their size.

6. Das Balkenflugzeug steht über der Böschung und gibt den Kindern die Illusion des Darüberschwebens.
7. Der Weg der aus einzelnen Betonelementen zusammengesetzten Eisenbahn führt durch den Kletterbogentunnel zum Röhrenbahnhof auf der gegenüberliegenden Seite des Platzes.
8. Blick von Südosten über den »Bahnhof« hinweg zum Schlittenhügel. Vom hochgelegenen Pavillon aus können die Mütter die spielenden Kinder im Auge behalten, ohne sie zu stören.
9. Kletterbaum für Schaukel- und Mutspiele. Im Hintergrund die Rutschbahn, die von der Böschungskante auf den Platz führt.
10. Der Planschbrunnen aus bunt bemalten, verschieden hohen Betonröhren. Vom Brunnenturm in der Mitte springt das Wasser zunächst in die höchste Betonschale und fließt dann von einem Becken zum anderen. Der Wasserstand in den einzelnen Becken beträgt 10 cm. Durch den ständigen Wasserlauf verschmutzt der Planschbrunnen weniger rasch als die üblichen Planschbecken, und die einzelnen Becken bieten den Kleinkindern eine ihren Größenmaßen entsprechende, gefahrlose Spielmöglichkeit.

**Playground for small children at the "Sulivan Court"
Housing Estate, Fulham, London**

Designed by the Architect's and Housing Department of the Borough
of Fulham

**Siedlungsspielplätze »Sulivan Court«,
Fulham, England**

Planung: Borough of Fulham Architect's and Housing Department

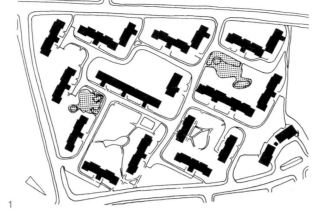

1

This housing estate comprising 432 units was built between 1949 and
1955. Two large playgrounds each of approximately 6600 square feet
were provided which show free shape outlines, in contrast to the rectangular spacing of the blocks of flats. This contrast is emphasised by
the 3-feet-high brick walls surrounding the playground. The hard
surface consists of concrete paving slabs of two colours in which
sandpits surrounded by dwarf walls have been set. The two playgrounds make provision mainly for street and action games. The
recessed parts of the curved outline are suitable for quieter groups
of children who prefer to keep apart from others. The position of the
mass-produced play equipment appears to be somewhat casual; it
causes breaks in the play-space rather than provision for a successive
flow of movement from one item to another. These playgrounds have
been incorporated in the entire housing scheme in a particularly
bold manner and their meticulous architectural detailing is of interest.

In der 1949–1955 errichteten Siedlung, die insgesamt 432 Wohnein-
heiten umfaßt, wurden zwei jeweils rund 600 qm große Spielplätze
ausgeführt, die als freie Formen in die lockere, rechtwinklig zuein-
andergeordnete Blockbebauung eingefügt sind. Dieser formale Gegensatz ist durch die Begrenzung mit etwa 90 cm hohen Backsteinmauern noch besonders betont. Die Platzfläche erhielt einen Hartbelag aus zweifarbigen Plattenelementen, in den einzelne Sandflächen mit etwas niedrigerer Klinkerummauerung eingelassen sind.
Im übrigen würden die beiden Plätze vor allem für Straßen- und Bewegungsspiele eingerichtet. Doch bieten die Ausbuchtungen der ge-
kurvten Umfassungsmauern auch einige Möglichkeiten für die Ab-
sonderung stillerer Spielgruppen. Die Aufstellung der bunt bemalten
serienmäßigen Spielgeräte scheint etwas zufällig; sie unterbricht die
Spielfläche mehr, als daß sie spieldramatische Zusammenhänge
schafft. Was die beiden Plätze jedoch besonders auszeichnet, ist die
Großzügigkeit, mit der sie in die Gesamtbebauung einbezogen sind,
und die sorgfältige Durchgestaltung der architektonischen Details.

2

3

1. Site plan of the "Sulivan Court" housing scheme. The two playgrounds are well protected by the flanking multi-storey blocks.
2. Aerial view from the east. Heavy traffic merely touches the fringe
of the estate; access roads alone lead right into it.
3. The playground in the north-western part of the estate. Because
of the adjoining access road the exit is obstructed by a number of
staggered railings.

1. Gesamtplan von »Sulivan Court«. Die beiden Kinderspielplätze
(gerasterte Flächen) liegen geschützt zwischen den locker verteilten,
mehrgeschossigen Baukörpern.
2. Luftansicht von Osten. Der Durchgangsverkehr tangiert das Wohn-
gebiet nur, ins Innere führen lediglich Zubringerstraßen.
3. Der langgestreckte Spielplatz im Nordwesten. Wegen der angrenzenden Erschließungsstraße ist der Ausgang durch verschiedene
Sperren verstellt.

4. The shape of this climbing structure has been developed from the stretched net type. For the sake of greater durability it was made of tubular steel. The whole structure was placed in a sandpit surrounded by a dwarf wall.

5. The playground in the south-eastern part of the estate, with sandpit, slide, swings and climbing structure.

6. The sandpit of the south-eastern playground with brick wall and raised concrete pad forming a "table".

4. Die Form dieses Klettergerätes ist von ausgespannten Kletternetzen hergeleitet, doch wurde es wegen der größeren Haltbarkeit in Stahlrohr ausgeführt. Das ganze Gerüst ist in eine ummauerte Sandfläche gestellt.

5. Der südöstliche Platz mit Sandfläche, Rutschbahn, Schaukeln und Klettergerüst.

6. Der Sandkasten des südöstlichen Spielplatzes mit Klinkermauer und Betonsockel als Tisch.

4

5

6

Playground for Jacob Riis Houses Plaza, Manhattan, New York, U.S.A.

Designed by Pomerance & Breines, architects
M. Paul Friedberg & Associates, landscape architects
Client: New York Housing Authority
Finance: The Astor Foundation

Siedlungsspielplatz Jacob Riis Houses Plaza, Manhattan, New York, USA

Planung: Pomerance & Breines, Architekten,
M. Paul Friedberg & Associates, Landschaftsarchitekten
Bauherr: New York City Housing Authority
Finanzierung: The Astor Foundation

1. The old "forbidden mall".
2. The area as transformed. Front right, part of the children's playground. Middle, between flower beds and raised borders, the garden courtyards with shady seats for older people and play facilities for small children. Top left, the pergola-lined amphitheatre.

1. Die abgeschrankte »Allee« im alten Zustand.
2. Das Areal nach dem Umbau. Vorn rechts ein Teil des Kinderspielplatzes. In der Mitte zwischen Blumenbeeten und erhöhten Pflanzenbecken die Felder der atriumartigen Gartenhöfe mit schattigen Bänken für ältere Leute und Spielgelegenheiten für Kleinkinder. Oben links das von Pergolen umgebene Amphitheater.

1

The tree-lined mall, stretching the length of two blocks between a 14-storey and 6-storey housing development, had become a dead area for the 8000 tenants of Jacob Riis Houses (built in 1947), who were forbidden to walk on the grass and were subject to other restrictions. Thanks to $ 900,000 from the Astor Foundation, this area of 3 acres was transformed into a highly attractive playground and recreation park for children and adults, which can be used almost throughout the year, for in summer the pools and maple trees (largely preserved) offer coolness and shade, while in winter the walls and sunk spaces give protection from the wind. Out of brick walls, wood artefacts and pergolas, raised flower beds, concrete steps, walls for climbing, paving stone mounds and pools of water, a "play-scape" was created, divided into various spaces and levels, in which four zones are distinguishable: a sitting area for grown-ups, an amphitheatre, an area of garden courtyards, and a plastically modelled children's playground.

Der alleeähnliche Grünstreifen, der sich auf die Länge von zwei Straßengevierten zwischen 14geschossigen Hochhäusern und 6geschossigen Wohnblöcken erstreckt, war für die 8000 Bewohner der 1947 erbauten Jacob Riis Houses durch Verbote, die Grasflächen zu betreten und entsprechende Abschrankungen zu einer toten Zone geworden. Mit 900000 $ Finanzhilfe der Astor Foundation wurde dieses 1,2 ha große Areal in einen höchst attraktiven Spiel- und Erholungspark für Kinder und Erwachsene verwandelt. Er kann fast das ganze Jahr über benützt werden, denn im Sommer bieten die Wasserbecken und die großenteils erhalten gebliebenen Ahornbäume Kühlung und Schatten, und im Winter schützen die Mauern und Vertiefungen vor dem Wind. Aus Backsteinmauern, Holzstrukturen und -pergolen, erhöhten Blumenbeeten, Betonstufen, Kletterwänden, Hügeln aus Pflastersteinen und Wasserbecken wurde eine in verschiedene Räume und Ebenen gegliederte Spiellandschaft geschaffen, in der vier Zonen zu unterscheiden sind: ein Sitzbereich für Erwachsene, ein Amphitheater, ein Bereich mit atriumartigen Gartenhöfen und ein plastisch modellierter Kinderspielplatz.

2

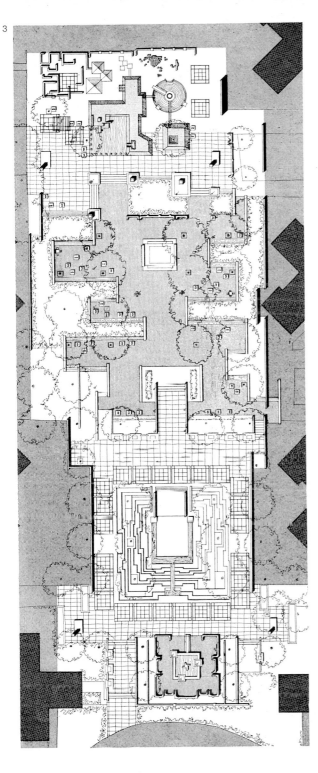

3

4

3. Site plan of the playground and recreation park. Top, the children's play area; below it, the islands and bays of the garden courtyards. In the lower half, the amphitheatre and sitting area with its pool.
4. "Mountain peaks", separate piles and trees for climbing, and white spherical lights, in the play area.
5. This picture, with its wooden piles and stone mounds to climb, illustrates the designers' aim to give the children continuous adventure in a playscape of horizontal and vertical movement.

3. Lageplan des Spiel- und Erholungsparks. Oben der Kinderspielplatz, darunter die Inseln und Buchten des atriumartigen Gartenhofes. In der unteren Hälfte das Amphitheater und der Sitzbereich mit dem zentralen Wasserbecken.
4+5. Diese Abbildungen mit Kletterpfählen und Steinhügeln machen die Absicht der Planer deutlich, den Kindern durch die horizontale und vertikale Entfaltung der Spiellandschaft ein kontinuierliches Spielerlebnis zu vermitteln.

5

6

7

8

9

10

11

6+7. The children's playground is conceived as "total play environment", spacious sanded surfaces with individual play elements horizontally and vertically integrated and interconnected. For example pile bridges lead from the tree house (ill. 7) to the stone mounds. The round igloo can be climbed through tunnels up to the escape hole in the "dome", from which a slide runs down to the sand. Climbing arches span ravines. Stone pyramids can be fortresses or houses. Sand, stone and wood give an exciting impetus to games, so mobile equipement could be dispensed with.

8+9. The amphitheatre provides space on its steps for 1000 people. In summer it can be transformed into a water-games zone with sprays and sprinklers.

10. Concrete sculpture (with reliefs) for climbing.

11. Brickwalls in the sitting area have passages for hiding games.

12. Even wooden frameworks and pergolas have their place in games.

13. The pool in the sitting area with its concrete slab fountain.

6+7. Der Kinderspielplatz ist als »totale Spielumgebung« konzipiert, als riesige Sandfläche, auf der die einzelnen Spielelemente horizontal und vertikal integriert und aufeinander bezogen sind. Zum Beispiel führen vom Baumhaus (Abb. 7 unten) Pfahlbrücken zu den Steinhügeln. Der runde Iglu läßt sich durch Tunnels bis zum Ausstiegloch auf der Kuppe durchklettern, von wo eine Rutsche in den Sand herunterführt. Kletterbögen überspannen »Schluchten«, Steinpyramiden sind »Burg« oder »Haus«. Sand, Stein und Holz ergeben einen dramatischen Spielablauf, so daß auf bewegliche Geräte verzichtet werden konnte.

8+9. Das Amphitheater bietet auf seinen Stufen 1000 Personen Platz. Im Sommer läßt es sich mit Düsen und Wassersprühern in eine Wasserspielzone verwandeln.

10. Eine Kletterplastik aus Beton mit Reliefs.

11. Die Backsteinmauern am Sitzbereich haben Durchlässe zum Versteckspiel.

12. Auch die Holzgerüste und Pergolen werden in das Spiel einbezogen.

13. Das Wasserbecken im Sitzbereich mit dem Brunnen aus Betonscheiben.

12

13

Playground for Public School 55, Richmond, Staten Island, N.Y., U.S.A.

Designed by Richard G. Stein and Associates, New York
Landscaping by Peter Rolland

Schulspielplatz der Public School 55, Richmond, Staten Island, N.Y., USA

Planung: Richard G. Stein and Associates, New York
Landschaftsgestaltung: Peter Rolland

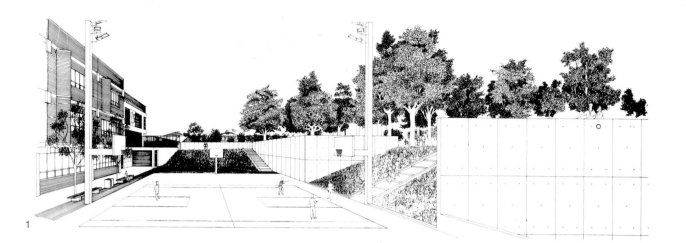

1

Instead of the more or less depressing asphalt surface of a schoolyard, a solution was sought which confounded the usual monotony by lively geometry and opportunities for a wide variety of games. In addition the scheme is so planned that it can be shared by people of all ages, while in form and materials, largely stone and concrete, it creates a unified whole with the school (also designed by Richard G. Stein). The long, somewhat irregular, site which falls sharply between the two roads along the long sides, was divided into two principal levels linked by an amphitheatre for 500 people. The upper area, where 40 existing oak trees have been preserved, comprises strong geometric modular "plazas" of brick or r. c. paving and equipment of concrete or steel tubing (climbing structures, swings, benches, tables). The lower area and the intermediate level directly bordering the school is provided with asphalt spaces for sidewalk games and group gatherings. The playgrounds are marked out on the asphalt in strong primary colours. The whole scheme is enclosed with iron fencing.

Statt der mehr oder weniger trostlosen Asphaltfläche eines Schulhofes wurde hier eine Lösung versucht, die der üblichen Monotonie eine lebendige Gliederung und vielseitige Spielmöglichkeiten entgegensetzt. Darüber hinaus ist die Anlage so geplant, daß sie von der Bevölkerung aller Altersgruppen mitbenutzt werden kann. In der Gestaltung und in den Materialien, vorzugsweise Backstein und Beton, bildet sie mit der Schule (ebenfalls von Richard G. Stein entworfen) eine Einheit. Das lange, leicht trapezförmige Grundstück, das zwischen den beiden Straßen an den Längsseiten ein starkes Gefälle aufweist, wurde in zwei Hauptebenen unterteilt, die durch ein Amphitheater für 500 Personen verbunden sind. Die obere Stufe, auf der ein alter Bestand von 40 Eichen erhalten blieb, enthält streng geometrisch geordnete Felder mit Backstein- oder Betonbelag und Geräten aus Beton oder Stahlrohr (Klettergerüste, Schaukeln, Bänke, Tische). Auf dem niedrigeren Niveau und auf der direkt an die Schule angrenzenden halbhohen Zwischenstufe werden asphaltierte Plätze für Straßenspiele und Schulversammlungen angelegt. Die Spielfelder sind auf dem Asphalt in starken Primärfarben markiert. Die ganze Anlage soll mit einem Eisenzaun umgeben werden.

2

1. Basket ball ground on the intermediate level next to the school.
2. The colour of the play areas on the lower and intermediate levels is brought out strongly in the view of the model.
3. View from the lower level towards the amphitheatre with its board-marked r. c. slab walls.
4. Geometrical play patterns, concrete shapes and metal structures under the old trees. The lamps along the paths are concrete as well.

1. Das Korbballfeld auf dem mittleren Niveau neben der Schule.
2. In der Modellansicht kommen die farbigen Spielfelder des unteren und mittleren Niveaus deutlich heraus.
3. Blick vom unteren Niveau auf das Amphitheater mit seinen Wänden aus schalungsrauhen Betonplatten.
4. Unter den alten Bäumen der oberen Stufe die geometrischen Spielfelder, Betonformen und Metallgeräte. Auch die Lampen an den Wegen sind aus Beton.

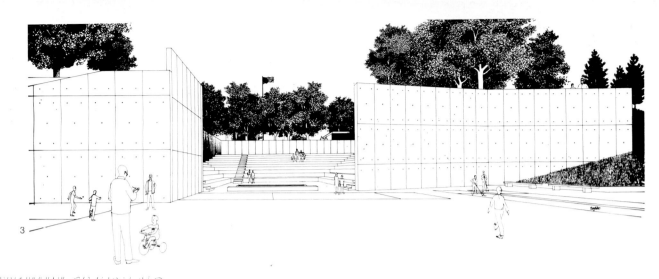

Playground for Public School 166, West 89th Street, New York City, U.S.A.

Designed by M. Paul Friedberg & Associates, New York

Schulspielplatz der Public School 166, West 89th Street, New York City, USA

Planung: M. Paul Friedberg & Associates, New York

1. Perspective from the East. Front right, the resilient spider's web; behind, the suspended rolling logs and concrete climbing elements. Front left, the amphitheatre. A large blackboard can be used by the children for drawing scenes for their theatre productions. Toilets are housed under the (grnite block) mound behind. The recessed parts of the wall are painted with bright coloured epoxy paints. The asphalted play area is depressed 3 ft below street level. Left, the space is specially equipped for small children. In the two geodesic domes of steel tubing, the larger with a diameter of 26 ft, cushion-like rubber shapes are hung as swings. The whole playground is surrounded with a black-painted tubular steel fence.

1. Perspektive von Osten. Vorn rechts das federnde Spinnennetz, dahinter die rotierend aufgehängten »Baumstämme« und die Betonkletterelemente. Vorn links das Amphitheater. Eine große Tafel kann von den Kindern selbst mit Szenen für ihr Theaterspiel bemalt werden. Im Block dahinter sind unterirdisch die Toiletten untergebracht. Die Basreliefs in der Wand werden mit Epoxydharz starkfarbig ausgemalt. Der asphaltierte Platzteil dahinter liegt 0,90 m unter Straßenniveau. Links der speziell für Kleinkinder eingerichtete Bereich. In die beiden geodätischen Kuppeln aus Stahlrohr, die größere mit einem Durchmesser von 8 m, sind kissenähnliche Gummiformen als Schaukeln eingehängt. Das ganze Areal wird mit einem Zaun aus schwarz gestrichenem Stahlrohr umgeben.

On a site of 100 ft by 165 ft the architect planned a playground for use both by the school and the neighbourhood. This double use is reflected in a separate play area for small children, where facilities are provided on a smaller scale. As with all Friedberg's playgrounds, the aim is to achieve an inviting and exciting atmosphere, in which the equipment is not disposed in a hap-hazard manner, but in a deliberately stimulating relationship. The playground has a paved perimeter area at street level, largely furnished with equipement for games of dexterity: a big spider's web with resilient cables to climb, rolling logs with ball-bearings for balancing, or concrete modular elements for making mountains or houses. The sunk amphitheatre can be transformed in summer into a spray-pool by jets recessed under the steps. Among other equipment the most interesting are two geodesic domes, in which swings with plastic cushions are suspended as seats.

Auf einem Grundstück von rund 30 x 50 m plante der Architekt einen Spielplatz, der sowohl von der Schule als auch von der Nachbarschaft genutzt werden soll. Dieser Doppelnutzung ist durch eine besondere Spielfläche für die Kleinkinder der Nachbarschaft Rechnung getragen, auf der die Geräte in verkleinertem Maßstab aufgestellt werden. Wie auf allen Plätzen Friedbergs ist auch hier versucht, eine einladende, anregende Atmosphäre zu schaffen, indem die Geräte nicht zufällig nebeneinander gestellt, sondern in einen spieldramatischen Zusammenhang gebracht werden. Der Platz hat einen gepflasterten Randstreifen auf Straßenniveau, der vorwiegend mit Geräten für Geschicklichkeitsübungen ausgerüstet ist: einem riesigen Spinnennetz mit elastischen Kabeln zum Klettern, in Kugellagern drehbare »Baumstämme« zum Balancieren oder modulare Betonelemente als »Berg« oder »Haus«. Das vertieft angelegte Amphitheater kann im Sommer durch Düsen unter den Stufen in ein Planschbecken verwandelt werden. Unter den übrigen Geräten sind die beiden geodätischen Kuppeln am interessantesten, in die Schaukeln mit Kunststoffkissen als Sitze eingehängt werden.

1

Playground for Public School 33, Queens, New York, U.S.A.

Designed by Richard G. Stein & Associates, New York

Schulspielplatz der Public School 33, Queens, New York, USA

Planung: Richard G. Stein and Associates, New York

1

In this project for a neigbourhood playground, jointly used by the school and the community, the planners aimed to create smaller areas, suitable for simultaneous activity by different age groups, without destroying the visual unity of the park. This was accomplished with a series of pergolas which zone the entire space, provide shade and greenery and seem to enlarge the comparatively small playground. The shape of the existing paved "field" has been altered and extended; with added facilities for basketball, handball, volleyball, etc., it can now be better used, both for the school's physical education classes and during out-of-school hours. The remainder of the site has been divided into smaller areas. The paved portions, with picnic and games tables, benches, spaces for pavement games and a young children's playground, are shaded with wisteria-covered trellises. The treed and grassy areas, the horseshoe pitches and boccie courts, and the seats (accessible by stepping stones) are open to the sky. For evening use the playground has comprehensive lighting.

Bei diesem Projekt für einen Nachbarschaftsspielplatz, der von Schule und Bevölkerung gemeinsam benutzt wird, war es den Planern wichtig, kleinere Flächen zu schaffen, die sich für die gleichzeitige Betätigung verschiedener Altersgruppen eignen, ohne dabei die visuelle Einheit des Parks zu zerstören. Diese Absicht wird mit einer Reihe von Pergolen verwirklicht, die den Gesamtraum unterteilen, Schatten und Grün bieten und den verhältnismäßig kleinen Platz optisch erweitern. Die Form des vorhandenen gepflasterten Spielfeldes wurde abgeändert und vergrößert. Zusammen mit den Feldern für Basketball, Handball, Volleyball usw. kann es nun besser ausgenützt werden, sowohl für den Turnunterricht der Schule als auch außerhalb der Schulstunden. Das übrige Grundstück wird in kleinere Flächen aufgeteilt. Die gepflasterten Bereiche mit Picknick- und Spieltischen, Bänken, Spielflächen für Straßenspiele und Kleinkinderspielplatz werden von Pergolen mit Glyzinien beschattet. Die baumbestandenen und grasbewachsenen Flächen, die Hufeisenwurfbahnen und Bocciabahnen und die über Tretsteine zugänglichen Sitzgelegenheiten sind offen. Abends ist der Platz überall beleuchtet.

Site plan: open playground (A), hard-surfaced area (1), softball (2), handball (3), basket ball (4), volley ball (5), play zone with trellises (B), benches under trees (6), benches under climbing plants (7), picnic and games tables (8), toilets (9), pavement games (10), shuffleboard (11), horseshoe pitch (12), boccie court (13), swings (14), sculpture (15) small children's playground (16), a benches, b play cubes, c small amphitheatre, d splashing pool, e pyramid fountain, f slide, g sanded surface

Lageplan: Offenes Spielfeld (A), Hartbelagplatz (1), Federball (2), Ballfeld (3), Korbball (4), Volleyball (5), Spielbereich mit Pergolen (B), Bänke unter Bäumen (6), Bänke unter Kletterpflanzen (7), Picknick- und Spieltische (8), Toilettengebäude (9), Straßenspiele (10), Shuffleboard (11), Hufeisenwerfen (12), Boccia (13), Schaukeln (14), Skulptur (15), Kleinkinderspielplatz (16); a Bänke, b Spielkuben, c Kleines Amphitheater, d Planschbecken, e Pyramidenbrunnen, f Rutsche, g Sandfläche.

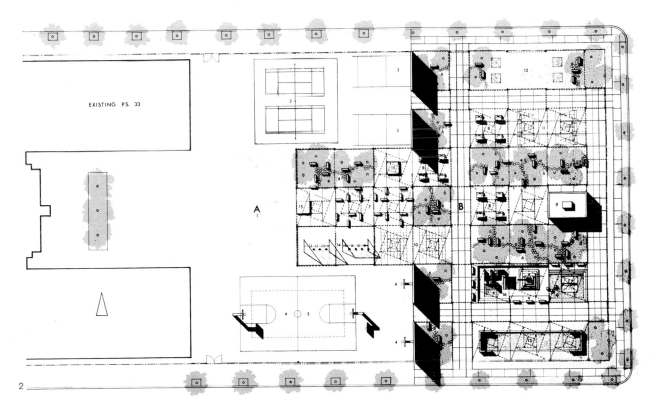

EXISTING P.S. 33

2

Playground for disabled children,
Eduardus-Hospital, Cologne-Deutz, Germany

Designed by Horst Calles, Köln-Müngersdorf

Spielplatz für versehrte Kinder,
Eduardus-Krankenhaus, Köln-Deutz, Deutschland

Planung: Horst Calles, Köln-Müngersdorf

1

The hospital playground of 19,300 square feet is bordered by roads on two sides, with a protective screen of densely planted shrubs. Previously, inquisitive passers-by had caused some inconvenience to nursing staff in charge of severely disabled children. On the third side, in front of the new wing, fire regulations had required a slightly sloping path, 10 ft wide, which was incorporated in the playground as a track for wheel-chairs and pedal cars. Of the three levels forming the playground, the lowest (a grassed area of 3200 square feet) is used for active games. The middle one is provided with sand and play equipment. For bedridden patients and children in wheel-chairs there is a sand play-table of two different heights. The hoops, with their 7 ft diameter, are big enough for children in bed to be pushed through. A swing, 5 ft high, with safety seat, a see-saw and rocking horses of stripped logs complete the equipment, which was evolved with the collaboration of doctors and nursing staff. The sloping ground offers a slide, which can be reached by a "suspension" bridge or by clambering up shallow wood steps. On the third level a paddle-pool is arranged, fed from a shallow trough.

Der 1800 m² große Krankenhaus-Spielplatz ist an zwei Seiten von Straßen begrenzt, an denen als Sichtschutz dichte Sträucher gepflanzt wurden. Neugierige Passanten hatten zuvor die Heilpädagoginnen bei der Betreuung der zum Teil schwer versehrten Kinder erheblich gestört. Auf der dritten Seite vor dem Neubautrakt war feuerpolizeilich ein 3 m breiter Weg mit leichtem Gefälle vorgeschrieben, der als Bahn für Roller und Tretautos in den Spielplatzbetrieb einbezogen wurde. Von den drei Ebenen des Platzes dient die unterste, eine 300 m² große Rasenfläche, für Bewegungsspiele. Die mittlere Stufe ist als Sand- und Gerätespielplatz eingerichtet. Für bettlägerige Patienten oder Kinder im Rollstuhl wurde ein Sandspieltisch mit zwei verschiedenen Höhen aufgestellt. Mit 2 m Durchmesser sind die Kriechrohre so groß, daß selbst Kinder in Betten hindurchgeschoben werden können. Eine nur 1,50 m hohe Schaukel mit Sicherheitssitz, Balancierbalken und Schaukelpferde aus geschälten Stämmen vervollständigen die Geräteausstattung, die zusammen mit den Ärzten und dem Pflegepersonal entwickelt wurde. Durch das Gefälle des Geländes ergab sich ein Rutschhügel, der über eine Schwingbrücke oder flache Holztreppen auch kriechend erreicht werden kann. Auf der dritten Ebene ist ein Planschbecken angelegt, das durch eine Wasserkanone gespeist wird.

2

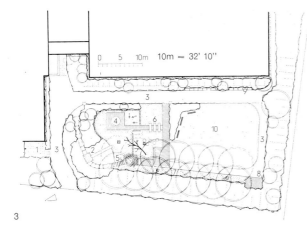

3

4

5

6

1. Sandpit on the middle level; left, the slide with its aluminium safety "track". The system of planting forces the children to use the steps at the side.
2. The playground under construction. Old tyres fastened on top of each other serve as tables. Above, the playing lawn.
3. Site plan: paddle-pool (1), slide (2), asphalt surface for street games (3), sand play-table (4), "suspension" bridge (5), concrete hoops (6), gravel of different grades for walking practice (7), games hut (8), hobby gardens (9), lawn (10).
4. Nurses and physiotherapists caring for children during play.
5. The bridge of planks, suspended on wire cables teaches balance.
6. Rocking horses of tree-trunks swing back and forth on two iron loops. Foot rests increase the children's safety.

1. Sandgrube auf der mittleren Ebene, links der Rutschhügel mit der Sicherheits-Wannenrutsche aus Aluminium. Die Bepflanzung zwingt die Kinder zur Benutzung der seitlichen Treppen.
2. Der Platz während der Bauzeit. Aufeinander genietete alte Autoreifen dienen als Tische. Oben die Spielwiese.
3. Lageplan: Planschbecken mit Wasserkanone (1), Rutschhügel (2), Asphaltfläche für Straßenspiele (3), Sandspieltisch (4), Schwingbrücke (5), Betonröhren (6), Kies mit verschiedener Körnung für Gehübungen (7), Spielhütte (8), Hobby-Gartenbeete (9), Rasen (10).
4. Schwestern und Heilpädagoginnen betreuen die Kinder beim Spiel.
5. Die Schwingbrücke aus Bohlen auf längsgespannten Drahtseilen schult das Gleichgewichtsempfinden.
6. Schaukelpferde aus Baumstämmen schwingen in zwei Eisenbügeln vor und zurück. Fußstützen erhöhen die Sicherheit der Kinder.

Playground for physically handicapped children, Bird S. Coler Hospital, Welfare Island, N.Y., U.S.A.

Designed by Richard Dattner, New York

Spielplatz für körperbehinderte Kinder, Bird S. Coler Hospital, Welfare Island, N.Y., USA

Planung: Richard Dattner, New York

The "Rehabilitation Unit" of the Bird S. Coler hospital will offer sick children various possibilities for play with which they can cope despite their physical handicaps, while providing play therapy that teaches perseverance and dexterity. It comprises six circular units of differing radius. Similarly rounded, but partly open, partition-walls give an appearance of protection to the centre, which is accessible from two directions. As the drawing shows, the scheme includes (beginning left foreground) a circle with a sandpit and planting area, both at waist height for children in wheel-chairs; a circle with climbing tower, through which children in wheel-chairs can pass; a raised, circular, swimmingpool; a small amphitheatre; an open sitting area with a gentle ramp for climbing, which leads to a bridge over the second entrance and terminates in another sitting area intended for older girls.

Das »Rehabilitation Unit« des Bird S. Coler Hospitals soll kranken Kindern Spielmöglichkeiten bieten, die sie trotz ihrer körperlichen Behinderung bewältigen können, und zugleich wird es dem therapeutischen Spiel dienen, das Ausdauer und Geschicklichkeit schult. Es besteht aus sechs kreisförmigen Einheiten von verschieden großem Radius. Ebenfalls kreisförmige zum Teil durchbrochene Wandscheiben schirmen andeutungsweise das Zentrum ab, zu dem zwei Zugänge hinführen. Wie die Zeichnung zeigt, sieht das Projekt (beginnend links vorn) einen Kreis mit Sandkasten und Gartenbeeten vor, beide hüfthoch für Kinder in Rollstühlen; einen Kreis mit Kletterturm, der von Kindern im Rollstuhl durchfahren werden kann; ein erhöhtes, kreisförmiges Schwimmbecken; ein kleines Amphitheater; einen Freisitzplatz mit einer sanft ansteigenden Rampe, die zu einer Brücke über den zweiten Zugang führt und in einem weiteren Sitzbereich endet, der für größere Mädchen gedacht ist.

1. The three upper drawings show sections through the approximately waist-high wall, which surrounds the entire play space. Slowly flowing water runs along the top in a shallow channel, so that children in wheel-chairs or beds can float little ships and be enticed to follow or guide them round. The wall also serves as a support for those with walking difficulties. The sandpits, too, and planting beds (left below) are within convenient reach and the walls are slanted, so that children in wheel-chairs can come close. To the right, the picture shows the bridge passing over the path below.
2. Perspective sketch of proposed playground.

1. Die drei oberen Abbildungen zeigen Querschnitte durch die ungefähr hüfthohe Mauer, die den ganzen Spielplatz umgibt. In ihre Oberkante ist eine Rinne mit langsam fließendem Wasser eingelassen, so daß die Kinder vom Rollstuhl oder Bett aus Schiffchen schwimmen lassen können und angeregt werden, ihnen nachzugehen oder -zufahren. Zugleich dient die Mauer als Stütze für gehbehinderte Patienten. Auch die Sandspielflächen und die Gartenbeete (Abbildung unten links) sind in bequeme Greifhöhe gelegt und ihre Mauern so abgeschrägt, daß die Kinder mit dem Rollstuhl ganz nahe heranfahren können. Die Abbildung unten rechts zeigt die Kreuzung zwischen Brücke und Unterführung.
2. Perspektivische Skizze des geplanten Spielplatzes.

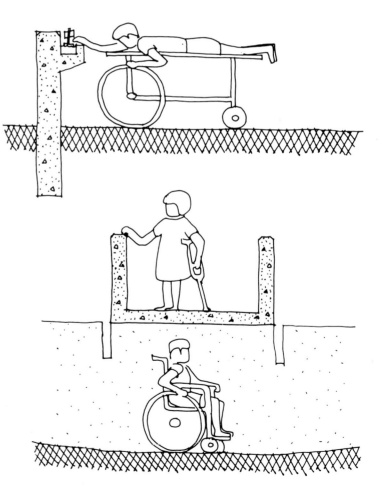

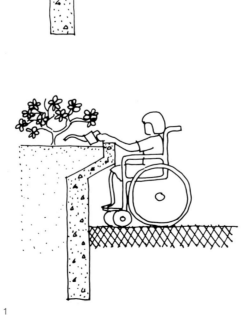

1

Water Playground, Central Park, New York City, U.S.A.

Designed by Richard Dattner, New York

Wasserspielplatz, Central Park, New York City, USA

Planung: Richard Dattner, New York

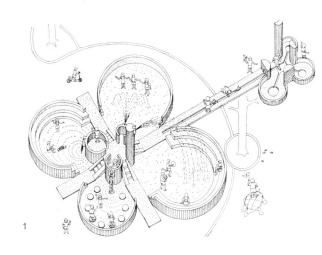

1. Perspective drawing of the preliminary design. Top right, the "channel" and "harbour" part (not carried out).
2–4. Various views. The children take particular delight in the water sprays of the "turrets". The central platform also serves as a stage for rockn' roll' evenings.

1. Perspektivische Zeichnung des Vorentwurfes. Rechts oben die nicht ausgeführten Teile von »Bach« und »Hafen«.
2–4. Verschiedene Ansichten. Besonders gerne spielen die Kinder an den Spritzdüsen der Kanzeln. Das zentrale Podest diente übrigens auch schon als Podium für eine abendliche Rock'n'Roll-Veranstaltung.

The architect planned a water playground at West 81st Street, with four splashing pools in the shape of a four-leaf clover. A platform, three steps high, forms the centre, from which three "turrets" (with water sprays) project outwards. At the fourth corner stands a higher column, also with a spray. The three-quarter circles of the pools have either sitting "stones", plain walls or stepped benches. The final version differs slightly from the original design. The circular form was made polygonal to simplify the formwork for the concrete walls. The "stalk" of the clover leaf was also sacrificed. It was to have contained a channel of running water on which children could guide their boats to a harbour. The latter was conceived as a counter attraction to the large clover leaf, with its semi-circular "turrets" and columns, but even without this extension the playground enjoys great popularity. As the pools have only a gentle slope to the centre, the water does not exceed ankle-depth, so the children can play in safety without supervision.

An der West 81st Street projektierte der Architekt einen Wasserspielplatz, dessen vier Planschbecken die Form eines vierblättrigen Kleeblattes haben. Das Zentrum bildet ein um drei Stufen erhöhtes Podest, aus dem nach drei Seiten verschieden große Kanzeln mit Wasserspeiern vorspringen; an der vierten Ecke steht eine höhere Säule, ebenfalls mit einer Wassersprühdüse. Die Dreiviertelskreise der Becken haben teils Sitzstufen, teils glatte Mauern mit eingekerbten Schwellen. Die Ausführung weicht vom Entwurf etwas ab: Die Kreisformen wurden wegen der einfacheren Schalung der Betonmauern polygonal gebrochen. Auch der »Stiel« des Kleeblattes fiel den Einsparungen zum Opfer. Er sollte eine Rinne mit strömendem Wasser aufnehmen, in dem die Kinder Schiffchen bis zum »Hafen« hätten treiben lassen können. Dieser Hafen war als Gegenform zu dem großen Kleeblatt gedacht, mit halbkreisförmigen Trommeln und Säulen. Aber auch ohne diese Ergänzung erfreut sich der Platz großer Beliebtheit. Da sich die Becken nur schwach zur Mitte hin neigen, steht das Wasser höchstens knöchelhoch, so daß die Kinder auch ohne Beaufsichtigung gefahrlos spielen können.

Playground at the spa of Grenchen, Switzerland

Designed by Alfred Trachsel, Zürich, in collaboration with B. Hefti
and the Pro Juventute Foundation, Zürich

Spielplatz im Gartenbad Grenchen, Schweiz

Planung: Alfred Trachsel, Zürich, in Zusammenarbeit mit B. Hefti
und der Stiftung Pro Juventute, Zürich

This playground forms part of an outdoor swimming pool. It was designed with water as its main element. Its chief attraction therefore is its stream which children can navigate in small boats. They can propel their boats with hands and feet. The round trip passes the lighthouse and leads to a small harbour passing through a climbing arch and a tunnel.

Continuing along the stream, children can moor their boats at the primitive village consisting of open huts on poles. Adjacent to it is the widest section of the stream called the "ocean". In this "ocean" of quite shallow water a larger boat is at anchor; this boat can be climbed with the help of rope ladders or via a series of stepping poles in the water. Further playground elements are the sandpit on the artificial hill away from the centre of activity, and the paddling pool near the bend of the stream. They have been well sited, adding to the liveliness of the ground and leading to playful activity.

Als Teil einer Freibadanlage wurde dieser Kinderspielplatz ganz vom Wasser her geplant. Seine Hauptattraktion ist der »Schiffchenbach«, auf dem die Kinder mit kleinen Schiffen, die sie mit Händen und Füßen vorwärtstreiben, fahren können. Die Rundfahrt führt am Leuchtturm vorbei, unter einem Kletterbogen und einem Tunnel aus Betonelementen durch, hinüber zum kleinen Hafen. Auf der Weiterfahrt können die Kinder am Pfahlbaudorf mit seinen offenen Hütten anlegen und schließlich in die Ausweitung des Baches, das »Meer«, hinaussteuern. In diesem Becken mit niedrigem Wasserstand ist ein größeres Schiff verankert, das mit Strickleitern oder über eingerammte Pfähle bestiegen wird. In diese spieldramatisch höchst lebendige Konzeption sind die weiteren Platzelemente geschickt einbezogen: der Sandplatz abseits neben dem aufgeschütteten Aussichtshügel, das Planschbecken an der Bachschleife.

Site plan: The stream (1), the island and the lawn (2), climbing arches bridging the stream (3), tunnel made of curved concrete castings (4), the harbour (5), village on poles (6), "ocean" with the larger boat (7), lighthouse and climbing tree (8), village green with Wendy houses and water trough (9), hill with slide (10), sandpit bordered with precast concrete elements. Circular concrete tables and crawling ducts (11), copse with seats for children (12), see-saws (13), paddling pool with sculpture (14), restaurant (15), swimming pool (16).

Lageplan: Der Schiffchenbach (1), die »Insel« und Liegewiese (2), Kletterbögen als Flußübergänge (3), Tunnel aus Betonbögen (4), der kleine Hafen (5), Pfahlbaudorf (6), das »Meer« mit dem großen Schiff (7), Leuchtturm und Kletterbaum (8), Dorfplatz mit Spielhütten und Brunnen (9), Aussichtshügel mit Rutschbahn (10), Sandplatz mit Einfassung aus Betonelementen, runden Betontischen und Kriechröhren (11), Wäldchen mit Kinderbänken (12), Balkenschaukeln (13), Planschbecken mit Plastik (14), Restaurant (15), Gartenbad (16).

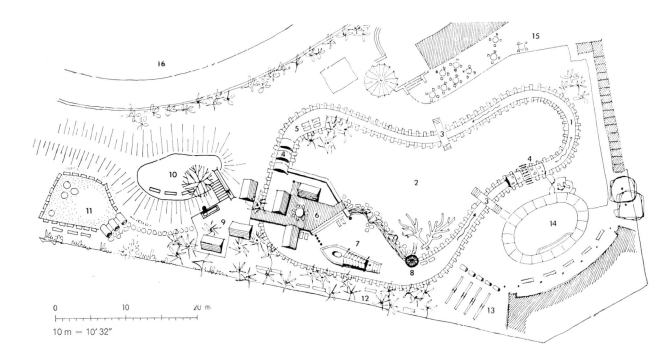

0   10   20 m

10 m = 10' 32"

Water playgrounds at Düsseldorf, Germany

Designed by the Municipal Gardens Department of Düsseldorf
(Ulrich Wolf)

Wasserspielplätze, Düsseldorf, Deutschland

Planung: Stadtgartenamt Düsseldorf (Ulrich Wolf)

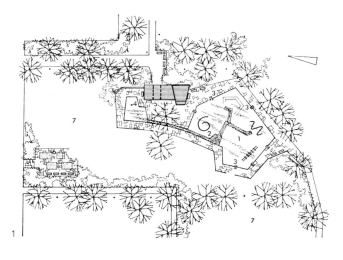

1. Site plan: water playground with equipment (1), drainage channel
(2), spray pipes (3), paddling pool for small children (4), shelter with
attendants' room, store and lavatories (5), sandpit (6), lawn (7).
2. Large climbing structure of tubular steel with jets inside and
below the supports (water curtain).

1. Lageplan: Wasserspielplatz mit Geräten (1), Abflußkanal (2), Spritzrohre (3), Kleinkinderbad (4), Unterstandhalle mit Wärter- und Geräte-
raum und Toiletten (5), Sandspielplatz (6), Liegewiesen (7).
2. Großes Klettergerüst aus Metallrohren mit Düsen in und unter den
Ständern (Wasservorhang).

Water has a great fascination for children: showers, paddling in
dirty water, fountains and sprays arouse ever-fresh enthusiasm. That
is why water should never be missing from any playground. As
paddling pools generally get dirty quickly and as they can only be
built and maintained at comparatively high cost, Düsseldorf Municipal Gardens Department made a new departure with its so-called
water playgrounds, several of which have been installed during
recent years. Areas, paved on a slight incline, have climbing and
hopping equipment which also discharges water by means of jets
and revolving sprays. The plant, which consists of galvanised or
painted steel tubes, is made up in different combinations for each
playground and is modified according to the age-group for which
it is intended. Movable sprays at the outer edge and a drainage
channel at the lowest point of the paving keep the whole installa-
tion constantly clean.

Wasser übt eine starke Anziehungskraft auf Kinder aus: Duschen,
Pfützen, Brunnen und Rasensprenger sind Anlaß zu immer neuer
Begeisterung. Deshalb dürfte Wasser eigentlich auf keinem Kinderspielplatz fehlen. Da Planschbecken im allgemeinen rasch ver-
schmutzen und zudem nur mit verhältnismäßig hohen Bau- und
Unterhaltungskosten erstellt werden können, ging das Stadtgartenamt von Düsseldorf neue Wege und entwickelte in den vergangenen
Jahren verschiedene sogenannte Wasserspielplätze. Auf leicht ge-
neigten, plattenbelegten Flächen werden Kletter- und Hüpfgeräte
aufgestellt, die durch Spritzrohre, Düsen und Dreharme Wasser aus-
stoßen. Die aus verzinkten oder gestrichenen Metallrohren zusammengesetzten Geräte werden für jeden Platz neu kombiniert und auf
die Spielbedürfnisse der verschiedenen Altersstufen abgestimmt.
Bewegliche Spritzrohre am äußeren Rand und ein Abflußkanal an
der tiefsten Stelle des Platzes sorgen für eine ständige Reinigung der
Anlage.

3. Curved horizontal bars with water jets. On the pavement are funnel jets.

4. One of the movable spray pipes at the edge of the water playground, with the help of which the paving slabs are kept clean by children having fun with the pipes.

5. Automatic splashing device. Water pouring into the bowl turns it over and returns it to its former position.

6. Circular pipe with jets directed to the outside and inside alternately.

3. Hangelgerät mit Düsen. Auf den Platten Trichterdüsen.

4. Eines der beweglichen Spritzrohre am Rande der Wasserfläche, mit denen die Platten »spielend« gereinigt werden.

5. Automatisches Kippgerät. Durch Wasserzulauf füllt sich die Schale, kippt um und kehrt wieder in die alte Lage zurück.

6. Stahlrohr-Spirale mit abwechselnd nach innen und außen gerichteten Düsen.

3

4

5

6

Playground in a Stockholm park, Sweden

Designed by the Parks Section of the Municipal Planning Department, Stockholm

Parkspielplatz, Stockholm, Schweden

Planung: Parkabteilung des Stadtplanungsamtes Stockholm

1

2

In Stockholm, through the Parks Section of the municipal administration, more than 70 playgrounds have been built. These are mostly parts of the extensive public parks and therefore are frequently designed on a generous scale, covering large areas. In Sweden a noticeable emphasis is laid on the separation of various age-groups, and on intensive leadership by qualified people. For instance, fenced areas are provided where mothers can leave their small children for a few hours in the care of a supervisor. Carefully trained female playground leaders and assistants, who are employees of the Parks Section, organise games and spare-time occupations for the older children; they also look after the equipment and material for constructional hobbies. Endeavours are being made to place these women on a footing equal to school teachers as regards remuneration. In spite of this extensive supervision by qualified staff the use of these playgrounds is free of charge. Often playground activities are continued all the year round. In the winter flat surfaces are transformed into ice rinks.

In Stockholm wurden durch die Parkabteilung der Stadtverwaltung mehr als 70 Spielplätze erbaut, die meist Bestandteile der großen öffentlichen Parkanlagen sind und deshalb vielfach sehr großzügig und weitläufig geplant werden konnten. Für die Verhältnisse in Schweden ist es bezeichnend, welch großer Wert auf eine intensive spielpädagogische Führung und auf dieTrennung der verschiedenen Altersstufen gelegt wird. So sind für Kleinkinder »Kindergitter« eingerichtet, wo die Mütter ihre Kinder für einige Stunden zur Beaufsichtigung abgeben können. Sorgfältig ausgebildete Spielplatzleiterinnen und -helferinnen, die Angestellte der Parkabteilung sind, organisieren für die Größeren Spiele und Freizeitbeschäftigungen und verwalten Spielgerät und Bastelmaterial. Es wird angestrebt, diese Helfer gehaltsmäßig den Schullehrern gleichzustellen. Trotz dieser vielfältigen pädagogischen Betreuung ist die Benutzung der Plätze kostenlos. Vielfach wird der Spielbetrieb das ganze Jahr über aufrechterhalten; im Winter werden die Spielflächen in Eisbahnen verwandelt.

3

1. Hard-surface area for ball games.

2. The fenced area for small children where experienced nursery school teachers look after children.

3. General view of a playground in a Stockholm park. The divisions by fences and shrubs are characteristic of many Swedish playgrounds. In the foreground is the fenced area for small children; behind on the left is the ground for constructional games – building blocks and boards are handed out by the playground leader – a sandpit and a slide form part of the equipment too. On the right one can see the more extensive hard-surfaced area for action and other games, with a separate enclosure for swings leading off it. In the background behind the row of trees are the paddling pool and the ground for ball games.

4. Work benches in the open air for the constructional hobbies of older children.

5. The playground assistants not only hand out equipment for sports and play but also the material for constructional hobbies and games played on by groups of children.

6. Issuing "building material" and play equipment.

1. Der Ballspielplatz mit Hartbelag.

2. Im Kleinkindergitter übernehmen erfahrene Kindergärtnerinnen die Betreuung.

3. Gesamtansicht eines Stockholmer Parkspielplatzes, dessen Aufteilung in verschiedene, durch Zäune und Grünstreifen voneinander getrennte Abteilungen charakteristisch für viele schwedische Spielplatzlösungen ist. Vorn das Kindergitter für die Kleinkinder, links dahinter das Areal für Sand- und Bauspiele (die Bauklötze und Bretter gibt der Spielplatzleiter aus), rechts davon die ausgedehntere Hartbelagfläche für Tummel- und Bewegungsspiele mit abgetrennter Schaukelnische. Im Hintergrund (hinter der Baumreihe) Planschbecken und Ballspielplatz.

4. Im Freien aufgestellte Werkbänke zum Basteln für größere Kinder.

5. Von den Spielplatzhelferinnen werden nicht nur Sport- und Spielgeräte, sondern auch Bastelmaterial und Brettspiele ausgegeben, mit denen sich die Kinder in kleinen Gruppen beschäftigen.

6. Bei der Ausgabe von Spielmaterial und Sportgeräten.

4

5

6

Playground in a park, Silver Spring, U.S.A.

Designed by Samuel Snyder, Stuart M. Armstrong and Wilbur C. Irving

Spielplatz im Park, Silver Spring, USA

Planung: Samuel Snyder, Stuart M. Armstrong, Wilbur C. Irving

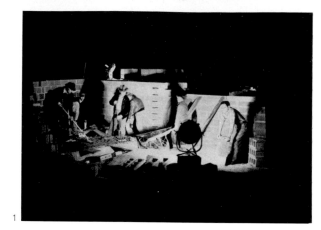

In order to provide their children with better facilities for play the parents at the Parkside School at Silver Spring joined forces and built this playground as a communal effort. The mothers raised the necessary finance by means of a bazaar, and the fathers volunteered at week-ends, in the evenings, and even at night for the building work. The ground, which caters for a large part of the 400 children at the elementary school, is mainly designed for action games and climbing. The centre is formed of ramps, steps, walls and towers made from hollow blocks for climbing and jumping. A surrounding zone, containing sandpit, concrete seats and walls for ball games, is for quieter activities. On the inner side of the curved ramp is the amphitheatre. The stage is the high-level gangway on the opposite side. The ground has been successfully divided up into individual zones by skilful placing of walls and towers.

Um für ihre Kinder bessere Spielmöglichkeiten zu schaffen, tat sich die Elternschaft der Parkside School in Silver Spring zusammen und baute in Gemeinschaftsarbeit diesen Spielplatz. Die notwendigen Geldmittel wurden von den Müttern durch einen Bazar aufgebracht und die Väter stellten sich an den Wochenenden, abends – und auch nachts – freiwillig für die Bauarbeiten zur Verfügung. Der Platz, der einen großen Teil der 400 Kinder der Elementarschule aufnimmt, ist in erster Linie auf Bewegungs- und Kletterspiele ausgerichtet. Rampen und Treppen, Kletterwände und Sprungtürme aus Hohlblocksteinen bilden das Zentrum, eine Randzone mit Sandkasten, Sitzblöcken und Ballwänden dient dem stilleren Spiel. In der Rundung der Zugangsrampe ist ein Amphitheater angelegt, als Bühne dient der gegenüberliegende Laufsteg. Die Platzfläche selbst wird durch geschickt gruppierte Sprungwände und Klettertürme aufgelockert und in einzelne Bezirke unterteilt.

1. Fathers at voluntary night work. Searchlights with generators were placed at their disposal by the fire brigade free of charge.
2. View of the whole playground. In the centre is the curved ramp around the amphitheatre, high-level gangway and steps; on the right is the jumping and climbing tower; on the left the climbing wall and sandpit.
3. "Fire station" with sliding pole which can be climbed from the ramp.
4. Amphitheatre for performances and gatherings.
5. Intersecting climbing walls of hollow blocks.
6. The tunnel under the ramp is extended by a few separate concrete drums.

1. Väter bei freiwilliger Nachtarbeit. Die Scheinwerfer und Beleuchtungsaggregate stellte die Feuerwehr kostenlos zur Verfügung.
2. Gesamtansicht. Im Zentrum die geschwungene Zugangsrampe mit dem Amphitheater, Laufsteg und Verbindungstreppen; rechts Sprung- und Kletterturm; links Kletterwand und Sandkasten.
3. »Feuerwache« mit Rutschpfahl, der von der Rampe aus erklettert wird.
4. Amphitheater für Vorführungen und Versammlungen.
5. Sich durchkreuzende Kletterwände aus Hohlblocksteinen.
6. Der in die Rampe eingelassene Betontunnel wird ergänzt durch eine Reihe frei aufgestellter Kriechröhren.

3

4

5

6

Adventure playground in Central Park, New York City, U.S.A.

Designed by Richard Dattner, New York

Abenteuerspielplatz im Central Park, New York City, USA

Planung: Richard Dattner, New York

This playground, laid out in Central Park close to West 67th Street and costing $85,000, is a gift of the Estée and Joseph Lauder Foundation. The architect designed an enormous sandbox, for which in place of the usual climbing and swinging equipment he developed a number of play innovations: a combination of amphitheatre and splashing pool, a water channel and dam for model ships, tree houses, a stone mound with "crawling passages", a castle with concrete walls and tower, and a real boat. Finely sieved sand is spread around the slides, and on other parts a mixture of sand and gravel, dustfree, which does not become mud in rain. Only the perimeter is asphalted for roller-skating and sidewalk games. Further play possibilities are offered by "moving" elements (planks and blocks for building, bamboo sticks, sacks, canvas, paper and paint) which children can manipulate as they like, for they should be able to exploit not only the obvious, "fixed", equipment for play, but also be creative. A supervisor and several assistants step in when needed.

Dieser im Central Park bei der West 67th Street gelegene Spielplatz, dessen Baukosten $ 85000.– betrugen, ist ein Geschenk der Estée and Joseph Lauder Foundation an die Stadt New York. Der Architekt entwarf eine riesige Sandkiste, für deren »Möblierung« er anstelle der üblichen Geräte wie Schaukeln, Wippen oder Kletterbögen neue Spielelemente entwickelte: eine Kombination aus Amphitheater und Planschbecken, Wasserrinne und Staudamm für Modellschiffe, Baumhäuser, Steinkegel mit Kriechgängen, eine Festung mit Beton-mauern und Turm und ein richtiges Schiff. An den Rutschbahnen liegt feingesiebter Sand, andere Teile sind mit einem Gemisch aus Sand und Kies belegt, das nicht staubt und bei Regen nicht zu Matsch wird. Lediglich die Randzone ist als Rollschuhbahn und Fläche für Straßenspiele asphaltiert. Diese Spielmöglichkeiten werden ergänzt durch bewegliche Elemente (Bretter und Klötze zum Bauen, Bambusstangen, Sackleinen, Leinwand, Papier und Farbe), die das Kind nach Belieben verändern kann. Es soll nicht nur die an-gebotenen, fest eingebauten Spielmöglichkeiten ausnutzen, sondern auch selbst schöpferisch gestalten können. Eine Aufsichtsperson und mehrere Assistenten greifen nötigenfalls helfend ein.

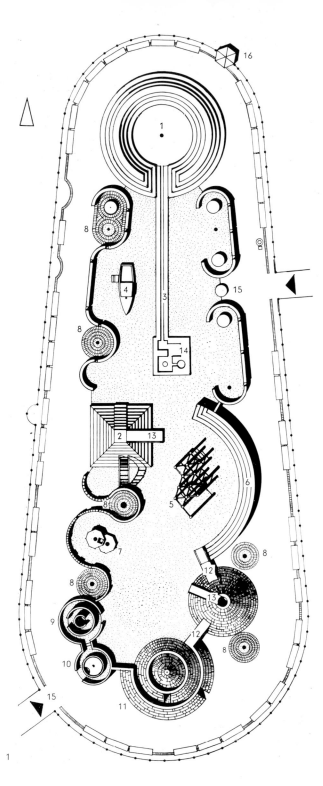

1. Site plan: splashing pool (1), climbing pyramid (2), water channel (3), boat (4), climbing structures (5), amphitheatre (6), tree houses (7), tree "pit" (8), castle (9), "stronghold" with tower (10), hill-in-a-hill (11), tunnel (12), slide (13), wading pool (14), entrance (15), pump house (16).
2. The moving elements include painted wood boards for building and hand barrows in bright colours.
3. View (from the climbing pyramid) of a tree pit and tree houses. Right background, the castle; middle background, the hill-in-a-hill; further left, the "volcano" with slides and crawling hoops; left, part of the amphitheatre.

1. Lageplan: Planschbecken (1), Kletterpyramide (2), Wasserrinne (3), Boot (4), Klettergerüst (5), Amphitheater (6), Baumhäuser (7), Baumgrube (8), Festung (9), Bollwerk mit Turm (10), Hügel im Hügel (11), Tunnel (12), Rutschbahn (13), Watbecken (14), Eingang (15), Pumpenhaus (16).
2. Zu den beweglichen Spielgeräten gehören bunt bemalte Sperrholz-bretter zum Bauen und Schubkarren in leuchtenden Farben.
3. Blick von der Kletterpyramide auf eine Baumgrube und Baum-häuser. Rechts hinten die Festung; hinten Mitte der »Hügel im Hügel«, weiter links der »Vulkankegel« mit Rutschbahnen und Kriechröhren, links ein Stück des Amphitheaters.

4+5. The water games area, which on plan looks like a large key, is fed from the round splashing pool (with rising "amphitheatre" sides and central spray). The channel broadens at the end into a small wading pool.

6. General view of the narrower, Northern, half of the playground with its water area. The metal paling fence was not the architect's idea, but mothers like it, because it keeps the children from straying.

4+5. Der Wasserspielbereich, der im Plan wie ein großer Schlüssel aussieht, hat seinen Zufluß aus dem kreisförmigen, amphitheatralisch ansteigenden Planschbecken, in dessen Zentrum das Wasser aus einer Düse sprüht. An seinem Ende erweitert er sich zu einem kleinen Watbecken.

6. Gesamtansicht der schmaleren, nördlichen Spielplatzhälfte mit dem Wasserbereich. Der 3 m hohe Staketenzaun war kein Vorschlag des Architekten; die Mütter finden ihn jedoch gut, weil er die Kinder am Weglaufen hindert.

7. Project for an extensible play area for small children. Left, swings; behind, maze; middle, sand box; at back, climbing pyramid with slide; right, ride-through gate for tricycles to the quiet games space; behind, two-floor play house with ladder, slide and sitting area below.
8. Climbing pyramid and slide of wood planks.
9. The igloo-like hill-in-a-hill; right, the "volcano".
10. Castle and stronghold with tower.

7. Entwurf für einen ergänzenden Kleinkinder-Spielplatzteil. Links Schaukeln, dahinter Irrgarten; Mitte Sandkiste, dahinter Kletterpyramide mit Rutschbahn; rechts Tordurchfahrten für Dreiräder zum Bereich für stille Spiele, dahinter zweistöckiges Spielhaus mit Leiter, Rutschbahn und unterem Sitzbereich.
8. Kletterpyramide und Rutschbahn aus Holzbohlen.
9. Der igluartige »Hügel im Hügel«, rechts der »Vulkan«.
10. Festung und Bollwerk mit Turm.

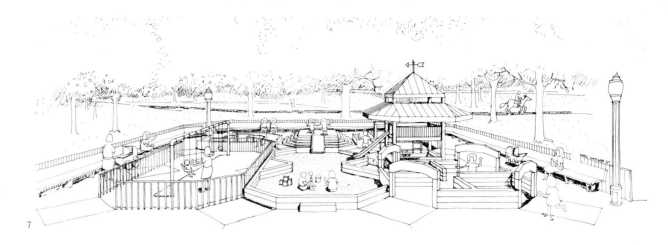

7

8

9

10

99

Krusi Park Playground at Alameda, U.S.A.

Designed by Royston, Hanamoto & Mayes, San Francisco

Spielplatz Krusi-Park, Alameda, USA

Planung: Royston, Hanamoto & Mayes, San Francisco

1. Site plan.
   1 Concrete paving
   2 Sandpit with mounds of concrete and surrounding shelf for sand pies
   3 Paddling pool
   4 Spiral slide of concrete
   5 Soft-surface area with swings, slide, vertical tree-trunks for climbing and play sculpture of tubular steel picked out in various colours (designed by Raymond Rice)
   6 Roundabout
   7 Garages
   8 Fly-over for pedal cars
   9 Workshop and petrol station
   10 Play shelter
   11 Pergola with seats for grown-ups
   12 Lattice fence

1. Lageplan.
   1 Hartbelag aus Betonplatten
   2 Sandplatz mit Kuchentisch und Sprungberg aus Beton
   3 Planschbecken
   4 Spiralrutschbahn aus Beton
   5 Weichbelagflache mit Kletter- und Bewegungsgeräten: Schaukeln, Rutschbahn, Kletterberg aus Holzstämmen und Spielplastik aus verschiedenfarbig akzentuiertem Stahlrohr (Entwurf: Raymond Rice)
   6 Karussell
   7 Garagen
   8 Fahrbahngürtel für Tretautos
   9 Reparaturwerkstatt und Tankstelle
   10 Spielpergola
   11 Pergola mit Sitzbänken für die Erwachsenen
   12 Lattenzaun

Scale and equipment of this playground is for childern of 3 to 10 years of age. Sand, water and equipment have been kept to clearly defined areas, which encourages the formation of small groups when children play. The main attraction of this ground is the hiring out of pedal cars which are kept in six small garages. These cars can use the paved area which is made of roundabouts, and streets through the sandpits and pools etc. In addition there are fly-overs and hairpin bends in scale with cars. The road surface is of concrete. As with all the other projects of this team of architects, this playground has been carefully detailed – as is apparent for example from the placing and design of the equipment and the curved lattice fence which surrounds the whole ground. The siting of a seat as an element of articulation in front of the play shelter, and the one-foot-high stepped concrete surround to the sandpit show the intensive design work that has been put into the scheme.

Im Maßstab und in der Geräteausstattung wurde dieser Platz auf Kinder im Vorschul- und Schulalter bis zu 10 Jahren zugeschnitten. Sand, Wasser und Geräte sind auf einzelne, formal klar abgegrenzte Felder verteilt, die die Bildung von kleineren Spielgruppen fördern. Ihren Hauptakzent erhält die Anlage durch den Verleih von Spielautos, die in sechs zeltförmigen Garagen auf engstem Raum untergebracht sind. Als Fahrbahn steht nicht nur die schleifenförmige, kunstgerecht ausgebaute Betonstraße mit ihren Kurven, Steigungen und Übergängen zur Verfügung, sondern auch die gesamte Hartbelagfläche des Spielplatzes, die zwischen den eingelassenen Sand- und Gerätefeldern weitere »Straßen« ergibt. Wie alle Projekte dieses Architektenteams ist der Platz bis in alle Details sorgfältig durchgestaltet, wie dies beispielsweise Form und Anordnung der Geräte zeigen. Auch die Aufstellung einer Sitzbank als trennendes Element vor dem Spielhäuschen und die kniehohe, abgetreppte Einfassung des Sandplatzes kennzeichnen die intensive Durcharbeitung des Planes.

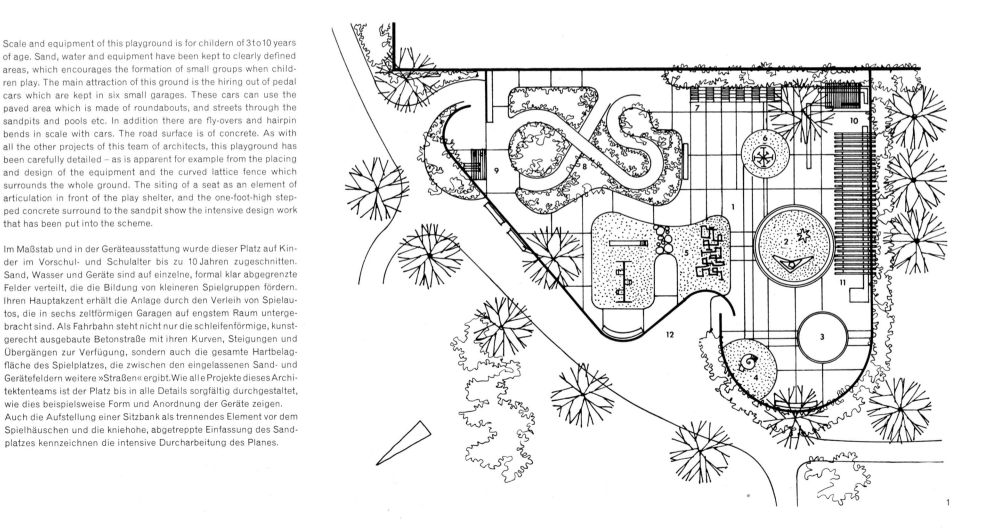

2. Sandpit with concrete mounds and shelf for sand pies.
3. Lock-up double garage.
4. Petrol station with roofover. A standard length of drainage pipe, a metal junction piece and a rubber hose are the simple components of this petrol pump.
5. The soft-surface area with play sculpture, wall and tree-trunks for climbing. In the background the hairpin bend.

2. Sandplatz mit Kuchentisch und Sprungberg.
3. Verschließbare Doppelgarage.
4. Tankstelle mit Schutzdach. Ein serienmäßiges Kanalisationsrohr, ein Metallverbindungsstück und ein Gummischlauch sind die einfachen Elemente der Tanksäule.
5. Blick über die Weichbelagfläche mit Spielplastik, Kletterwand und Holzberg auf die Haarnadelkurve des Fahrbahnhügels.

2

3

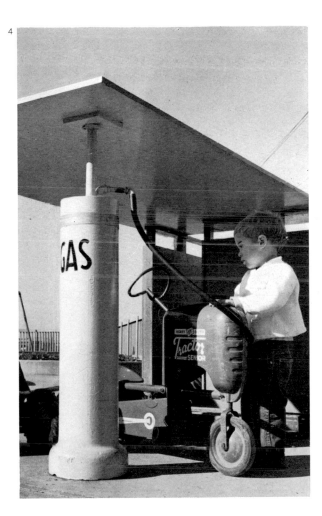

4

5

6. Tubular steel sculpture, sandpit and pergola.
7. The road leads to the petrol station and repair shop in the background on the left.
8. The climbing wall with rounded corners and holes.
9. The swings have special safety devices in the form of triple attachments for each seat and braking bars for the feet.
10. Sandpit with surrounding concrete shelf for making sand pies. In the background the roundabout and garages.

6. Stahlrohrplastik, Sandplatz und Pergola.
7. Die gut ausgebaute Fahrbahn führt am Halteschild vorbei zu Reparaturwerkstatt und Tankstelle im Hintergrund.
8. Die Kletterwand mit Steiglöchern und abgerundeten Kanten.
9. Die Kettenschaukeln bieten durch dreifache Aufhängung und Fußhaltestangen erhöhte Sicherheit.
10. Blick vom Sandplatz über die als Kuchentisch ausgebildete Mauer auf Karussell und Garagen.

7

8

9

10

103

"...parken" miniature traffic area and playground
...r blocks of flats at Mørkhøj, Denmark

Designed by Erik and Agnete Mygind, Virum

Haus- und Verkehrsspielplatz »Pileparken«, Mørkhøj, Dänemark

Planung: Erik und Agnete Mygind, Virum

A long stretch of grassland in front of the informally grouped blocks of flats (see illustration 2) has been divided up into a number of small patches with either a sandpit or play equipment in them. These patches are linked by groups of small bushes. The architects have created an excellent network of playgrounds for small children, in close proximity to the playgrounds at Herlev Byvænge (see page 58). The most interesting part of this playground is the miniature traffic area which is an example of a good solution obtained for very little expenditure. A system of "streets" of concrete paving, occasionally widening into "squares", leading through tunnels of concrete drums, over undulating stretches, passing signals, waiting-shelters, garages and petrol stations, provides a stimulating run for scooters and alternative possibilities for a great variety of games. All elements of this playground are of the most simple materials – tree-trunks, boards, concrete slabs – which, in spite of their improvised nature, afford ample scope for play, when approached with a child's imagination.

Ein Grünstreifen, der an den Stirnseiten der locker hintereinandergereihten Wohnblocks entlangzieht (Abbildung 2), ist in verschiedene Geräte- und Sandspielnischen unterteilt, die von niedrigen Buschgruppen eingereiht werden. Ähnlich wie bei den Hausspielplätzen in Herlev Byvænge (siehe Seite 58) schufen die Architekten auch hier ein dichtes Netz von Kleinkinderspielplätzen, die in unmittelbarer Nachbarschaft zu den Häusern liegen. Den interessantesten Teil dieses Spielplatzsystems bildet der Verkehrsspielplatz, der zeigt, wie sich gute Lösungen auch mit geringen Kosten erzielen lassen. Ein Straßensystem aus Betonplatten, das sich gelegentlich zu Plätzen weitet, ergibt eine vielseitige Rollerbahn, die mit ihren Wellenstrecken, Tunnels aus Betonröhren, Signalen, Garagen und Tankstellen abwechslungsreiche Spielmöglichkeiten bietet. Alle Elemente dieses Platzes bestehen aus einfachsten Materialien – Rundhölzer, Bretter, Betonplatten –, die jedoch trotz ihres improvisierten Charakters der kindlichen Vorstellungskraft genügend Raum geben.

1. The undulating "road" along the edge of this ground. Simple railings keep the children on the track. As the ground is purely for play and not for giving traffic instruction, no traffic signs have been provided.
2. The stretch of grassland along the blocks of flats. Behind the miniature traffic area are pergolas and climbing equipment of another playground.
3. The large crossing with double-track roads and the real traffic lights in the centre. At the "stops" in the background are small Wendy houses.
4. The road to the tunnel passes a signal.
5. Garage of simple boards and tree-trunks.
6. Petrol station made of a telephone pole; a wire spiral serves as the supply pipe.

1. Die gewellte Fahrbahn auf der Längsseite des Platzes. Einfache Schranken halten die Kinder auf der Spur. Da der Platz reines Spielgelände ist und nicht zum Verkehrsunterricht dient, wurde auf die Ausstattung mit Verkehrszeichen verzichtet.
2. Der Grünstreifen entlang den Häuserzeilen. Hinter dem Verkehrsspielplatz Spielpergolen und Klettergeräte eines weiteren Spielplatzes.
3. Die große Kreuzung mit den zweispurigen Hauptverkehrsstraßen und der drehbaren Verkehrsampel in der Mitte. An den »Haltestellen« im Hintergrund kleine Spielhäuschen.
4. Am Signal vorbei führt die Strecke zum Tunnel aus Betonröhren.
5. Die Garage aus einfachen Brettern und Rundhölzern.
6. Tankstelle mit einer Telegrafenstange als Zapfsäule und einem Füllschlauch aus Drahtspiralen.

4

5

6

Traffic playground in the Lordship Recreation Ground, Borough of Tottenham, London

Designed by G. E. Paris in collaboration with the Tottenham Borough Council

Verkehrsspielplatz im Lordship Erholungspark, Tottenham, England

Planung: G. E. Paris in Zusammenarbeit mit dem Tottenham Borough Council

Site plan.
1 Play spaces with Wendy houses and climbing equipment
2 Green areas with seats
3 Roads with traffic lights and road signs
4 Zebra crossings for pedestrians
5 Paddling pool
6 Sandpit
7 Boating pool for model ships

Lageplan.
1 Spielareale mit Klettergeräten und Spielhäuschen
2 Grünanlagen mit Sitzgelegenheiten
3 Straßen mit Ampeln und Verkehrszeichen
4 Fußgängerübergänge
5 Planschbecken
6 Sandfläche
7 Teich für Modellboote

The design provides children with a playground where they can drive their pedal cars, and cycle without disturbing visitors to the recreation ground. At the same time the playground is meant to make children aware of traffic danger. The whole ground incorporates, in addition to a number of play-spaces with climbing equipment and Wendy houses, such things as a stream with a pond and a boating pool. When children cross over from one area to the other they have to take notice of the "road traffic", which consists of hired pedal cars and cycles. Traffic signs are half size. The network of roads consists of two intersecting main roads and a number of side roads. Particular emphasis has been laid on planting shrubs and trees at bends and traffic islands. This not only helps to preserve the park-like character of the whole ground but creates obstructions which give a sense of reality to traffic problems.

Der Plan ging davon aus, den Kindern ein Spielgelände zu schaffen, in dem sie ungehindert mit ihren Autos und Rädern fahren können, ohne die erwachsenen Besucher des Erholungsparkes zu stören. Dabei sollten ihnen zugleich die Gefahren des Verkehrs bewußt gemacht werden. In die Gesamtanlage sind neben einer Reihe von Spielarealen mit Klettergeräten und Spielhäuschen auch ein Bachlauf und ein Teich für Modellboote einbezogen. Gehen die Kinder von einem Spielareal zum anderen, so müssen sie Rücksicht auf den »Straßenverkehr« nehmen, für den mietweise Autos und Räder zur Verfügung stehen. Die Anlage ist mit Verkehrszeichen in halber natürlicher Größe ausgestattet. Das »Straßennetz« besteht aus zwei sich kreuzenden Hauptstraßen und einer Reihe von Nebenstraßen. Besonderer Wert wurde auf die Bepflanzung an Kurven und Straßeninseln gelegt. Dadurch konnte nicht nur der parkartige Charakter gewahrt werden, sondern es ließ sich auch das Spiel durch die Unübersichtlichkeit der Verkehrssituation interessanter gestalten.

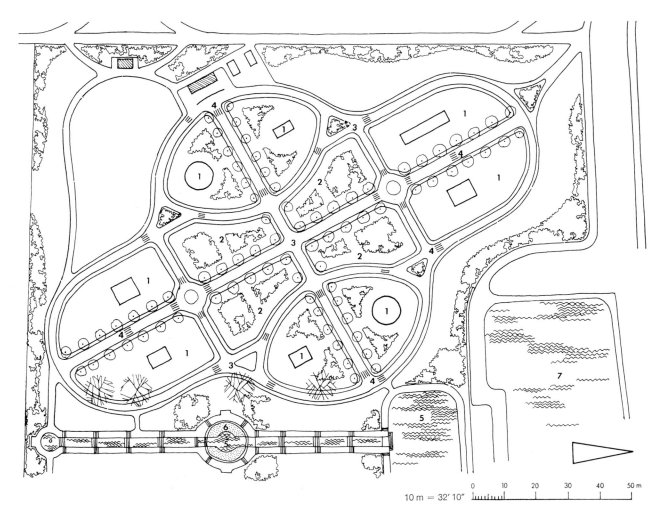

10 m = 32' 10"   0 10 20 30 40 50 m

Traffic playground at Stuttgart, Germany

Designed by the Department for Public Works of the Municipal Administration of Stuttgart

Verkehrsspielplatz Stuttgart, Deutschland

Planung: Stadt Stuttgart, Amt für Öffentliche Ordnung

This playground was built to supplement the theoretical instruction given by the schools. The ever-increasing density of traffic and the number of road accidents made the need for such a ground urgent. It is the first of its kind in Western Germany. Built on top of a former air-raid shelter, it forms a flat area of about 264 feet × 264 feet, on which have been constructed asphalt roads including bends, cross-roads and roundabouts of altogether some 2,000 feet in length. There are special pedestrian and cycling paths, and some 70 traffic signs have been erected with two control posts and traffic lights. Pedal cars and horse-teams, miniature motor-scooters, bicycles and scooters were donated mostly by oil companies and car manufacturers. Specially trained policemen give lessons to school classes in the mornings, and in the afternoons supervise and teach the 7- to 13-year-olds who attend voluntarily. Outside the fixed play hours the vehicles are kept in a store and are maintained in good repair by a retired policeman.

Die stetige Zunahme des Straßenverkehrs und die Steigerung der Verkehrsunfälle führten zur Errichtung dieser Anlage, die als erste westdeutsche Jugendverkehrsschule den theoretischen Unterricht in den Schulen ergänzt. Über einem ehemaligen Luftschutzbunker sind auf einer Fläche von rund 80 × 80 m asphaltierte Straßen von insgesamt 600 m Länge mit Kurven, Kreuzungen und Kreisverkehr, Einbahnstraßen, Rad- und Fußwege angelegt und mit etwa 70 Verkehrszeichen, zwei Signalanlagen und einer Verkehrsampel versehen. Tretautos, Tretpferdegespanne, Kindermotorroller, Fahrräder und Roller wurden zum großen Teil von Öl- und Kraftfahrzeugfirmen gestiftet. Besonders geschulte Polizisten unterrichten vormittags Schulklassen und beaufsichtigen und belehren am Nachmittag die freiwilligen 7–13jährigen Verkehrsteilnehmer. Die Fahrzeuge sind außerhalb der Spielstunden in einer Halle untergebracht und werden von einem pensionierten Polizeibeamten instand gehalten.

Children's town for street games and road safety instruction at Zürich-Buchegg, Switzerland

Designed by the Building Department of the municipal administration of Zürich (Alfred Trachsel) and Hans Litz and Fritz Schwarz, in collaboration with the Parks Division, the traffic police, the Swiss Touring Club and the Pro Juventute Foundation

Kinderstadt für Straßenspiele und Verkehrsunterricht, Zürich-Buchegg, Schweiz

Planung: Hochbauamt der Stadt Zürich (Alfred Trachsel) und Hans Litz und Fritz Schwarz in Zusammenarbeit mit Gartenbauamt, Polizeiamt, Touring Club und der Stiftung Pro Juventute

1. The buildings of the children's town are constructed of U-shaped prefabricated concrete elements.
2. The town area seen from the pedestrian bridge. In the foreground, the terminus made of concrete ducts.
3. View towards the eastern part with rural landscape and "long distance" traffic.
4. Traffic demonstration. In the background, instruction and store rooms below the bridge.
5. Here the U-shaped concrete elements are used as benches.

1. Die Gebäude bestehen aus U-förmigen Betonfertigteilen.
2. Der Stadtbezirk von der Fußgängerbrücke aus gesehen. Vorn der Bahnhof aus Betonröhren.
3. Blick nach Osten auf den Überlandbezirk.
4. Beim Verkehrsunterricht. Im Hintergrund die Instruktions- und Magazinräume unter der Brücke.
5. Die U-förmigen Betonelemente hier als Sitzbänke.

A children's town as part of a "Robinson Crusoe" playground has been designed for the north-east side of the Recreation Centre mentioned on pages 146–149. This town is meant to fulfil the twofold task of teaching traffic rules and regulations to children of all ages during school hours, demonstrations being given by police instructors in a systematic way as close to real life as possible; and also of providing a variety of possibilities for street and traffic games. Through this combination the one-sidedness of many a "traffic garden", which is only too often schoolmasterly and not childlike at all, has been avoided. A playground has been created which through its dual-purpose functions justifies its comparatively high costs. A pedestrian bridge with viewing bay enables an entire class to watch the traffic on the streets and crossroads of this children's town. The vehicles and the removable traffic signs are kept in a special store. For games outside actual instruction hours the signs will be removed so that the children do not get accustomed to driving carelessly past traffic sings while playing.

Auf der Nordostseite der Freizeitanlage Zürich-Buchegg (siehe Seite 146–149) wurde als Teil des »Robinson«-Spielplatzes eine Kinderstadt errichtet, die eine doppelte Aufgabe zu erfüllen hat: einmal dient sie dazu, Klein- und Schulkindern während der Schulstunden durch Verkehrsinstruktoren des Polizeiamtes einen systematischen und wirklichkeitsnahen Verkehrsunterricht zu erteilen, und zweitens bietet eine derartige Anlage außerhalb der Verkehrsschulung die vielgestaltigsten Möglichkeiten für Straßen- und Verkehrsspiele. Durch diese Kombination wird die Einseitigkeit mancher allzu »schulmeisterlicher« und unkindlicher Verkehrsgärten vermieden und zugleich ein Platz geschaffen, der durch seinen doppelten Effekt den verhältnismäßig hohen finanziellen Aufwand rechtfertigt. Eine Fußgängerbrücke mit Aussichtskanzel gibt ganzen Schulklassen Gelegenheit, den Verkehr zu beobachten. Die Kinderfahrzeuge und die abnehmbaren Verkehrszeichen sind in einem besonderen Magazin untergebracht. Für das Spiel außerhalb der Instruktionsstunden werden die Schilder entfernt, damit die Kinder nicht achtlos an den Verkehrszeichen vorbeifahren.

6. Plan. The pedestrian bridge (1) divides the ground into two parts of similar size: the western with the actual children's town, and the eastern with the rural landscape and "long distance" traffic. The miniature railway (2) leads into the town. The egg-shaped concrete elements of the train are let into the ground in such a way that the children can drive through the train. The track leads through a tunnel to the terminus made of concrete ducts (3). The station square with its fronts of houses blocking the view at dangerous crossings creates life-like traffic situations. The house fronts (4) not only block the view but serve as scenery for police quarters, information bureau etc. Streets for two-line traffic are 10' 0" wide with pavements of 3' 4" width. A petrol station (5), car parks, footpaths, traffic islands at "train" stops, a traffic roundabout (6) and long-distance roads (7), all add to the varied possibilities for games. Bollards (8) separate the ground

from a footpath (9). West of the "town" is a playground for small children (10) and a footpath to the "Robinson Crusoe" playground (11). Garage and store (12) are provided for hired vehicles and traffic signs. A pedestrian subway (13) is planned below the street east of the grounds leading to the school nearby and to the ring road.

6. Plan. Die Fußgängerbrücke (1) trennt die Anlage in zwei ungefähr gleich große Teile: den westlichen mit der Kleinkinderstadt und den östlichen mit der freien Landschaft und dem Überlandverkehr. In die Stadt hinein führt die Kindereisenbahn (2), deren eiförmige Betonelemente so in den Boden eingelassen sind, daß die Kinder durch den Zug hindurchfahren können. Die Strecke geht weiter durch den Tunnel zum Betonröhren-Bahnhof (3). Der Bahnhofsplatz mit seiner ge-

fährlichen Kreuzung und den unübersichtlichen Häuserfronten läßt wirklichkeitsnahe Verkehrssituationen entstehen. Die Hausattrappen (4) verstellen nicht nur die Sicht, sie dienen zugleich als Spielwände für Rollenspiele (Polizeiwache, Verkehrsbüro usw.). Die Straßen mit zwei Fahrbahnen haben eine Breite von 3 m, die Gehwege sind 1 m breit. Eine Tankstelle (5), Parkplätze, Gehwege, Straßenbahninseln, ein Verkehrskreisel (6) und Überlandstraßen (7) bieten weitere Spielmöglichkeiten. Begrenzungssteine (8) schließen den Platz gegen einen Spazierweg (9) ab. Auf der Westseite des Areals schließen sich ein Kinderspielplatz (10) und ein Verbindungsweg zum »Robinson«-Spielplatz (11) an. Garage und Magazin (12) nehmen Leihfahrzeuge und Verkehrszeichen auf. Unter der Straße am Ostrand ist eine Fußgängerunterführung (13) und Verbindung zur benachbarten Schule und Ringstraße geplant.

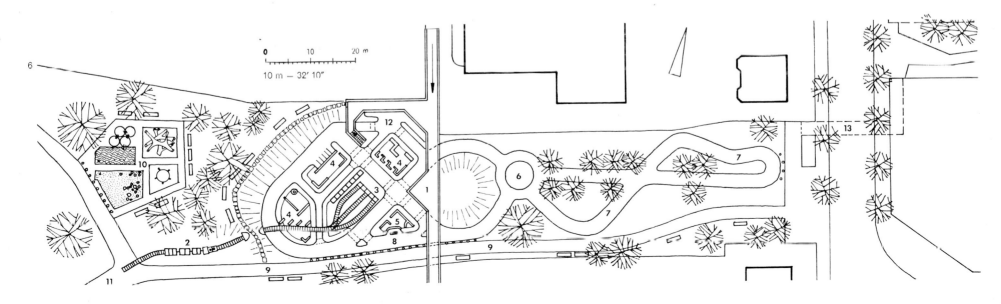

Building playground (Skrammellegeplads), Copenhagen-Emdrup, Denmark

Based on ideas of C. Th. Sørensen

Bauspielplatz (Skrammellegeplads), Kopenhagen-Emdrup, Dänemark

Ausgeführt nach Ideen von C. Th. Sørensen

The first Danish Skrammellegeplads, a playground using building materials to encourage children's constructional activities, was built in 1943 on the initiative of a worker's co-operative building society. The idea is based on a suggestion by C. Th. Sørensen, the landscape architect who as early as 1931 advocated the provision of playgrounds with building and demolition materials. The ground at Emdrup is approximately 70,000 square feet in size, and, being surrounded by a six-feet-high dam of earth planted with rose hedges, it is hardly visible from without. There are about 100 small "houses" with gardens built by children in all shapes and sizes of brick or wood. There is a group of permanent buildings, erected by fathers and children together, which comprises a common room, two workshops with benches and vices, and a pergola with tables where modelling and constructional hobbies can be pursued. All other "buildings" are dismantled before the winter starts. A playground leader, who has to look after about 100 children per day from April to November, is also in charge of the building material and makes suggestions without forcing ideas on the children.

Der erste dänische »Gerümpelspielplatz« (Skrammellegeplads) entstand 1943 auf Initiative einer Arbeitersiedlungsgenossenschaft. Als Idee geht er auf einen Vorschlag des Gartenarchitekten Sørensen zurück, der schon 1931 dafür eingetreten war, Spielplätze mit Bau- und Abbruchmaterial auszurüsten. Der Platz in Emdrup ist ungefähr 6300 qm groß. Von einem mannshohen, mit Rosenhecken bepflanzten Erdwall umgeben, ist er von außen kaum sichtbar. Auf dem Gelände stehen rund 100 von den Kindern gebaute Häuschen mit Gärten in allen Formen und Größen, Backstein- und Holzbauten. Ein größerer Gemeinschaftsraum, von Vätern und Kindern gemeinsam gebaut, zwei Werkstatträume mit Hobelbänken und Schraubstöcken und schließlich eine Pergola, an deren Tischen gezeichnet, gebastelt und modelliert werden kann, bilden eine Gruppe von festen Bauten, während die Spielhäuschen im Herbst fast alle wieder abgebrochen werden. Eine Spielplatzleiterin, die von April bis November täglich etwa 100 Kinder zu betreuen hat, verwaltet das Baumaterial und gibt Anregungen, ohne autoritär einzugreifen.

1. This sculpture made of concrete is an example of the artistic endeavours of the children.

2. When the playground is opened in April the children are assigned their "building sites" and are handed material which consists partly of the demolished play-houses of the previous year and partly of the replenished stock of boxes, boards and bricks.

3. As the children come each successive year to the playground they gradually develop technical faculties to an astonishing degree. This is evident in the diversity of form shown by these erections with their bays and annexes as well as in the technique of laying bricks and the standard of comfort of the interior.

4. When the houses have been finished, fences are erected and gardens laid out. A large flower-garden which forms part of the grounds supplies the children with plants for their own little gardens. Not much play goes on in the finished houses; the most important thing is the building activity itself.

1. Zementplastik als Beispiel für die musische Beschäftigung.

2. Wenn im April der Bauspielplatz geöffnet wird, bekommen die Kinder von der Spielplatzleiterin ihre Parzellen zugewiesen und das Baumaterial zugeteilt, das zum Teil aus Abbruchresten von den Vorjahrsbauten, zum Teil aus den neu beschafften Kisten, Brettern und Steinen besteht.

3. Da die Kinder alljährlich wieder auf den Bauspielplatz kommen, entwickeln sie allmählich erstaunliche technische Fähigkeiten, die sich sowohl in der Vielgestalt der Häuschen mit ihren Erkern und Anbauten als auch in der »Mauertechnik« und dem komfortablen Innenausbau zeigen.

4. Wenn die Häuschen im Lauf des Sommers fertig sind, werden Zäune errichtet und Gärten angelegt. Ein größerer Blumengarten, der zum Spielplatz gehört, liefert den Kindern die Pflanzen für ihre eigenen Gärtchen. In den endgültig fertiggestellten Häuschen wird nur wenig gespielt; das Wichtigste ist das Bauen selbst.

5. Wooden huts propped high up on poles can be found on this kind of playground too. During the first couple of years the ground was financed entirely by the co-operative housing estate. Now the Social Welfare Department of the Copenhagen city administration subsidises it with an annual payment of 10,000 crowns, which amounts to 80% of the entire running costs, including the salary of the playground leader. The remaining 20% is contributed by the co-operative, and raised by means of a modest levy on the rents.

6. This underground shelter shows the variety of form these playhouses can take.

5. Auch Pfahlbauten aus Stangen und Brettern sind auf dem »Skrammellegeplads« zu finden. In den beiden ersten Jahren wurde er von der Siedlungsgenossenschaft allein finanziert; jetzt gibt die Sozialbehörde der Stadt Kopenhagen eine jährliche Subvention von 10000 Kronen, das sind etwa 80% der Gesamtbetriebskosten einschließlich des Gehalts für die Spielplatzleiterin. Die restlichen 20% werden von der Genossenschaft durch einen bescheidenen Mietaufschlag gedeckt.

6. Auch diese Erdhütte zeigt die Vielgestalt der Bautypen.

5

6

7. In the common room and under the pergola activities such as drawing, constructional hobbies and modelling are pursued. Parents often take part.
8. Girl learning basket work. Encouragement for such activity is given by the playground leader.
9. Puppet show on the stage which was made by the children themselves.

7. Im Gemeinschaftsbau und unter der Pergola wird gezeichnet, gebastelt und modelliert. Oft helfen die Eltern mit.
8. Mädchen beim Korbflechten. Anregungen für solche Freizeitbeschäftigungen kommen von der Spielplatzleiterin.
9. Beim Kasperlespiel vor dem selbstgebauten Puppentheater.

Playground for the Children's Creative Centre, Canadian Federal Pavilion, Expo '67, Montreal, Canada

Design: Cornelia Hahn-Oberlander, Landscape Architect, Vancouver

Spielplatz des Creative Centre für Kinder, Kanadischer Pavillon, Expo '67, Montreal, Kanada

Planung: Cornelia Hahn-Oberlander, Gartenarchitektin, Vancouver

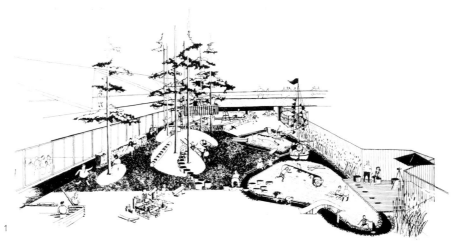

1

The Creative Centre introduced to the visitors of the Canadian Pavilion advanced methods in teaching music, art, drama and in nursery education. It consisted of four classrooms, and all activities could be observed through one-way screens. The playground designed on the adjacent open space of modest dimensions offered a variety of possibilities for active and creative play. A covered area of 60 by 40 feet for quiet play contained a manipulative wall with a series of Op Art puzzles which the children could arrange in infinite ways; free-standing screens made up of different musical instruments, strings, bells, drums and xylophones; as well as play tables, climbing net and a story-telling area with a movable bookshelf. A hexagonal nursery area, separated from the rest by a cedar hedge, lead to the open area, 60 by 120 feet in size, which was divided into a sand and canal area and a mound area with tunnel, slide and treehouse; it also included a flat area for building games.

Das Creative Centre machte die Besucher der kanadischen Pavillons mit fortschrittlichen Methoden der musischen Ausbildung und Beschäftigung bekannt. In Unterrichtsräumen, die von außen durch Ein-Weg-Scheiben beobachtet werden konnten, wurden für 6–11 jährige Kurse in Musik, Theaterspiel und Kunst veranstaltet; ein weiterer Bestandteil war ein Muster-Kindergarten für 3–5 jährige. Das anschliessende Freigelände bot auf kleinstem Raum einen vielseitigen Platz mit den verschiedensten Möglichkeiten für aktives Spiel. Ein überdachter Bereich von 18 × 12 m für stille Spiele enthielt neben Spieltischen, Kletternetz und einer durch Bücherborde abgetrennten Erzählecke eine Reihe von Op-Art-Wandbildern, die von den Kindern verändert werden konnten, sowie freistehende Schirmwände mit Musikinstrumenten wie Glocken, Trommeln und Xylophonen. Der von einer Zedernhecke umgebene, sechseckige Kindergarten-Spielplatz leitete zu dem offenen, rund 18 × 36 m großen Spielgelände über, das in einen Sand- und Kanalbereich unterteilt war und in eine grasbewachsene, über 3 m hohe Hügelzone mit Tunnel, Rutsche und Baumhaus, dazu kam noch ein flacher Teil für Bauspiele.

2

1. Perspective drawing of playground. Basic ideas of design: Interesting modeling of site; attractive play areas and equipment; restful, garden-like atmosphere with groups of bushes and pine trees.
2. Overall view from a look-out. In the background, below the bridge, the quiet play area; to the left, mound and treehouse; to the right, sand and canal area.
3. The covered area with manipulative wall and musical screens designed by Gordon Smith.
4. The treehouse. Access by ladder, rope ladder and climbing tree; sliding pole for getting down quickly.
5. Between the two sand islands a boat. Getting on board requires skill and courage.
6. Site plan: Covered play area (1), Nursery area (2), Mound with slide and treehouse (3), Sand and canal area (4), Building games (5), Nursery school (6), Music (7), Drama (8), Art (9).
7. Mound with slide and tunnel. Sliding surface covered in plastic.
8. Beams and boards for all kinds of building games.

1. Perspektive des Spielplatzes. Grundgedanken der Gestaltung: möglichst plastisch modelliertes Terrain; interessante Geräte und Spielbereiche; ruhige gartenähnliche Atmosphäre durch Buschgruppen und Kiefern.
2. Gesamtüberblick von einer Beobachtungskanzel aus. Im Hintergrund unter der Brücke die ruhige Spielzone, links Hügel und Baumhaus, rechts Sandflächen und Kanal.
3. Der überdachte Bereich mit den von Gordon Smith gestalteten Op-Art-Wänden und Musik-Schirmwänden.
4. Baumhaus. Strickleiter, Sprossenleiter und Steigbaum als Aufstieg.
5. Zwischen den beiden Sandinseln im 10 cm tiefen Kanal ein locker angekettetes Ruderboot. Das Einsteigen erfordert Geschicklichkeit.
6. Lageplan: Überdachter Spielbereich (1), Kleinkinderspielplatz (2), Hügel mit Rutsche und Baumhaus (3), Sandplatz- und Kanalbereich (4), Bauspiele (5), Kindergarten (6), Musik (7), Theater (8), Kunst (9).
7. Hügel mit Rutsche und Tunnel. Rutsche mit Kunststoffbelag.
8. Bauspiele mit vorbereiteten Balken und Brettern.

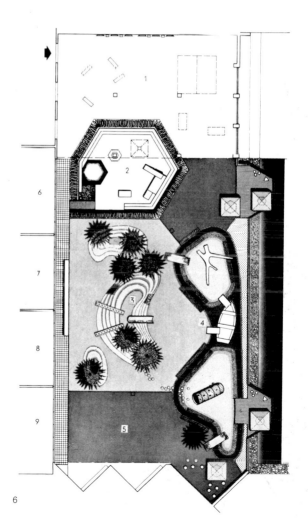

Red Indian Playground at Mannheim, Germany

Designed by Fritz Häfelinger, Mannheim, in collaboration
with U. S. and German authorities

Indianerspielplatz, Mannheim, Deutschland

Planung: Fritz Häfelinger, Mannheim, in Zusammenarbeit
mit amerikanischen und deutschen Dienststellen

1. The ground from the south-west, with the surrounding buildings.
2. Site plan.
   1 Meeting-place and grass area for games
   2+3 Huts made of stone and clay, covered with reeds
   4 Cave of 55 cubic yards capacity built with debris
   5 Climbing tree
   6 Pond with stream
   7 Large pond
   8 Waterfall (13 feet high)
   9 Grottoes
   10 Suspension bridge
   11 Shelters
   12 Climbing tower made of tree-trunks
   13 Youth house with kindergarten
   14 Playground for small children

A flat stretch of waste land measuring about 130,000 square feet was
transformed into a playground which is outstanding on account of
its conception and execution. It is mainly due to the initiative of a
youth leader that the playground came into being. It forms part of a
youth centre, to which there is attached a youth house, a playground
for small children and a grass area for playing. Using debris, stones,
clay, reeds and rushes, nearly 200 children and voluntary helpers of
the "International Voluntary Service for Peace" – mostly students
from 27 nations – contoured the ground in hills of varying height, up
to 46 feet, and planted the whole with trees and shrubs. Caves,
tunnels, places for camp fires, paths for creeping games and ponds
were created. A number of firms and a U. S. Army Engineers' unit
gave assistance by lending equipment and vehicles, and by donations
of building materials, thus cutting expenses to a minimum. The idea
of placing on this playground disused vehicles or mechanical equipment was dismissed as not in keeping with its character.
The wild nature of the ground offers sufficient stimulus and opportunities for games of all kinds.

Der Initiative eines Jugendleiters ist es zu verdanken, daß auf einer
brachliegenden, völlig ebenen Fläche von rund 12 000 qm ein Spielplatz entstand, der in Idee und Ausführung vorbildlich ist. Er ist ein
Teil eines Jugendzentrums, zu dem ein Jugendhaus, ein Kleinkinderspielplatz und eine Spielwiese gehören. Aus Trümmerschutt und
alten Steinen, aus Lehm und Schilf schufen nahezu 200 Kinder und
freiwillige Helfer des »Internationalen Zivildienstes« (zumeist Studenten aus 27 Nationen) ein stark bewegtes Gelände von 14 m Hö-
hendifferenz mit Bäumen und Sträuchern, Höhlen, Grotten, unterirdischen Gängen, Feuerstellen, Schleichpfaden und Seen. Verschiedene Firmen und eine US-Pioniereinheit halfen durch leihweise
Überlassung von Geräten und durch Schenkung von Baumaterial die
Unkosten auf ein Mindestmaß herabzudrücken. Es wurde bewußt
darauf verzichtet, mechanische Geräte oder ausgediente Fahrzeuge
aufzustellen. Allein die Vielgestaltigkeit des Geländes bietet eine
Fülle von Spielmöglichkeiten.

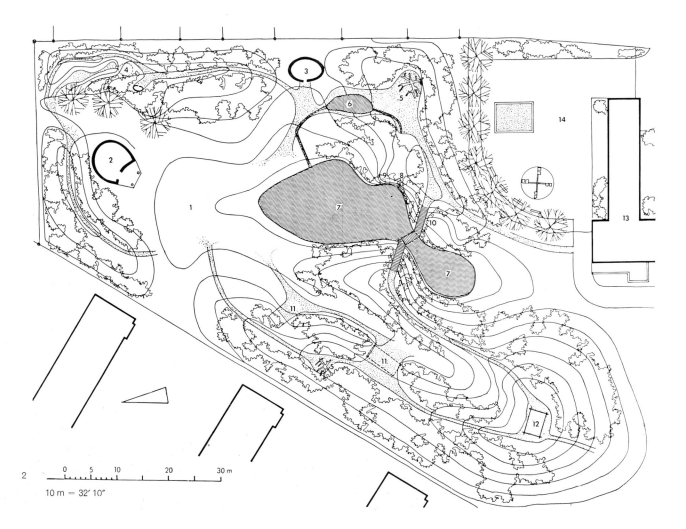

0 5 10   20   30 m

10 m = 32' 10"

1. Blick von Südwesten auf den Platz und die umgebende Bebauung.
2. Lageplan.
   1 Versammlungsplatz und Spielwiese
   2+3 schilfgedeckte Hütten aus Stein und Lehm
   4 42 cbm große Höhle aus Trümmersteinen
   5 Kletterbaum
   6 Wasserbecken mit Bachlauf
   7 großer See
   8 Wasserfall mit 4 m Gefälle
   9 Grotten
   10 Hängebrücke
   11 Unterstände
   12 Kletterturm aus Rundstämmen
   13 Jugendheim mit Kindergarten
   14 Kleinkinderspielplatz

3

3. The small pond, meeting-place and huts.
4. The wild and romantic scenery stimulates the adventurous spirit of children.
5. The large pond is an ideal skating rink in the winter. It is surrounded by two stepped rows of stone seats. In the background is the suspension bridge.

3. Kleines Wasserbecken, Versammlungsplatz und Hütten.
4. Das wildromantische Gelände regt die schöpferische Phantasie der Kinder zu den verschiedensten Abenteuern an.
5. Der große See, im Winter eine ideale Schlittschuhbahn, ist mit zwei verschieden hohen Sitzmauern aus Steinen eingefaßt. Im Hintergrund die Hängebrücke.

4

5

6. By means of crawling tunnels one can enter the "enemy's" camp unnoticed.

7. The climbing tower of tree-trunks. Being at the highest point of the ground, it provides a good look-out-post.

8. The 53-feet-long suspension bridge spanning a deep gorge forms a link between two hills.

9. Walls and supports were decorated by the children themselves.

10. The incised and painted clay blocks show the range of the children's imagination.

11. The grass area with the climbing tower and the suspension bridge in the background as seen from inside the large hut.

6. Durch unterirdische Kriechgänge kommt man unbemerkt ins feindliche Lager.

7. Der Kletterturm aus Rundstämmen an der höchsten Stelle des Geländes bietet eine gute Übersicht.

8. Die 16 m lange Hängebrücke führt von Bergrücken zu Bergrücken über eine tiefe Schlucht.

9. Wände und Pfähle dieser Hütte wurden von den Kindern selbst ausgeschmückt.

10. Die bemalten Tonplatten zeigen den Reichtum der kindlichen Phantasie.

11. Blick aus der großen Hütte über die Spielwiese auf Kletterturm und See mit Hängebrücke.

9

10

11

Weißenburgpark Play and Recreation Ground, Stuttgart, Germany

Designed by Stuttgart City Parks Department
(Director: Dr. Werner Kaufmann)

Spiel- und Erholungsanlage »Weißenburgpark«, Stuttgart, Deutschland

Planung: Gartenbauamt der Stadt Stuttgart,
Gartenbaudirektor Dr. Werner Kaufmann

Central Stuttgart lies in a deep hollow which imposes a need for supplementary green spaces, because the light prevailing winds provide scarecely adequate air circulation. Therefore, in addition to their function of reaching as far as possible into the city and of offering pedestrians traffic-free communications, these green spaces have the special task of supplying channels of fresh air. Thus from the predominantly wooded heights down to the densely built-up "cauldron" below radial green features converge, which are comprehensively equipped for play and recreation. A typical example is the Weißenburgpark, forming a connecting link, between the Southern inner city and the woods round the television tower, out of land which was once private gardens, 7 1/2 acres in size and with a drop in level of 230 ft. A footbridge enables mothers with children to reach the park, with its many play spaces, undisturbed by wheeled traffic. The design of the park skilfully exploits in countless ways the topographical opportunities of the slope.

Die Kessellage der Stuttgarter Innenstadt stellt an die Grünplanung zusätzliche Anforderungen, weil die geringe Windgeschwindigkeit kaum zur genügenden Durchlüftung ausreicht. Deshalb haben die Grünanlagen neben der Funktion, so weit wie möglich in die City hineinzureichen und den Fußgängern verkehrsfreie Verbindungen in der Fallinie zu bieten, noch die besondere Aufgabe, als Frischluftschneisen zu dienen. So ziehen sich von den großenteils bewaldeten Höhen in den dicht bebauten Talkessel radiale Grünzüge hinunter, die in großzügiger Weise zu Spiel- und Erholungsparks ausgestaltet wurden. Ein typisches Beispiel ist der Weißenburgpark, der auf einem ehemals privaten Gartengelände von 3 ha Größe mit einem Höhenunterschied von rund 70 m das Bindeglied zwischen der südlichen Innenstadt und dem Wald beim Fernsehturm bildet. Über eine Fußgängerbrücke können die Mütter mit Kindern ungehindert vom Fahrverkehr den Park mit seinen vielen Spielbereichen erreichen, deren Gestaltung vielfach sehr geschickt die topographischen Gegebenheiten des Hanggeländes ausnutzt.

1

1. The main features of the playground are the large sanded play pit, adjoining on the right the water games space (not seen in picture), and the climbing steps and slide. Top right, the observation platform on the highest point of the site; top left, the round pavilion of the milkbar.

2. Air view, showing the system of ramifying paths disposed at various levels and the varied possibilities for play distributed over the grounds.

1. Kernstück des Spielparks sind der große Sandspielplatz, an den rechts (im Bild nicht sichtbar) der Wasserspielplatz anschließt, und der Kletterhang mit den Rutschen. Rechts oben die Aussichtsplattform auf dem höchsten Punkt des Geländes, links oben der Rundpavillon der Milchbar.

2. Luftansicht mit dem verzweigten Wegesystem in verschiedenen Steigungsgraden und den über das Areal verteilten Spielmöglichkeiten.

Key to air view / Legende zum Luftbild
1 Rest area / Liegewiese
2 Water games, milkbar / Wasserspiele, Milchbar
3 Observation terrace / Aussichtsterrasse
4 Toboggan run / Rodeln
5 Climbing causeway and slides / Kletterhang mit Rutschen
6 Water games / Wasserspielplatz
7 Playground shelter / Spielplatzgebäude
8 Ball games, soft ball / Ballspielplatz, Federball
9 Cowboys and Indians / Indianerspiele
10 Chess / Schach
11 Skittles / Kegeln
12 Table tennis / Tischtennis
13 Dolls' and fairy-tale houses / Spielhäuschen für Märchen- und Puppenspiele
14 Parking / Parkplatz
15 Footbridge / Fußgängerbrücke
16 Sanded play pit / Sandspielplatz

3. The water games place with its splashing pool and the stream, like a meandering brook, which feeds it.

4. View from the observation path over the climbing causeway of the large sanded play space and, a little higher up, of the splashing pool fed by a serpentine channel; behind, the playground shelter, containing W.C.s and equipment. The climbing slope is studded with round wood blocks, rammed in vertically, which make a stairway for those going up. The hill is less steep at the top, so the slide must be reached by climbing a ladder, although at the bottom it is embedded in the hillside.

5. The easily damaged nets, which at first served as handrails (ill. 1+4), were later replaced by palings. Tree trunks inserted vertically in the ground, planks laid horizontally, and stone slabs make steps. The two slides each describe a quarter-circle. Top right, the pathway becomes an observation terrace.

3. Der Wasserspielplatz mit dem Planschbecken und der wie ein Bach sich windenden Zulaufrinne.

4. Blick vom Aussichtsweg über den Kletterhang auf den großen Sandspielplatz und das etwas höher gelegene Planschbecken mit der mäanderförmigen Watrinne als Zufluß, dahinter das Spielplatzgebäude, das Toiletten und Geräteräume enthält. Der Kletterhang ist mit senkrecht eingerammten Rundhölzern befestigt, die beim Aufstieg als Treppen dienen. Im oberen Teil ist die Hangneigung flacher, so daß die Rutsche hier über eine Leiter bestiegen werden muß, während sie im unteren Teil in den Hang gebettet ist.

5. Die verschleißanfälligen Netze, die anfangs als Geländer dienten (Abb. 1+4), wurden später durch Palisaden ersetzt. Senkrecht eingelassene Rundstämme, waagerecht verlegte Bohlen und Felsplatten als Treppenstufen. Die Rutschen beschreiben jeweils einen Viertelskreis. Rechts oben der Aussichtsweg als Zuschauerterrasse.

3

4

5

6. Crow's nest with round wooden rung steps and safety net stretched beneath.
7. Basket-work play hut and shady seats for grown-ups.
8. A combination of climbing net and trampolin, suspended from a totem pole.
9. Weather-resistant concrete table-tennis "court"; left, open-air skittle alley with stop fence. The games equipment is issued by the milkbar staff.

6. Der Mastkorb mit Stufen aus Rundhölzern und untergespanntem Schutznetz.
7. Spielhäuschen aus Korbgeflecht und Sitzplätze für Erwachsene.
8. Eine Kombination aus Kletternetz und Trampolin, aufgehängt an einem Totempfahl.
9. Wetterfeste Tischtennisplatten aus Beton, links die Freiluft-Kegelbahn mit einer Kugelfangpalisade. Die Spielgeräte werden vom Personal der Milchbar ausgegeben.

6

7

8

9

Playgrounds in the Isar Valley, Munich, Germany

Designed by Munich City Building Authority, Municipal Parks Department (Director: Josef Höllerer)

Parkspielplätze in den Isarauen, München, Deutschland

Planung: Baureferat der Stadt München, Gruppe Stadtgartendirektion, Stadtgartendirektor Josef Höllerer

The surroundings of the Isar Valley, lying to the South of Munich, consist of dense residential districts, developed with few exceptions before the first world war and containing neither public nor private green spaces. The propitious location of the valley, its extent (about 190 acres) and the increasing difficulty of reaching in ever worsening traffic conditions by congested roads, places for recreation further afield, led to the decision of making this wild tract of country into a park. 35–40,000 people live on its perimeter, and for those driving from more distant homes, spacious parking lots are provided. By thinning out the trees, open parkland has resulted with play areas and meadows, which summer and winter offer all ages infinitely varied opportunities for recreation. A well devised system of paths for pedestrians and bicyclists makes the whole park accessible.

Die Umgebung der im Süden von München gelegenen Isarauen besteht aus dichten Wohngebieten mit einer Bebauung, die mit wenigen Ausnahmen vor dem ersten Weltkrieg entstanden ist und weder öffentliche noch private Grünflächen enthält. Die günstige Lage des Auengeländes, seine große Ausdehnung (etwa 76 ha) und die mit wachsender Verkehrsdichte zunehmende Schwierigkeit der Bevölkerung, an den Wochenenden auf überfüllten Ausfallstraßen weiter entfernte Erholungsgebiete zu erreichen, gaben den Anstoß, dieses verwilderte Gebiet zum Naturpark umzugestalten. In seinem Einzugsbereich leben 35–40000 Menschen, für weiter entfernt wohnende Autofahrer sind großflächige Parkplätze eingerichtet. Durch Ausholzen entstand eine lichte Parklandschaft mit Spielplätzen und Wiesenflächen, die im Sommer und Winter allen Altersstufen die verschiedenartigsten Spiel- und Erholungsmöglichkeiten bieten. Ein gut ausgebautes Fuß- und Radwegnetz sorgt für die Erschließung des gesamten Parkgeländes.

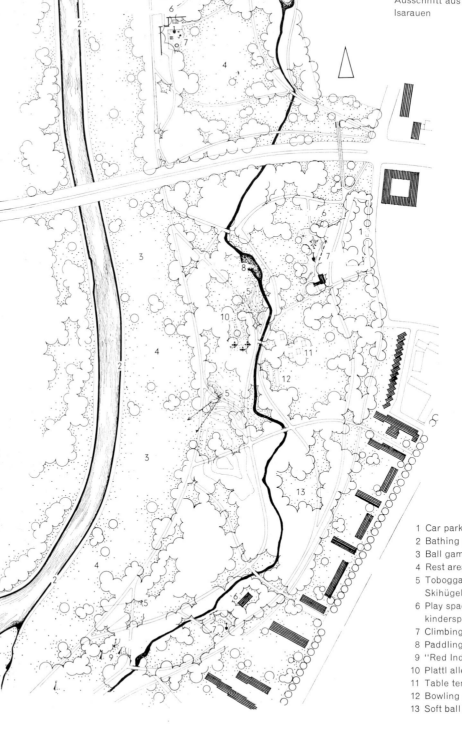

1. Section of site plan of Isar Valley, Munich / Ausschnitt aus dem Lageplan der Münchener Isarauen

1 Car park / Parkplatz
2 Bathing / Baden
3 Ball games / Ballspiele
4 Rest areas / Liegewiese
5 Tobogganing and ski run / Rodel- und Skihügel
6 Play space for small children / Kleinkinderspielplatz
7 Climbing structures / Gerätespielplatz
8 Paddling pool / Bade- und Floßweiher
9 "Red Indian" village / Indianerdorf
10 Plattl alleys / Plattlplätze
11 Table tennis / Tischtennis
12 Bowling / Bocciabahnen
13 Soft ball / Federball

1

2. Several smaller sanded play places are distributed over the grounds for little children, with shady benches for their mothers. The animals are made out of rough-cut tree trunks.

3. Wigwams of branches in the Red Indian playground.

4. Weather-resistant table-tennis "courts" in artificial stone on solid wooden legs.

5. Even the larger play spaces, mainly intended for children 6–14 years old, are largely equipped with wooden figures and toys. Here is a train of hollow tree trunks. Meadows for games surround the play spaces.

2

3

4

2. Über das Gelände sind mehrere Kleinkinder-Sandspielplätze mit schattigen Sitzbänken für die Mütter verteilt. Die Fabeltiere bestehen aus rohbehauenen Baumstämmen.

3. Wigwams aus Rundhölzern auf dem Indianerspielplatz.

4. Wetterfeste Tischtennisplatten aus Kunststein auf stabilen Holzgestellen.

5. Auch die größeren Sandspielplätze, die vorwiegend für Kinder von 6–14 Jahren gedacht sind, wurden hauptsächlich mit Holzgeräten und Holzfiguren ausgestattet, hier eine Eisenbahn aus hohlen Baumstämmen. Große Spielwiesen umgeben die Spielplätze.

5

6

6. The Isar bed with a breadth at high water of about 500 ft offers ideal open-air bathing in summer. As bathers have spacious fields close to the banks at their disposal, the overcrowding usual with open-air bathing seldom occurs. Scattered plantations of trees give form to the landscape and enable visitors to split up into conveniently small groups.

7. By widening and damming an existing stream, a pool for paddling and boats has been formed, which in winter can be used for skating.

8. Tobogganing and skiing are the lively rule on the hillsides in winter.

6. Das Hochwasserbett der Isar mit einer Breite von etwa 150 m bietet im Sommer ideale Freibademöglichkeiten. Da den Badenden auch die ufernahen großen Liegewiesen zur Verfügung stehen, kommt es kaum zu solchen Menschenballungen wie in den üblichen Freibädern. Locker verteilte Gehölze gliedern die Parklandschaft und gestatten eine Aufteilung der Besucher in kleine und kleinste Gruppen.

7. Durch Ausweiten und Aufstauen eines vorhandenen Bachlaufs ergab sich ein Plansch- und Floßweiher, der im Winter zum Schlittschuhlaufen dient.

8. Auf den angeschütteten Aussichtshügeln herrscht im Winter reger Betrieb mit Rodeln und Skilaufen.

7

8

9

10

11

9+10. Some examples of recreation opportunities for adults in the Isar Valley park. Tho "Plattl alleys" are used summer and winter. "Plattln" is a traditional throwing game in Upper Bavaria, played with small metal discs. It bears some resemblance to bowling or curling.
11. As with all playing areas in the Isar Valley Park, the bowling alleys are fitted into the countryside in such a way that any group of players can easily be extended, while leaving enough room for spectators, even exceptional crowds.
12. Skat and chess tables are always surrounded by onlookers.

9+10. Einige Beispiele für die Spielmöglichkeiten der Erwachsenen im Erholungsgebiet Isaraue. Die Plattlplätze werden sommers wie winters benutzt. Plattln ist ein in Oberbayern althergebrachtes Wurfspiel mit kleinen Eisenplatten, dem Bocciaspiel oder Eisstockschießen ähnlich.
11. Die Bocciabahnen sind, wie alle Spielplätze in den Isarauen, so in die Landschaft eingegliedert, daß jede Spielgruppe leicht erweitert werden kann und selbst bei größtem Andrang noch genügend Platz für die Zuschauer bleibt.
12. Die Skat- und Schachspieltische sind ständig von einer großen Schar Zuschauer umstanden.

12

Play and Recreation Park at Corte Madera, U.S.A.

Designed by Royston, Hanamoto & Mayes, San Francisco

Spiel- und Erholungspark, Corte Madera, USA

Planung: Royston, Hanamoto & Mayes, San Francisco

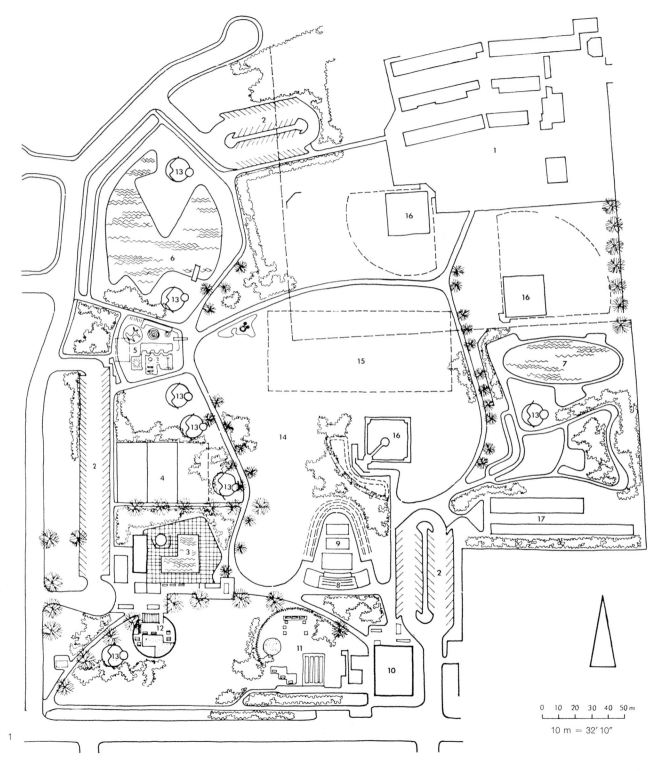

The large lawn for games forms the centre of this play and recreation park at Corte Madera. Together with the sports grounds of the school north of the site there is ample space for ball and action games. Around the central lawn are grouped the zones for other games and various forms of recreation, from a playground for small children to a park for adults. The differentiation of the whole area into various zones is achieved by park-like landscaping which is emphasised by extensive contouring. For instance around the auditorium of the open-air theatre (8+9) a mound has been built and planted with shrubs in order to separate the theatre from other sporting activities. A particular attraction in addition to the swimming pool (3) is the large paddling and boating pool (6) at the north-west and the anglers' practice pond (7) at the east side of the grounds. Three large car parks (2) are provided for teen-agers and grown-ups who frequently come to the playground by car.

Mittelpunkt des geplanten Spiel- und Erholungsparkes in Corte Madera ist die große Spielwiese. Sie bildet zusammen mit den Sportfeldern der im Norden gelegenen Schule ein weitläufiges Areal für Ball- und Bewegungsspiele, um das sich die Zonen für die verschiedensten Spiel- und Erholungsmöglichkeiten – vom Kleinkinderspielplatz bis zum Park für Erwachsene – gruppieren. Die Gliederung des Gesamtareals in verschiedene Zonen wird durch parkartige Landschaftsgestaltung erreicht, die noch durch Aushub und Aufschüttung von Erde betont ist. So wurde beispielsweise um die Zuschauerfläche des Freilichttheaters (8+9) ein Erdwall aufgeschüttet und mit Büschen bepflanzt, um so das Theater vom übrigen Spielbetrieb abzusondern. Als besondere Bereicherung der Anlage sind außer dem Schwimmbad (3) noch der im Nordwesten angeordnete große Plansch- und Bootsteich (6) und der im Osten liegende Übungsteich für Angler (7) zu nennen. Da das Areal auch von Jugendlichen und Erwachsenen besucht wird, die vielfach mit dem Wagen kommen, sind drei große Parkplätze (2) vorgesehen.

0 10 20 30 40 50 m

10 m = 32′ 10″

1. Site plan.
   1 School
   2 Car parks
   3 Swimming pool
   4 Tennis courts
   5 Playground for small children
   6 Paddling and boating pool
   7 Anglers' practice pond
   8 Open-air theatre
   9 Hard-surfaced auditorium available for ball and street games
   10 Recreation centre
   11 Area where grown-ups may play or relax
   12 Play-space for teen-agers
   13 Picnic area with barbecue facilities
   14 Lawn
   15 Football field
   16 Baseball fields
   17 Archery ranges

2. Aerial perspective of the park from the south. The sketch gives
an impression of the spaciousness of the grounds and shows clearly
the varous zones for play, sports and recreation in their skifully
landscaped settings.

1. Lageplan.
   1 Schule
   2 Parkplätze
   3 Schwimmbad
   4 Tennisplätze
   5 Kleinkinderspielplatz
   6 Plansch- und Bootsteich
   7 Übungsteich für Angler
   8 Freilichttheater
   9 Zuschauerfläche mit Hartbelag, auch für Ball- und Straßen-
     spiele benutzbar
   10 Gemeinschaftshaus
   11 Spiel- und Ruheplatz für Erwachsene
   12 Spiel- und Aufenthaltsplatz für Jugendliche
   13 Picknickplätze mit offenen Feuerstellen
   14 Wiese
   15 Fußballfeld
   16 Baseballfelder
   17 Bahnen für Bogenschießen

2. Perspektive des Parks von Süden. Die Skizze vermittelt einen guten Eindruck von der ungeheuren Weiträumigkeit des Geländes und
zeigt deutlich die verschiedenen, durch geschickte gärtnerische Gestaltung in sich geschlossenen Spiel-, Sport- und Erholungszonen.

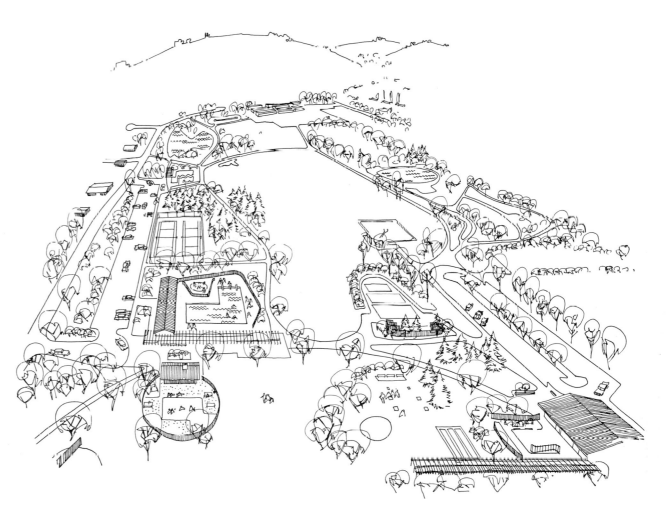

Recreation centre for all age-groups in Zürich-Wipkingen, Switzerland

Designed by the Building Department of the municipal administration of Zürich (Alfred Trachsel) in collaboration with the Pro Juventute Foundation, Zürich
Architect: Hannes Troesch, Zürich

Freizeitanlage für alle Altersstufen, Zürich-Wipkingen, Schweiz

Planung: Hochbauamt der Stadt Zürich (Alfred Trachsel) in Zusammenarbeit mit der Stiftung Pro Juventute, Zürich
Architekt: Hannes Troesch, Zürich

1

This first Swiss recreation centre is the prototype of those centres which cater for all age-groups. Since its opening in the summer of 1954 observations have been made which lead to an increasingly clear understanding of this type. After two enlargements, the centre now includes a site for building activities for older children with appropriate accommodation, training accommodation for staff members, a quieter zone with enclosure for theatrical and musical performances adjoining theater and social club, which have rooms for games, music and reading with an adjacent library; there is also a hard-surface area for street games, the lawn, and a playground for small children. For grounds of this size a leader is required. The centre has strong associations with the district through the voluntary assistance given by parents, youth organizations, local firms, and particularly, of course, through the children, who administer the ground as far as possible through their Robinson Crusoe Council.

Dieses erste schweizerische Freizeitzentrum darf als Prototyp einer Anlage für alle Altersstufen gelten. Seit der Eröffnung im Sommer 1954 wurden hier die Erfahrungen gesammelt, die zur immer klareren Profilierung dieses Typs führten. Nach zwei Erweiterungen umfaßt die Anlage heute einen Werkplatz für die größeren Kinder mit dem zugehörigen Werkstättenbau, ein weiteres Werkstattgebäude für die Ausbildung der Freizeitleiter, dann den musischen Bereich: den Hof für Theaterspiel und Musikaufführungen in Verbindung mit Theaterbau und Clubraum, die Spiel-, Musik- und Lesebereiche und eine Bibliothek enthalten, weiter die Hartbelagfläche für Straßenspiele, die Spiel- und Liegewiese und schließlich den vielgestaltigen Kleinkinderspielplatz.
Selbstverständlich braucht eine so große Anlage einen Freizeitleiter. Zudem ist der ganze Platz stark im Quartier verankert durch die aktive Mitarbeit der Eltern, der Jugendorganisationen, der ortsansässigen Firmen und besonders der Kinder, die durch ihren »Robinsonrat« die Anlage soweit als möglich selbst verwalten.

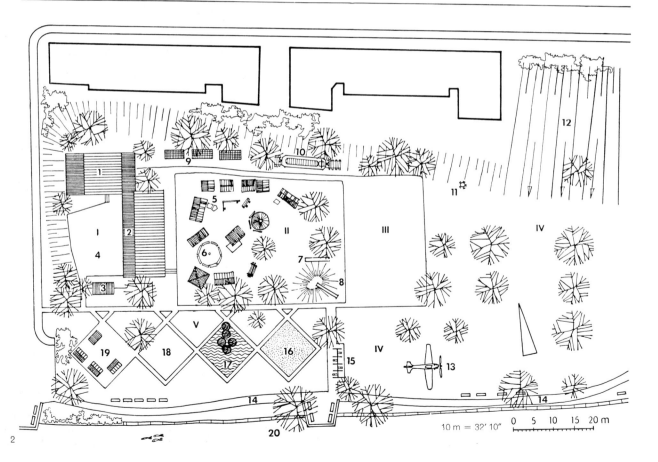

2

10 m = 32' 10"   0 5 10 15 20 m

3+4. The buildings for social purposes provided by the municipal authorities. Illustrations show the intermediate stage, which was later modified by adding training accommodation for recreation leaders (site plan, fig. 8).

3+4. Die von der Stadtverwaltung erstellten Gemeinschaftsbauten. Die Abbildungen zeigen den Zwischenzustand vor der Errichtung des Seminargebäudes für Freizeitleiter (siehe Grundriß, Abb. 8), das erst später hinzukam.

3

1. Model of the original design. Due to modifications to the buildings the design was later somewhat altered (see site plan).
2. Site plan (intermediate stage).
   I. Buildings for common use during summer and winter. Block containing library and large multi-purpose room (1), workshop and hobbies room (2), lavatories (3), enclosure for theatrical and musical performances (4).
   II. Space for building activities. Wendy houses constructed by the children themselves (5), meeting place for the "Robinson Crusoe" Council (6), crawling duct through hill (7), slide (8), children's zoo (9), old tramcar (10).
   III. Hard-surface area for street games. During the winter it is used for ice-skating.
   IV. Lawn with roundabout (11), slope for sledging (12), areoplane (13), and proposed foot path along the riverside (14).
   V. Playground for small children with swings (15), sandpit (16), paddling pool (17), space for equipment (18), hamlet of Wendy houses (19), and the river Limmat (20).

1. Modell des ersten Zustandes von Süden. Durch den Ausbau der Gemeinschaftsbauten ergaben sich einige Veränderungen (s. Plan).
2. Lageplan (Zwischenzustand).
   I. Gemeinschaftsbauten für Sommer- und Winterbetrieb: Mehrzweckgebäude mit Bibliothek, Lese- und Spielraum (1), Werkbau mit Werkstätte und Bastelraum (2), Toiletten (3), Hof für Theater- und Musikaufführungen (4).
   II. Bau- und Werkplatz: selbstgebaute Spielhäuschen (5), Besprechungsplatz des »Robinsonrates« (6), Kriechröhren durch Kletterberg (7), Rutschbahn (8), Kinderzoo (9), alter Straßenbahnwagen (10).
   II. Platz mit Hartbelag für Straßenspiele. Im Winter als Eisfeld zum Schlittschuhlaufen benutzbar.
   IV. Spiel- und Liegewiese mit Rundlauf (11), Schlittenbahn (12), Flugzeug (13) und projektiertem Uferweg (14).
   V. Kleinkinderspielplatz: Seilschaukeln (15), Sand (16), Planschbecken (17), Geräte (18), Spieldörfchen (19), Limmatfluß (20).

4

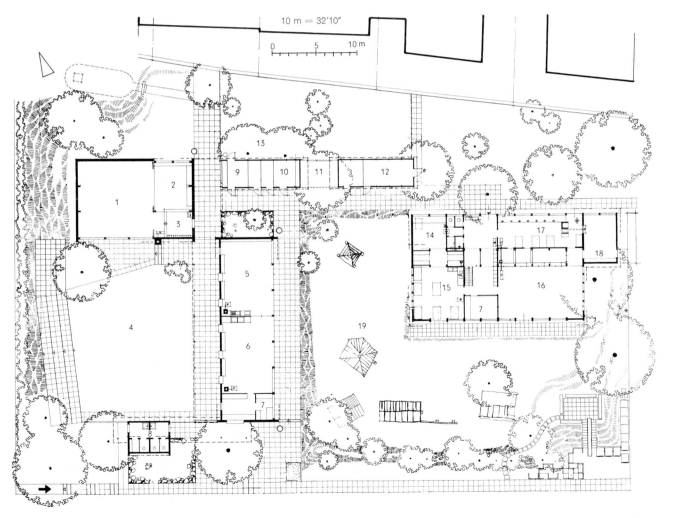

5. The large clubroom, a trussed construction of glued timber. Grown-ups of all ages come here for lectures, music and social gatherings. Children use it particularly in bad weather and in winter for rest, reading and games.

6. The library is fitted into one corner.

7. The workshop for larger jobs is available to everyone. Courses in all types of practical work are also given here.

8. Site plan (final version): theatre building (lectures, films, music, etc.) (1), stage (2), entrance and cloakroom (3), theatre courtyard (4), clubroom with tea bar and library (5), handicrafts (6), club leader (7), W.C. (8), stable and fodder store (9), deck-chair store (10), aviary (11), wood store (12), animals (pets) enclosure (13), leader training building (14), weaving shop (15), woodwork shop (16), metalwork shop (17), machine shop (18), workyard for construction hobbies (19).

5. Der große Clubraum, eine Holzkonstruktion aus verleimten Bindern, die Erwachsenen und alte Leute kommen hier zu Vorträgen, Musik und Geselligkeit zusammen. Die Kinder benutzen ihn vor allem bei schlechtem Wetter und im Winter als Aufenthaltsraum, Lese- und Spielzimmer.

6. In einer Ecke ist die Bibliothek eingerichtet.

7. Die Werkstatt für gröbere Arbeiten ist für jedermann benutzbar. Außerdem finden hier Werkkurse aller Art statt.

8. Lageplan (endgültiger Zustand): Theaterbau (Vorträge, Film, Musik usw.) (1), Bühne (2), Eingang und Garderobe (3), Theaterhof (4), Clubraum mit Teeküche und Bibliothek (5), Bastelraum (6), Freizeitleiter (7), WC (8), Stall und Futterraum (9), Magazin für Liegestühle (10), Volière (11), Holzlager (12), Tiergarten (13), Werkgebäude für Leiterausbildung: Webraum (14), Textilwerkstätte (15), Holzwerkstätte (16), Metallwerkstätte (17), Maschinenraum (18), Werkhof und Bauspielplatz (19).

9. In good weather, library users can come out on to the terrace in front of the clubroom to read.
10. View into the theatre courtyard and playground between the club and workshop premises.
11. A wood sculpture, presented by another Zürich recreation centre, in course of erection at a local ceremony.

9. Bei schönem Wetter lassen sich die Bibliotheksbenutzer auf der Terrasse vor dem großen Clubraum zum Lesen nieder.
10. Blick in den Theater- und Spielhof zwischen Club- und Werkstatt-gebäude.
11. Bei einem Quartierfest wird eine Holzskulptur, Geschenk einer anderen Zürcher Freizeitanlage, aufgerichtet.

9

10

11

12. Larger buildings like this bakery are built by small teams.
13. For a small village of Wendy houses, gardens are a necessity.
14. On the space for building activities a great variety of huts is erected from old materials, boxes, tree-trunks and boards. These are not particularly beautiful buildings in the eyes of grown-ups, but for the children they provide an ideal and stimulating opportunity for creative handiwork.
15. The last touches are put to a little house on stilts. The material was donated by building contractors in Zürich.

12. Größere Bauten wie diese Bäckerei werden in kleinen Arbeitsgemeinschaften erstellt.
13. Zum Ausbau des Spieldörfchens gehört auch das Anlegen von kleinen Gärten.
14. Auf dem Bauspielplatz entstehen aus Altmaterial, Kistenbrettern, Rundhölzern und Latten die verschiedensten Bauten, die für Erwachsenenaugen sicher nicht besonders ansehnlich sein mögen, für die Kinder jedoch eine ideale Gelegenheit bieten, ihre handwerklichen und gestalterischen Fähigkeiten auszubilden.
15. An ein Pfahlbauhäuschen wird die letzte Hand gelegt. Das Baumaterial wird von Zürcher Baufirmen zur Verfügung gestellt.

16. The trees on the lawn were carefully preserved when the playground was built. Mothers and children can withdraw to the sheltering trees, which also divide up the ground into smaller zones so that several groups can play simultaneously.

17. A special attraction is the disused aeroplane on the lawn.

18. At the west side of the lawn, adjoining the playground for small children, are five swings which are very popular.

19. In addition to the actual hard-surface area the paved paths serve as a substitute for the "street". They are used not only for scooters and tricycles but also for other street games such as skipping, marbles, roller-skating.

16. Der Baumbestand der Spielwiese wurde sorgfältig erhalten. So können sich Mütter und Kinder unter die Bäume zurückziehen, und das Gelände ist zugleich in kleinere Spielbereiche aufgeteilt, auf denen sich mehrere Gruppen gleichzeitig betätigen können.

17. Eine besondere Attraktion ist das auf der Spielwiese aufgestellte ausgediente Militärflugzeug.

18. Am Rande der Spielwiese, zum Kleinkinderspielplatz hin, sind fünf vielbenutzte Seilschaukeln aufgestellt.

19. Neben der eigentlichen Hartbelagfläche, die sich auf der Ostseite des Bauspielplatzes anschließt, dienen auch die Plattenwege als Straßenersatz. Sie werden nicht nur für Dreirad- und Rollerfahrten, sondern auch für alle anderen Straßenspiele (Hüpfen, Marmeln, Rollschuhlaufen) benutzt.

20

21

22

23

20. On the first of the four squares which form the playground for small children is a hamlet of three Wendy houses and a little shop. The houses are furnished with tables and chairs.

21. At the "grocer's shop" the children buy old tins and dummy packages.

22. The sandpit is one single area of 1100 square feet. Sailing boats made of concrete slabs, rocks, and blocks of concrete serving as play tables characterize this part of the playground. In the background, left, a group of mothers in deckchairs which are part of the equipment.

23. The paddling pool for small children is combined with a paddling fountain which consists of five concrete drums of 6 feet 8 inches diameter set into the ground. The water flows continuously from one basin to the other, thereby reducing the danger of pollution.

20. Auf dem ersten der vier Quadrate, die den Kleinkinderspielplatz bilden, steht das Spieldorf aus drei Wohnhäuschen und dem Kaufladen. In den mit Kindergartentischen und -stühlen ausgestatteten Holzhäuschen spielen die Kinder.

21. Was die Puppenmütter zum Kochen brauchen, kaufen sie im Konsumladen ein, wo alte Konservendosen und leere Schaufensterattrappen zum Verkaufen bereitstehen.

22. Der Sandspielplatz besteht aus einer einzigen 100 qm großen Fläche. Segelboote aus Betonplatten, Felsbrocken und Spieltische aus Betontrommeln beleben diesen Teil des Platzes. Hinten links eine Gruppe von Müttern in Liegestühlen, die zur Ausstattung des Platzes gehören.

23. Das Planschbecken des Kleinkinderspielplatzes ist mit einem Planschbrunnen kombiniert, der aus fünf verschieden tief eingelassenen und bunt bemalten Betonrohren von je 2 m Durchmesser besteht. Das Wasser läuft von einer Brunnenschale zur anderen über. Durch die ständige Bewegung des Wassers ist die Verschmutzungsgefahr weit geringer als bei den üblichen Becken.

24

25

24+25. The space for building activities is also an outdoor workshop. At the benches and tables such things as model ships or clay models are made. Sometimes parents give a helping hand as they do here with the painting of puppet heads.

26+27. In addition to constructional activities the "Robinson Crusoe" playground provides for artistic expression. Where appropriate, blackboards have been fixed for drawing and scribbling with chalk.

24+25. Der Bauspielplatz dient auch als Bastelwerkstatt im Freien. An den draußen aufgestellten Hobelbänken und Werktischen entstehen Holzschiffchen, Keramikarbeiten usw. Manchmal helfen auch Eltern mit, wie hier beim Bemalen von Kasperlfiguren.

26+27. Neben der handwerklichen Beschäftigung bietet sich auch Gelegenheit für musisches Spiel. Wo es anging, wurden zum Beispiel Malflächen (Wandtafeln, Eternitplatten) angebracht.

26

27

28

29

28. Weather permitting, children may take books from the library and read them on the lawn.
29. Old disused vehicles provide new adventures.
30–32. The animals and birds are looked after by the children themselves in their zoo which their fathers built for them.

28. Bei gutem Wetter können sich die Kinder mit dem Lesestoff aus der Kinderbibliothek auf die Spielwiese zurückziehen.
29. Alte Fahrzeuge bringen neue Spielabenteuer.
30–32. Die Tiere des Kinderzoos, der von Vätern aus der Nachbarschaft erbaut wurde, werden von den Kindern selbst versorgt.

31

30

32

33. The outdoor stage for theatrical performances has been built on a disused horse-cart. Spectators have to sit on the lawn.

34. With equally simple means – boards and boxes – the puppet theatre has been built, where the children give performances with puppets made by themselves.

35. Once a week the "Robinson Crusoe" Council meets. Children over ten years old who regularly play on the ground are Council members. With the assistance of the playground leader all matters concerning the running of the ground, the acquisition of materials, performances and supervision are discussed. In the background is the tram-car which was given by the city of Zürich.

33. Die Freilichtbühne für Theateraufführungen bei Quartierfesten ist auf einem ausgedienten Pritschenwagen aufgebaut. Die Zuschauer sitzen davor auf der Wiese.

34. Mit den gleichen einfachen Mitteln, Brettern und Kisten, ist das Kasperltheater improvisiert, aus dem die Kinder mit selbstgebastelten Puppen Vorstellungen geben.

35. Jede Woche kommt einmal der »Robinsonrat« zusammen, dem die Spielplatzkinder vom zehnten Jahr an zugehören. Er berät unter Assistenz des Spielplatzleiters alle Fragen des Spielplatzbetriebes wie Materialbeschaffung, Veranstaltungen, Ordnungsdienst. Im Hintergrund der von der Stadt Zürich geschenkte Trambahnwagen.

Heuried open-air baths, sports grounds and recreation centre, Zürich-Wiedikon, Switzerland

Planned by Municipal Building Department of Zürich (Alfred Trachsel), in cyllaboration with the Pro Juventute Foundation, Zürich
Architects: Hans Litz and Fritz Schwarz, Zürich

Freibad-, Sport- und Freizeitanlage Heuried, Zürich-Wiedikon, Schweiz

Planung: Hochbauamt der Stadt Zürich (Alfred Trachsel) in Zusammenarbeit mit der Stiftung Pro Juventute, Zürich
Architekten: Hans Litz und Fritz Schwarz, Zürich

On the site of a former clay pit of over 16 acres combined facilities have been provided for leisure, sports and recreation in a scheme forming a central feature for an urban district, now grown to 30,000 inhabitants, and accessible from any part of it on foot in 15 minutes. The spatial programme takes care of all the needs of a town population for active recreation, from competitive sport to casual relaxation. Every age group from small children to elderly walkers can find a wide variety of possible activities. All-the-year-round, and not merely seasonal, use has proved feasible. Instead of specialization and decentralization, the architects were able to create interesting spatial combinations between the various areas. Open-air bathing with several pools, an artificial ice rink and various sports installations were accommodated in the public green spaces and grouped about the centrally placed recreation building (with its rooms for games, handcrafts and intellectual pursuits). The sharpedged concrete cubes contrast strongly with the plastically modelled sports grounds.

Auf dem Gelände einer ehemaligen Lehmgrube von über 6,5 ha Fläche wurde eine kombinierte Freizeit-, Sport- und Erholungsanlage errichtet, die den Mittelpunkt eines auf 30000 Einwohner angewachsenen Stadtteils bildet und von allen Seiten in 15 Minuten zu Fuß erreicht werden kann. Das Raumprogramm berücksichtigt alle Wünsche einer modernen Stadtbevölkerung nach aktiver Freizeitgestaltung, vom reinen Leistungssport bis zum ungezwungenen Spiel. Jede Altersgruppe vom Kleinkind bis zum betagten Spaziergänger findet vielfältige Betätigungsmöglichkeiten. Statt Saisonbetrieb konnte eine Ganzjahresnutzung erreicht werden; statt Spezialisierung und Dezentralisation schufen die Architekten interessante räumliche Kombinationen zwischen den verschiedenen Bereichen. Eine Freibadeanlage mit mehreren Becken, eine Kunsteisbahn und diverse Sporteinrichtungen wurden in die öffentliche Grünanlage eingebettet und rings um das zentral gelegene Freizeitgebäude mit Räumen für Spiel, handwerkliche und geistige Beschäftigung gruppiert. Die scharfkantigen Betonkuben stehen in kraftvollem Kontrast zu dem plastisch modellierten Terrain.

1. Site plan.
Key: entrance to baths (1), cloak (changing) rooms for baths and ice rink (2), schoolchildrens' cloak (changing) rooms (3), swimming pools for learners (4), underground garage entrance (5), tennis courts (6), roller-skating or artificial ice rink (7), restaurant (8), changing-rooms (other sports) (9), swimmers (10), non-swimmers (11) recreation building (12), "building" play-yard (13), sports field (14), school playground (15), school (16), kindergarten (17).
2. Air view. On rising ground the dramatically stepped and terraced cloakrooms block for 3350 visitors. In centre, the retaurant with seating for 140 and garden terrace. Beneath the four tennis courts and roller-skating rink, two-tier parking for 342 vehicles. Fences are kept to a minimum; after the bathing or skating seasons every part of the entire area is readily accessible. The green spaces are interlaced with a network of footpaths with play areas for small children, benches and observation points.

1. Lageplan. Legende: Eingang zum Freibad (1), Garderoben für Bad und Eislaufbahn (2), Garderoben für Schüler (3), Lehrschwimmbekken (4), Einfahrt zur Tiefgarage (5), Tennisplätze (6), Rollschuhbahn oder Kunsteisbahn (7), Restaurant (8), Sportlergarderoben (9), Schwimmer (10), Nichtschwimmer (11), Freizeitgebäude (12), Bauspielplatz (13), Spielwiese (14), Schulspielwiese (15), Schule (16), Kindergarten (17).
2. Luftansicht. Auf ansteigendem Gelände die reich gestaffelten und abgetreppten Garderobengebäude für 3350 Besucher. Im Zentrum das Restaurant mit 140 Plätzen und Gartenterrasse. Unter der Plattform mit den vier Tennisplätzen und der Rollschuhbahn die zweigeschossige Tiefgarage mit 342 Einstellplätzen. Umzäunung auf ein Minimum reduziert, nach Ende der Bade- beziehungsweise Eislaufsaison ist die ganze Anlage mit allen ihren Bereichen frei zugänglich. Die Grünflächen sind von einem Netz von Fußgängerwegen durchzogen mit Kleinkinderspielplätzen, Bänken und Aussichtspunkten.

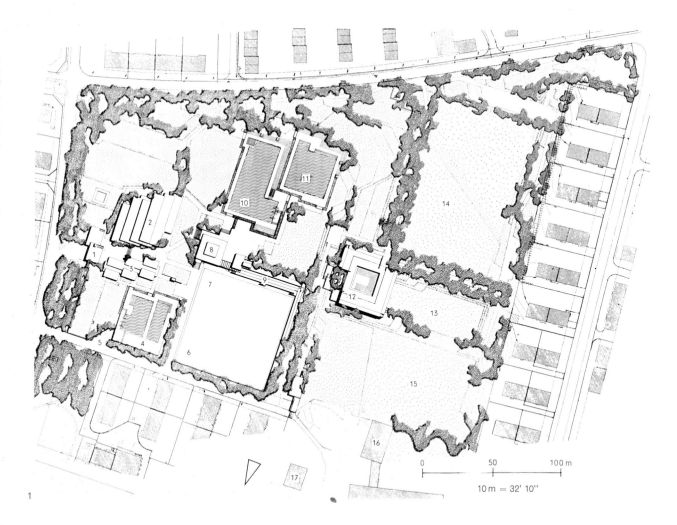

0   50   100 m

10 m = 32' 10''

1

3. The recreation building encloses with its two angular "wings" a terraced courtyard forming the theatre. Windowless façades; light enters through the inner court and by tringular roof lights.

4. The blind cube of the recreation building is the dominant feature of the scheme. Grey exposed concrete surfaces; the unglazed external side of the roof lights is faced with blue tiles.

5–7. Recreation building. Section and plans of upper and lower floors.

Key: theatre court (1), entrance and stairs to workroom on lower floor (2), hobby room (3), children's library (4), library for adults (5), library administration (6), cloakroom (7), open gallery (8), void above large clubroom (9), gallery of large clubroom (10), clubroom (11), toilets (12), large clubroom (13), kitchen (14), scenery store (15), storeroom (16), cloakrooms for men and women (17), garden departement stores (18), air-raid shelter (used as play room) (19), medical room (20), large workroom (21), materials (22), clubleader (23) photographic laboraties (24), "building" play-yard (25).

3. Mit zwei winkelförmigen Bauteilen umschließt das Freizeitgebäude atriumartig den abgetreppten Theaterhof. Fensterlose Fassaden, Belichtung über den Innenhof und über dreieckige Oberlichter.

4. Der geschlossene Kubus des Freizeitgebäudes als Dominante der ganzen Anlage. Graue Sichtbetonflächen, unverglaste Außenseite der Oberlichter mit blauen Ziegeln gedeckt.

5–7. Freizeitgebäude. Schnitt, Grundriß von Obergeschoß und Untergeschoß. Legende: Theaterhof (1), Eingang und Treppe zum Werkraum im Untergeschoß (2), Bastelraum (3), Bibliothek für Kinder (4), Bibliothek für Erwachsene (5), Bibliotheksverwaltung (6), Garderobe (7), Offene Galerie (8), Luftraum über großem Clubraum (9), Galerie des großen Clubraums (10), Clubraum (11), Toiletten (12), großer Clubraum (13), Teeküche (14), Magazin für Theaterkulissen (15), Materialraum (16), Garderoben für Männer und Frauen (17), Magazin des Gartenbauamts (18), Luftschutzraum, als Spielkeller benutzt (19), Sanitätsraum (20), großer Werkraum (21), Material (22), Leiter der Freizeitanlage (23), Photolabor (24), Bauspielplatz (25).

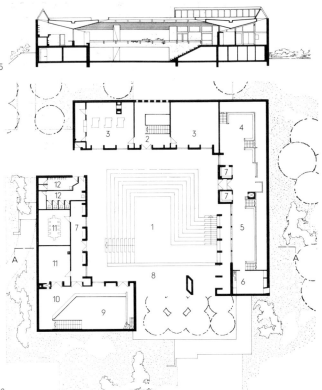
5

3

6

7

4

10 m = 32' 10''

8.

9.

10.

8. The large clubroom for dances, concerts, lectures, local festivities, with gallery and fireplace.
Materials: board-marked concrete, lime-washed brick partition walls, doors and ceiling facings of dark teak. Light enters through a triangular sky-light construction over the heavy timber beams of the roof truss.

9. The library of the Pestalozzi Association, its walls lined with white bookshelves, the upper half accessible from a narrow gallery.

10. One of the hobby rooms — it also serves as a clubroom. Solid furniture, spacious storage for materials, lighting from above.

11. The theatre court bounded on three sides by stepseats, above which the timber roof trusses form a continuous covered way with a kind of cornicelike projection. This covered way provides access to adjacent rooms. An observation gallery offers an extensive view over the ice rink, baths and city.

8. Der große Clubraum für Tanzabende, Konzerte, Vorträge, Quartierfeste mit Galerie und Kamin. Materialien: schalungsrauher Beton, weiß gekalkte, gemauerte Wände, Türen und Deckenverkleidung aus dunklem siamesischem Holz. Belichtung durch dreieckigen Oberlichtaufsatz über den schweren Holzbindern der Dachkonstruktion.

9. Die Bibliothek der Pestalozzigesellschaft, die an den Außenwänden mit weißen Büchergestellen, zur Hälfte von einer schmalen Galerie aus erreichbar, verkleidet ist.

10. Einer der Bastelräume, die zugleich als Clubzimmer dienen. Stabile Möblierung, geräumige Materialschränke, Belichtung durch Oberlichtaufsatz.

11. Der auf drei Seiten von Sitzstufen umgebene Theaterhof, über dem die hölzernen Dachbinder einen geschützten Umgang mit einer Art Kranzgesims bilden. Von diesem Umgang aus werden die anliegenden Räume erschlossen. Eine Aussichtsgalerie bietet einen weiten Blick über Eisbahn, Schwimmbad und Stadt.

11.

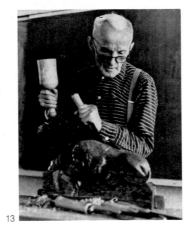

12. Drawing and painting in the hobby room. The older ones help the younger.
13. The oldest user of the woodwork shop.
14. Pre-Christmas activity in the woodwork shop. One of the three leaders issues materials, tools and guidance.
15. The metalwork shop is also provided with welding equipment.
16. Youth group meeting room in the hut (built by themselves) on the building playyard.
17 + 18. Building work with a father's experienced help.
19 + 20. The building play-yard in a hollow on the West side of the recreation building. A "homemade" town of packing cases, planks and scrap materials in a perpetual state of construction and demolition, displaying a surprising sense of instinctive design in its wealth of forms. The children have their own parliament to supervise their "town" and leisure activities.

12. Zeichnen und Malen im Bastelraum. Die Größeren helfen den Kleinen.
13. Der älteste Benutzer der Holzwerkstatt.
14. Vorweihnachtlicher Hochbetrieb in der Holzwerkstatt. Material, Werkzeug und Bastelanleitungen gibt einer der drei Freizeitleiter aus.
15. Zur Ausrüstung der Metallwerkstatt gehört sogar ein Schweißgerät.
16. Der Gruppenraum einer Jugendgruppe in der selbstgebauten Hütte auf dem Bauspielplatz.
17 + 18. Bauarbeiten unter sachverständiger Hilfe eines Vaters.
19 + 20. Der Bauspielplatz in der Mulde auf der Westseite des Freizeitgebäudes. Eine ständig im Auf- und Abbau befindliche, selbstgezimmerte Stadt aus Kisten, Brettern und Abbruchmaterial, die durch ihre spontane Gestaltung und den Reichtum an Formen überrascht. Ein eigenes Kinderparlament verwaltet »Stadt« und Freizeitanlage im wesentlichen selbst.

Recreation Centre, Zürich-Buchegg, Switzerland

Designed by Municipal Building Department (Alfred Trachsel) and Parks Department of Zürich in collaboration with the Pro Juventute Foundation, Zürich
Architects: Hans Litz and Fritz Schwarz, Zürich

Freizeitanlage, Zürich-Buchegg, Schweiz

Planung: Hochbauamt (Alfred Trachsel) und Gartenbauamt der Stadt Zürich, in Zusammenarbeit mit der Stiftung Pro Juventute, Zürich
Architekten: Hans Litz und Fritz Schwarz, Zürich

1

This scheme is an excellent example of the equipment of a public park as a community, play, and recreation centre for young and old. It comprises a rest-field with paths for walking and deck chairs for families and older people, a playing-field for all ball and field games, two playgrounds for small children, a children's "town" for traffic practice and road instruction (see page 108–109), and a building play-yard, as well as the building of the centre itself for various artistic, craft and social activities. These buildings are grouped about an inner court (with a hard surface for street games), which is separated by concrete "play" walls from the theatre space. Boardmarked concrete surfaces, which are disposed in a wide variety of cubic shapes of different heights, define the buildings' general character. The later extension of the workshop and library wing also reflects this impression. The clubrooms are used throughout the day by children for games and reading, and in the evening for youth group activities or adult education.

Diese Anlage ist ein vorzügliches Beispiel für die Ausgestaltung eines öffentlichen Parks zu einem Quartier-, Spiel- und Erholungszentrum für jung und alt. Sie umfaßt eine Liegewiese mit Spazierwegen, Ruhebänken und Liegestühlen für Familien und ältere Leute, eine Spielwiese für alle Ball- und Rasenspiele, zwei Spielplätze für Kleinkinder, eine Kinderstadt für Verkehrsspiele und -unterricht (siehe Seite 108–109), einen Bauspielplatz sowie die Gebäude des eigentlichen Zentrums für die verschiedensten musischen, handwerklichen und geselligen Freizeitaktivitäten. Diese Gebäude gruppieren sich um einen Innenhof mit Hartbelag für Straßenspiele, der durch Spielwände aus Beton vom Theaterplatz abgetrennt ist. Schalungsrauh belassene Betonflächen, die zu reich differenzierten, auch in der Höhe variierten Kuben zusammengefügt wurden, bestimmen den Gesamteindruck der Bauten. Auch die spätere Erweiterung des Werkstatt- und Bibliotheksflügels fügt sich in diesen Grundcharakter ein. Die Clubräume werden tagsüber von den Kindern zum Spielen und Lesen, abends von Jugendgruppen für ihre Zusammenkünfte oder von Erwachsenen als Elternschule usw. benutzt.

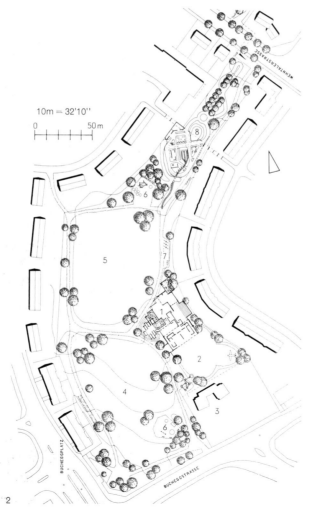

10m = 32'10''

0   50m

2

1. View from the North across the playing field towards the multipartite recreation centre.
2. Site plan: recreation building (1), building play-yard (2), kindergarten (3), rest-field and toboggan slope (4), playing-field (5), small children's playgrounds (6), swings (7), children's "town" for traffic instruction and road practice (8).
3. "Play" walls of the inner court of the recreation centre serve also as theatre wings. Right background, wall surfaces with blackboards at various heights.

1. Blick von Norden über die Spielwiese auf das Freizeitzentrum.
2. Lageplan: Freizeitgebäude (1), Bauspielplatz (2), Kindergarten (3), Liegewiese und Schlittenhügel (4), Spielwiese (5), Kleinkinderspielplätze (6), Schaukeln (7), Kinderstadt für Verkehrsunterricht (8).
3. Spielwände im Innenhof des Freizeitzentrums dienen zugleich als Theaterkulissen. Im Hintergrund rechts Wandflächen mit Zeichentafeln in verschiedenen Höhen.

3

4. The workshops section, a composition of cubes.
5. Plan of recreation centre: internal courts (1), "play" walls (2), wings for theatrical performances (3), stepped seats for theatre audience (4), large recreation room (5), small recreation room (6), forecourt and stairs to cellar theatre (7), kitchen (8), clubroom (9) library (10), recreation leader (11), modelling room (12), sports changing-rooms (13), ceramics workshop with baking-ovens and paint alcove (14), storage (15), photographic laboratory (16), hobby rooms (17), building play-yard (18).
6. View from workshop building over library wing towards the traffic practice ground behind.

4. Der aus Kuben zusammengesetzte Bauteil mit den Werkstatträumen.
5. Grundriß der Freizeitanlage: Innenhöfe (1), Spielwände (2), Kulisse für Theateraufführungen (3), Stufen für Theaterzuschauer (4), großer Freizeitraum (5), kleiner Freizeitraum (6), Vorplatz und Treppe zum Kellertheater (7), Küche (8), Clubraum (9), Bibliothek (10), Freizeitleiter (11), Modellierraum (12), Sportgarderoben (13), Keramikwerkstatt mit Brennöfen und Spritzkabine (14), Lager- und Abstellräume (15), Fotolabor (16), Bastelräume (17), Bauspielplatz (18).
6. Blick vom Werkstattgebäude über den Bibliotheksflügel auf den Verkehrsspielplatz im Hintergrund.

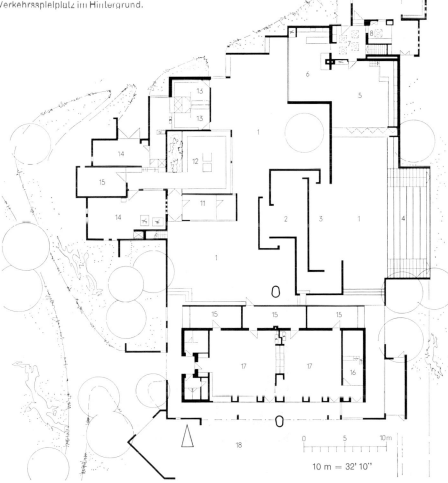

5

10 m = 32' 10''

7

8

9

10

11

12

13

7+8. The zoo, looked after by the children themselves, is one of the main attractions of the recreation centre.

9. Mother and son on their first "test-run".

10. As they walk past the workshops' wing, mothers can find out what is going on.

11. Samples of work are displayed in the show windows of the workshops' building. Musical instruments in this case.

12. Musical instrument making is a speciality of the Buchegg recreation centre. Young and old take part.

13. Learning to play the instruments which they have made.

7+8. Der von den Kindern selbst betreute Zoo ist einer der Hauptanziehungspunkte der Freizeitanlage.

9. Mutter und Sohn beim ersten prüfenden Rundgang.

10. Beim Spazierengehen am Werkstattflügel entlang informieren sich die Mütter aus der Nachbarschaft, was hier geschieht.

11. In den Schaufenstern des Werkstattgebäudes sind Arbeitsproben ausgestellt, hier Musikinstrumente.

12. Das Selbstbauen von Musikinstrumenten ist eine Spezialität der Freizeitanlage Buchegg. Jung und alt beteiligen sich daran.

13. In kleinen Gruppen lernt man auf den selbstgebastelten Instrumenten spielen.

14

15

14. Dancing in the clubroom.
15. The band at work in the practice room.
16. The cellar theatre, built by volunteers in the air-raid shelter.
17. The model railway, built jointly by young people and grown-ups.
18–21. Besides musical instrument making, the ceramics studio is a special hobby attraction. Potters' wheels, spray-painting facilities and two electric ovens are available under expert supervision.

14. Ein Tanzfest in den Clubräumen.
15. Die Musikband im Übungszimmer.
16. Eine Probe im Kellertheater, das von freiwilligen Helfern im Luftschutzkeller eingebaut wurde.
17. Ausschnitt aus der von Jugendlichen und Erwachsenen gemeinsam gebauten Modelleisenbahnanlage.
18–21. Für Bastler ist neben dem Instrumentenbau die Keramikwerkstatt eine besondere Attraktion. Unter fachmännischer Leitung stehen Töpferscheiben, Spritzkammern und zwei Brennöfen zur Verfügung.

16

17

18

19

20

21

Recreation Centre at the Falletsche School, Zürich-Leimbach, Switzerland

Municipal Building Department of Zürich (Alfred Trachsel), in collaboration with the Pro Juventute Foundation, Zürich
Architect: Oskar Bitterli, Zürich

Freizeitzentrum in der Schule Falletsche, Zürich-Leimbach, Schweiz

Planung: Hochbauamt der Stadt Zürich (Alfred Trachsel), in Zusammenarbeit mit der Stiftung Pro Juventute, Zürich
Architekt: Oskar Bitterli, Zürich

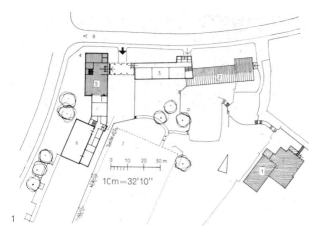

1. Site plan. Key: old school buildings (1), single-storey pavilion of primary school (2), three-storey secondary school range (3), recreation building (4), concert room (5), gymnasium (6), playground (7), to the "building" play yard (about 500 ft.) (8).
2. View from East (and direction of the old school) toward the new buildings. In the angle between the three-storey classroom block and the West cross wing lies the recreation building.
3. Recreation building from North, showing library and clubroom.

1. Lageplan. Legende: Altes Schulhaus (1), eingeschossiger Pavillon der Primarschule (2), dreigeschossiger Trakt der Sekundarschule (3), Freizeitgebäude (4), Singsaal (5), Turnhalle (6), Spielfläche (7), zum Bauspielplatz ca. 150 m (8).
2. Blick von Osten aus Richtung des alten Schulhauses auf die Neubauten. Im Winkel zwischen dem dreigeschossigen Klassentrakt rechts und dem westlichen Quertrakt das Freizeitgebäude.
3. Das Freizeitgebäude von Norden Bibliothek und Clubraum.

In collaboration with the school authorities and Pro Juventute Foundation, this scheme was carried out as an "open school" available to all age groups, with multipurpose facilities not only for teaching but also for the leisure requirements of the whole population. A covered passage links the single- and three-storey wings with the recreation building placed in the righthand corner, adjoined by the gymnasium on the South side. While the classroom blocks are not accessible to everyone, the gymnasium, school workshops and concert room in the West (transverse) range of buildings are for general use. The basement of the three-storey recreation building contains a hobby room, as well as woodwork and metalwork shops. The ground floor accommodates the concert room, which is designed, with an eye to leisure activities for 200–250 people and provided with a stage. If needed, it can be combined (by retracting a sliding partition) with the entrance foyer, which becomes an extension to the concert room and connects with a clubroom (with tea bar). The lending library for children and adults is on the top floor.

In Zusammenarbeit zwischen der Schulbehörde und der Stiftung Pro Juventute wurde diese Schulanlage zu einem »Offenen Schulhaus« ausgebaut, das als Mehrzweckeinrichtung nicht nur dem Unterricht, sondern auch den Freizeitbedürfnissen der Bevölkerung dient und allen Altersgruppen offensteht. Eine gedeckte Passage verbindet die ein- und dreigeschossigen Klassenzimmerflügel mit dem im rechten Winkel dazu gestellten Freizeitgebäude, an das sich im Süden die Turnhalle anschließt. Während die Klassengebäude nicht allgemein zugänglich sind, werden Turnhalle, Schulwerkstatt und Singsaal im westlichen Quertrakt gemeinsam benutzt. Das Untergeschoß des dreistöckigen Freizeitgebäudes enthält einen Bastelraum sowie eine Holz- und Metallwerkstatt. Im Erdgeschoß befindet sich der Singsaal, der im Hinblick auf den Freizeitbetrieb für etwa 200–250 Personen dimensioniert und mit einer Bühne ausgestattet wurde. Bei Bedarf kann er mit einer Schiebewand zum Eingangsfoyer hin geöffnet werden, das als Saalerweiterung dient und an einen Clubraum mit Teeküche anschließt. Im Obergeschoß liegt die Freihandbibliothek für Kinder und Erwachsene, die von Mitarbeitern der Pestalozzigesellschaft betreut wird.

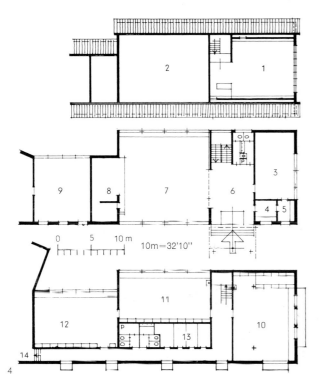

4. Recreation building. Plans of upper storey, ground floor and basement. Key: lending library (1), void above concert room (2), clubroom (3), leader's office (4), tea bar (5), foyer (6), concert room (7), stage (8), girls' handcrafts (9), hobby room (10), woodwork shop (11), metalwork shop (12), store rooms (13).
5. Concert room with stage and sliding partition opening to foyer.
6. Lending library in roof storey with open-access shelves.
7. Clubroom on ground floor during play time.
8. Schoolchildren and visitors share the basement workshops of the recreation building. Only their tools are kept apart.
9. The recreation-building hobby-room serves without restriction as an extension to the school workshops.
10. The basement also has space for table tennis.

4. Freizeitgebäude. Grundrisse von Obergeschoß, Erdgeschoß und Untergeschoß. Legende: Freihandbibliothek (1), Luftraum über dem Singsaal (2), Clubraum (3), Büro des Freizeitleiters (4), Teeküche (5), Foyer (6), Singsaal (7), Bühne (8), Handarbeitsraum (9), Bastelraum (10), Holzwerkstatt (11), Metallwerkstatt (12), Materialräume (13).
5. Der Singsaal mit Bühne und Schiebewand zum Foyer.
6. Die Freihandbibliothek mit frei zugänglichen Regalen.
7. Der Clubraum im Erdgeschoß während einer Spielstunde.
8. Schüler und Besucher des Freizeitzentrums benutzen die Werkstätten gemeinsam. Nur ihre Werkzeuge werden getrennt verwahrt.
9. Der Bastelraum des Freizeitzentrums dient beim offenen Betrieb als Ergänzung der beiden Schulwerkstätten.
10. Auch für das Tischtennisspiel ist im Untergeschoß Platz.

Plastic playthings of the Pepsi-Cola indoor playground, New York City, U.S.A.

Designed by Jerry Lieberman, New York
Distribution by Playscape Incorporated, New York

Kunststoff-Spielgeräte des Pepsi-Cola »Indoor«-Spielplatzes, New York City, USA

Entwurf der Geräte: Jerry Lieberman, New York
Vertrieb: Playscape Incorporated, New York

With the support of the Pepsi-Cola Company, a graphics and exhibition designer, Jerry Lieberman, devoted two years' work to developing novel playthings which consist entirely of standard products of the plastics industry. A temporary indoor playground was arranged with these objects, in association with the National Recreation and Park Association, in the entrance hall of the Pepsi-Cola office building on Park Avenue. Equally adaptable at reasonable cost to open-air playgrounds, one of their main advantages is that they offer the maximum safety and a minimum need for care and supervision, since the materials – polyethylene and plastic foam – are soft and yielding and cannot cause physical harm. The indoor playground provided 6500 sq ft of brand new play possibilities, like the trampoline effect of plastic foam sheets, fastened together into huge snail shells and tunnels to wriggle through, or the spring-back resilience of climbing poles or "one-man" fibre glass seesaws. Plastic beads (as substitutes for sand) and little houses (to clamber into) made of plastic containers make interesting experiments with new materials, too.

Mit Unterstützung der Pepsi-Cola Company entwickelte der Graphiker und Ausstellungsgestalter Lieberman in zweijähriger Arbeit neuartige Spielgeräte, die ausschließlich aus Fertigteilen der Kunststoffindustrie bestehen. In Verbindung mit der National Recreation and Park Association konnte aus diesen Geräten für einige Zeit in der Eingangshalle des Pepsi-Cola-Verwaltungsgebäudes an der Park Avenue ein »Indoor«-Spielplatz gestaltet werden. Inzwischen stehen sie zu erschwinglichen Kosten auch für Spielplätze im Freien zur Verfügung. Einer ihrer wichtigsten Vorteile ist, daß sie ein Höchstmaß an Sicherheit bieten und ein Minimum an Pflege und Überwachung brauchen, da ihr Material – Polyäthylen und Schaumstoff – sehr unempfindlich ist und jede Verletzungsgefahr ausschließt. Der »Indoor«-Spielplatz bot auf 600 m² neuartige Spielmöglichkeiten, so etwa der Trampolineffekt der Schaumstoffplatten, die zu großen Schneckenhäusern und Kriechröhren zusammengeklebt worden waren, oder die Federkraft der Kletterstangen und Ein-Personen-Wippen aus Fiberglas. Aber auch die Kunststoffperlen als Sandersatz oder die Kletterhäuschen aus Plastikbehältern sind interessante Versuche mit neuen Materialien.

1. The indoor playground in the hall of the Pepsi-Cola building at a busy moment.
2. Slide of revolving plastic rollers between plastic bars, originally components of a conveyor belt.
3 + 4. "One-man" seesaw. The toughened fibre glass shaft can carry adults.
5. A mountain range (with a trampoline effect) to climb over, made of rolls of foam material of various lengths placed on end.
6. Foam plastic sheets manipulated into snail shells and winding tunnels. Several layers (on top of each other) increase the elasticity.
7. A fibre glass pole, inserted vertically into the floor, makes a tree to climb and spring in every direction. (design by Robert Boggild).
8 + 9. The "sand boxes" normally serve as coverings for the jet-engines of DC 9 aircraft. Here they are filled with plastic beads of various sizes and colours, which American farmers mix with poultry food to prevent hens from over-eating.

1. Der »Indoor«-Spielplatz in der Halle des Pepsi-Cola-Gebäudes bei starkem Besuch.
2. Eine Rutschbahn aus drehbaren Plastikrollen zwischen Plastik-holmen, ursprünglich Bestandteile eines Förderbandes.
3 + 4. Eine Einmannwippe. Die verstärkte Fiberglasstange trägt sogar Erwachsene.
5. Ein Klettergebirge mit Trampolineffekt aus senkrecht stehenden, verschieden langen Schaumstoffrollen.
6. Schaumstoffplatten, zu Schneckenhäusern und Kriechtunnels zusammengeklebt. Mehrere Lagen erhöhen die Federung.
7. Senkrecht in den Boden eingelassen, federt die Fiberglasstange als Kletterbaum nach allen Seiten (Entwurf Robert Boggild).
8 + 9. Die Sandkastenbehälter dienen eigentlich als Abdeckung für die Düsenmotoren von DC-9-Maschinen. Hier sind sie mit unterschiedlich großen, farbigen Plastikperlen gefüllt, wie sie amerikanische Farmer unters Futter mischen, damit sich die Hühner nicht überfressen.

5

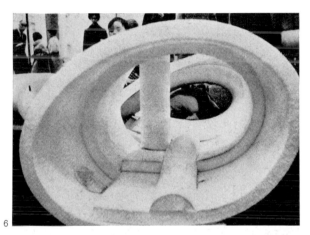

6

7

8

9

10

10–12. Rectangular, polyethylene containers in bright colours, as used by the textile industry for storing fibres, are arranged as a play town. Fibre glass cylinders in three lengths form bases of different heights and tubes to climb through. A variety of openings have been cut in the sides to make windows and doors. As the next picture shows, this "cityscape" was further developed with hexagonal containers.

10–12. In verschiedenen leuchtenden Farben gehaltene, rechteckige Behälter aus Polyäthylen, wie sie die Textilindustrie für die Aufbewahrung von Fasern verwendet, wurden zu einer Spielstadt zusammengestellt. Fiberglaszylinder in drei Längen bilden unterschiedlich hohe Sockel und Verbindungsröhren zum Durchkriechen. Als Fenster und Türen sind die verschiedenartigsten Öffnungen in die Wände eingeschnitten. Wie das nebenstehende Bild zeigt, wurde die »Cityscape« später mit sechseckigen Behältern weiterentwickelt.

11

12

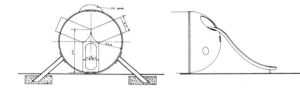

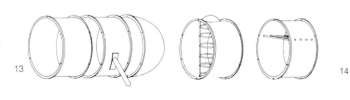

13

14

13–16. A onetime petrol tank of transparent coloured fibre glass (with multicoloured acrylic glass bulges) for children to play in and climb about. A later version (13 + 14) is composed of various rings of 8 feet diameter with a multiplicity of fittings. Hemispherical endpieces enclose the cyclinders, which are laid flat.

13–16. Beim Spieltank, einem Benzintank aus farbigem, transparentem Fiberglas mit verschiedenfarbigen Acrylglaskuppeln, können die Kinder im Inneren spielen und klettern. Die weiterentwickelte Ausführung (Abb. 13+14) wird aus beliebig vielen Ringen von 2,44 m Durchmesser mit unterschiedlicher Ausstattung zusammengesetzt. Halbkugelförmige Endstücke schließen den liegenden Zylinder ab.

15

16

Modular system of prefabricated elements for demountable playing equipment

Designer: M. Paul Friedberg & Associates, New York

Modulares System aus vorgefertigten Teilen für demontable Spielgeräte

Entwurf: M. Paul Friedberg & Associates, New York

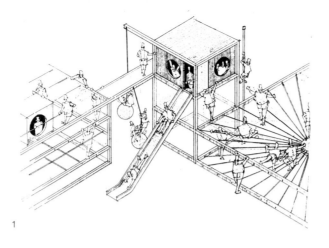

1+3. Play structure of wooden logs, pipe and cable units, combined with slide, playhouse, sliding pole and rubber ball swing.
2. Climbing structure of wooden logs of different lengths with crossed members; playhouse constructed of precast concrete parts.
4. A play structure of tubular steel elements.
5. Wood construction with rubber ball swings.

1+3. Ein Spielgerüst aus Holzbalken, Kabeln und Stahlrohrstangen, kombiniert mit Rutsche, Spielhaus, Kletterstange und Gummiballschaukel.
2. Klettergerüst aus verschieden langen, über Eck gekreuzten Balken, dazu Spielhäuschen aus vorfabrizierten Betonelementen.
4. Eine Spielstruktur aus zusammengesteckten Stahlrohrteilen.
5. Balkenkonstruktion mit Gummiballschaukeln.

1

Under the auspices of the United States Department of Housing and Urban Development and in conjunction with the Experimental Park Program, New York City Department of Parks, M. Paul Friedberg developed a simple, flexible system of demountable and portable play equipment with the help of which twelve vacant city lots have already become novel playgrounds. The elements do not require any foundations – therefore all of the investment will be above ground – and they are adaptable to odd sized lots of different terrains, even with trees. Temporarily vacant lots, as small as 20 by 75 feet, can be converted into play areas for a two- or three-year period. The basically rectangular elements are bolted together in a very simple manner, are easily assembled and demounted, quickly transferred from one site to another or stock-piled without requiring much space. Many of the objects can be moved or adjusted by the children during play, therefore they leave their playground somewhat different. With this equipment, a playground is not a fixed arrangement of structures, but constantly changing; and any designer using these elements may determine a form of his own choosing.

Mit Hilfe des United States Department of Housing and Urban Development und in Verbindung mit dem Experimental Park Program des New York City Department of Parks entwickelte M. Paul Friedberg ein ebenso einfaches wie flexibles System für demontable und leicht zu transportierende Spielgeräte, mit denen bereits ein Dutzend Plätze eingerichtet ist. Sie brauchen keinerlei Fundamente, so daß teure Erdbewegungen entfallen. Es können Grundstücke jeden Zuschnitts, auch mit Bäumen, verwendet werden. So ist es beispielsweise möglich, unbebaute Grundstücke in Baulücken bis zu einem Mindestmaß von 6 × 22,5 m für 1–2 Jahre als Spielplatz einzurichten. Die durchweg rechtwinklig anzuschließenden Elemente werden lediglich mit Bolzen zusammengesteckt. Sie lassen sich rasch auf- und abbauen, leicht transportieren und raumsparend lagern. Viele Geräte lassen sich während des Spielens verändern, so daß die Kinder ihren Spielplatz selbst umgestalten können. Ein Platz ist also niemals endgültig fertig, sondern ständig im Wechsel. Auch der Entwerfer, der mit diesen Elementen plant, hat viele Möglichkeiten, zu einer individuellen Lösung zu kommen.

2

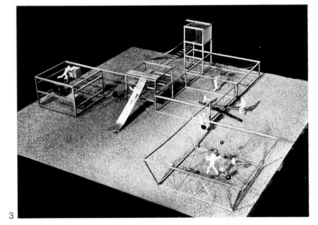

4

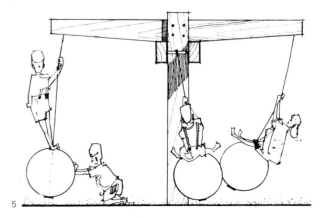

5

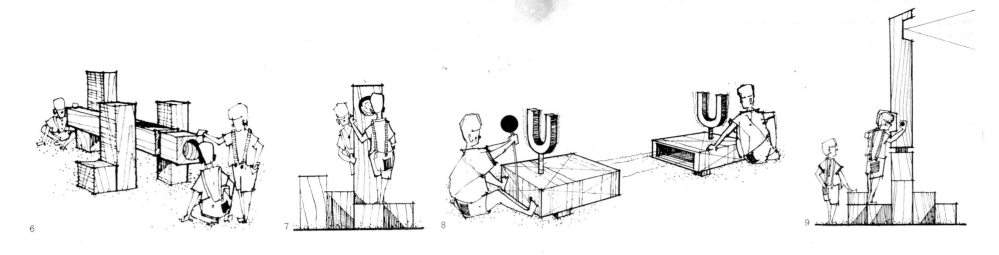

6 7 8 9

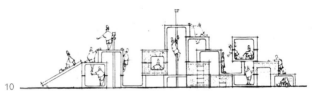

10

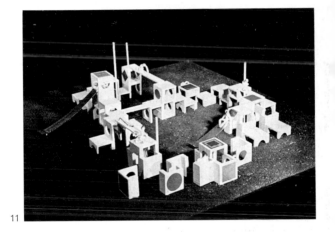

11

6–9. For the Nature Study Parks (see page) 54 Mr. Friedberg developed sturdy, simple equipment which may also be used for portable playgrounds. From left to right: Kaleidoscope, magnifying glass, tuning-fork and sounding-box, periscope.

10–13. Apart from prefabricated modular climbing structures and space defining frames of wooden logs (Figs. 1–3) and steel tubing (Fig. 4), there are U- and V-shaped precast concrete pieces that can be put together form climbing "mountains" and even villages. All parts are painted in many colors and have various kinds of holes or steps. Wooden and concrete elements can of course be combined (Fig. 12).

6–9. Für die Nature Study Parks in New York (siehe Seite 54) entwickelte Friedberg einfache, robuste Geräte, die auch auf den mobilen Spielplätzen aufgestellt werden können. Von links nach rechts: Kaleidoskop, Vergrößerungsglas, Stimmgabel und Resonanzkiste, Periskop.

10–13. Neben den vorfabrizierten modularen Klettergerüsten und raumbildenden Rahmen aus Holzbalken (Abb.1–3) und Stahlrohren (Abb. 4) stehen auch U- und L-förmige, ebenfalls vorfabrizierte Betonteile zur Verfügung, die zu Klettergebirgen und ganzen Dörfern zusammengestellt werden können. Die einzelnen Typen sind verschiedenfarbig bemalt und haben unterschiedliche Öffnungen oder Stufen. Selbstverständlich können die Holz- und Betonelemente auch kombiniert werden (Abb. 12).

12

13

Wendy houses made of pre-fabricated reinforced concrete components

Designed by Virginia Dortch Dorazio
Manufactured by Creative Playthings, Inc., New York, U. S. A.

Spielhäuschen aus Stahlbeton-Fertigteilen

Entwerfer: Virginia Dortch Dorazio
Hersteller: Creative Playthings, Inc., New York, USA

The "fantastic village" was the prize-winning design in a competition for play equipment held by the Museum of Modern Art in conjunction with a play equipment firm and a parents' journal. The village consists of five different types of house, each 5 feet high. The pre-fabricated parts of reinforced concrete can be assembled in a variety of combinations as roof or wall elements and can thereby be adapted to the various age-groups. The openings, which serve as doors and windows as well as giving convenient holds to foot or hand in climbing, are carefully positioned and related in shape. In conjunction with ladders and climbing bars they encourage the child's imagination. The irregular colour treatment accentuates the openings and projecting bars.

Das »phantastische Dorf«, das aus fünf verschiedenen Haustypen von 1,50 m Höhe besteht, wurde bei einem Wettbewerb für gute Spielgeräte – veranstaltet vom Museum of Modern Art, einer Elternzeitschrift und einer Spielgerätefirma – mit dem 1. Preis ausgezeichnet. Die vorfabrizierten Einzelteile aus Stahlbeton lassen sich als Wand- und Dachelemente in vielfältigen Kombinationen zusammenstellen und damit den verschiedenen Altersstufen anpassen. Die Öffnungen, die als Türen, Fenster, Ausstiege, Griff- und Trittlöcher dienen, sind in Form und Verteilung sorgfältig aufeinander abgestimmt und bieten, ergänzt durch Leitern und Kletterstäbe aus Stahlrohr, der kindlichen Phantasie viele Anregungen. Die unregelmäßige Bemalung der Wände korrespondiert mit den Öffnungen und Stahlrohrteilen, die auf diese Weise noch verschiedenfarbig akzentuiert werden.

Wooden Wendy Houses

Spielhäuschen aus Holz

Wendy houses are important elements of playground equipment for the quieter games and those where fantasy is an integral part of play. Besides the simple, tent shaped huts which one frequently finds in Switzerland (see page 89) and in Denmark (see illustration 1), complete fully-furnished little houses are sometimes used as at the "Robinson Crusoe" playground in Switzerland (see page 136) and in Sweden (see illustration 2). The Swedish examples, which normally consist of two-roomed houses of 5 feet 3 inches ceiling height, are often grouped together to form a hamlet. They are let by the hour to groups of up to four children by the playground leader when too many children want to play at the same time. These miniature houses imitate the world of grown-ups as accurately as is possible on a small scale. On the other hand box-like play houses (see illustration 3), which are cubist editions of a Wendy house, offer greater stimulus towards adventurous hide and seek games and to games which call for courage. They were erected on the playground of the H 55 Exhibition at Hälsingborg, and are accentuated by colourful exteriors. Raised on tubular steel supports of varying height, they are interconnected by narrow wooden bridges.

Spielhäuschen für Rollenspiele sind ein wichtiges Element der Spielplatzgestaltung. Neben einfachen, zeltförmigen Hütten, wie sie in der Schweiz (siehe Seite 89) und in Dänemark (Abbildung 1) häufig anzutreffen sind, werden auch vollständig eingerichtete Spielhäuschen verwendet, so etwa auf dem »Robinson«-Spielplatz in Wipkingen (Seite 136) und in Schweden (Abbildung 2). Die schwedischen Typen, die jeweils zwei Zimmer mit einer Raumhöhe von 1.60 m enthalten, sind vielfach zu kleinen Spieldörfchen zusammengefaßt und werden von der Spielplatzleiterin je nach Andrang stundenweise Gruppen von vier Kindern zugeteilt. Während diese Miniaturhäuschen die Welt der Erwachsenen möglichst genau im verkleinerten Maßstab zu wiederholen suchen, regen die Kastenhäuschen (Abbildung 3), die auf dem Spielplatz der Ausstellung H 55 in Hälsingborg erstellt worden waren, mehr zu abenteuerlichen Mut- und Versteckspielen an. Farbig stark akzentuiert, sind sie auf verschieden hohe Stahlbeine gestellt und miteinander durch Holzstege verbunden.

Wendy houses and Red Indian tents made of wood

Spielhäuschen und Indianerzelte aus Holz

1. Swedish tent house with "furniture" of wooden blocks.
2. Cheap, sturdy tent houses with roofs of unplaned boards on a playground in Stuttgart. (Design: Parks Department of Stuttgart)
3. A well-designed Danish Wendy house. On the roof, poles give holds to foot and hand in climbing.
4. A "village" between mounds on the playground of Biegerhof in Duisburg, Germany. (Design: Georg and Rosemarie Penker, Landscape Architects)

1. Ein schwedisches Zelthaus mit »Möbeln« aus Holzklötzen.
2. Billige und robuste Zelthäuser mit Dächern aus rohen Brettern auf einem Stuttgarter Spielplatz. (Entwurf: Gartenbauamt Stuttgart)
3. Ein dänisches Spielhaus. Auf dem Dach Griff- und Trittstangen.
4. Das zwischen Erdwällen eingebettete Dorf des Spielplatzes Biegerhof in Duisburg, Deutschland. (Planung: Georg und Rosemarie Penker, Gartenarchitekten)

Wendy houses normally have to meet two requirements: They should offer seclusion and shelter from sudden showers of rain, and they should be sturdy enough to be used for climbing and as a look-out. This second demand is frequently met in Denmark by equipping the roof with climbing poles (see illustration 3). The simple tent has achieved success as a sturdy and cheap construction with sufficient stability for climbing. Roofs consist of planed or rough boards (see illustration 2), or even of wooden poles nailed one above the other horizontally (see illustration 4).

For the typical round tent on Red Indian playgrounds, the Parks Department of the City of Stuttgart developed a series of different solutions (see illustrations 8–10), but neither the wickerwork version nor the one held together by ropes withstood the constant hard wear; only the construction using vertical poles which are screwed onto heavy metal rings (see illustration 10) proved strong enough for permanent use. Besides sturdy wooden pyramids (see illustration 5), the series includes a very popular palisade fort (see illustration 7).

Spielhäuschen haben fast immer eine doppelte Funktion. Sie sollen in ihrem Inneren Geborgenheit bieten und auch einmal einen Regenguß überstehen helfen, und zugleich sind sie als Klettergerät und als Aussichtsturm einer ziemlich rauhen Beanspruchung ausgesetzt. Dieser zweiten Aufgabe trägt man in Dänemark häufig dadurch Rechnung, daß das Dach von vornherein mit Kletterstangen ausgerüstet wird (Abb. 3). Als robuste und billige Konstruktion hat sich die einfache Zeltform bewährt, die auch als Klettergerüst genügend Stabilität bietet. Die Dachflächen werden mit gehobelten oder auch rohen Brettern (Abb. 2) verkleidet, vielfach verwendet man auch nur waagrecht übereinandergenagelte Stangen (Abb. 4).

Für das Rundzelt auf Indianerspielplätzen entwickelte das Gartenbauamt in Stuttgart eine Variantenreihe (Abb. 8–10), wobei allerdings weder die geflochtene noch die mit Seilen bespannte Ausführung auf die Dauer der Beanspruchung standhielt. Erst die Konstruktion mit senkrechten Stangen (Abb. 10), die an starken Metallreifen verschraubt werden, war widerstandsfähig genug. Neben stabilen Holzpyramiden (Abb. 5) zeigt diese Zusammenstellung noch ein Palisadenfort (Abb. 7), das bei den Kindern sehr beliebt ist.

5

6

7

5. Sturdy pyramid-shaped huts covered with wooden poles cut in halves lengthwise on the Red Indian playground "Aquilagelände"; in Leverkusen, Germany

6. Hexagonal Red Indian tents covered with rough boards.

7. A palisade fort with penetrating sitting poles; below, entrance to a crawling tunnel. (Design: Parks Department of the City of Stuttgart)

8+9. Red Indian tents: Wickerwork and ropes. (Design: Parks Department of the City of Stuttgart)

10. Red Indian tent made of vertical wooden poles screwed onto strong metal rings .(Design: Parks Department of the City of Stuttgart)

11. Even swings may well be hung from wooden structures; in this example, they are connected by long metal bolts. (Design: Parks Department of the City of Stuttgart)

5. Stabile Pyramidenhütten mit einer Verkleidung aus halbierten Holzstangen auf dem Indianerspielplatz Aquilagelände in Leverkusen, Deutschland.

6. Sechskantige Indianerzelte, mit rohen Brettern verkleidet.

7. Eine Palisadenburg mit durchgesteckten Sitzstangen, darunter der Eingang eines Kriechtunnels. (Entwurf: Gartenbauamt der Stadt Stuttgart)

8+9. Aus Weiden geflochtene und mit Seilen bespannte Indianerzelte. (Entwurf: Gartenbauamt der Stadt Stuttgart)

10. Indianerzelt aus senkrecht stehenden Stangen, die mit starken Eisenbändern verschraubt sind. (Entwurf: Gartenbauamt der Stadt Stuttgart)

11. Auch Schaukelgerüste können durchaus mit Holzstämmen ausgeführt werden. Hier sind sie durch lange Metallbolzen miteinander verbunden. (Entwurf: Gartenbauamt der Stadt Stuttgart)

8

9

10

11

Simple playground equipment made of wood and concrete drums

Einfache Spielgeräte aus Holz und Beton

1

2

The illustrations show how play elements can be created at comparatively small cost; these, because of their simplicity, leave the greatest scope for a child's imagination. It is evident too how one can achieve, with the help of skilful grouping, a lively and stimulating variety of games (see illustrations 3+6). Timber is usually quite easy to obtain and in the form of a balancing trunk, with the bark left on, can assume the most adventurous shapes, as shown in illustration 2. The climbing tree which is placed more or less horizontally, with its branches touching the ground, is part of the equipment of a great number of playgrounds. But, as shown in illustration 7, tree tops with the bark pealed off can be erected vertically so that the element of height becomes part of the game. Stepped pyramids made of closely placed tree-trunks of different heights are a challenge to climbing and jumping prowess, especially when the heights to be climbed are placed in a sandpit (see illustration 5).

Die Beispiele zeigen, wie mit verhältnismäßig geringen Kosten Spielelemente geschaffen werden können, die gerade durch ihre Einfachheit der kindlichen Vorstellungswelt weitesten Spielraum lassen. Es wird auch deutlich, wie bei geschickter Gruppierung eine abwechslungsreich bewegte und spieldramatisch anregende Platzgestaltung zu erreichen ist (Abbildung 3+6). Holz ist meist leicht zu beschaffen und kann als ungeschälter Balancierstamm die abenteuerlichsten Gestalten annehmen (Abbildung 2). Der Kletterbaum, der mehr oder weniger horizontal mit dem Geäst auf dem Boden aufliegt, gehört zur Geräteausstattung zahlreicher Plätze. Er kann aber auch als geschälte Baumkrone senkrecht eingegraben werden (Abbildung 7), damit das Element der Höhe ins Spiel kommt. Stufenpyramiden aus eng gestellten, verschieden hohen Stämmen fordern zum Besteigen wie zum Absprung heraus, besonders dann, wenn das Klettergebirge mit einem Sandplatz kombiniert ist (Abbildung 5).

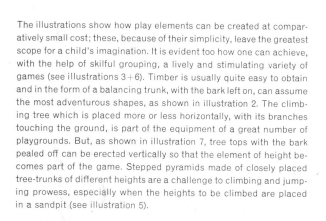

3

The concrete drum is cheap and a versatile equipment for playing. It can be used as a tunnel through a hill (see illustration 4) or, when laid above, ground its inside becomes challenging and dark in contrast to the brightness of the open grounds (see illustration 8).

Die Industrie liefert mit Betonröhren ein billiges und vielseitiges Spielgerät: es wird zum Tunnel durchs Gebirge (Abbildung 4), und frei gelagert ist es zugleich »Innen« und »Außen« (Abbildung 8). Sein dunkler Gang läßt das Kind das Unterirdische im Kontrast zur Helle des Spielplatzes erleben.

4

5

6

7

8

Slides, climbing walls and climbing equipment

Rutschbahnen, Kletterwände und Klettergeräte

1

1–3. "All Metal" slides on playgrounds designed by Mary Mitchell, landscape architect, in Birmingham, Borough of Nuneaton and County Borough of Blackburn. The mound 21 feet high has been formed from rubbish on the site and was built up layer by layer, consolidated and surfaced by concrete.
4. Water slide on a playground in the Buerscher Stadtwald, Gelsenkirchen, Germany.
5. This slide on the playground Södra Elineberg in Hälsingborg, Sweden, has a length of 60 feet.

1–3. Ganzmetallrutschbahnen auf Spielplätzen der Gartenarchitektin Mary Mitchell in Birmingham, Borough of Nuneaton und County Borough of Blackburn. Auf den 6,4 m hohen, schichtweise aus Aushub aufgeschütteten Hügel wurde eine Betonschicht aufgespritzt.
4. Wasserrutschbahn auf einem Spielplatz im Buerschen Stadtwald in Gelsenkirchen, Deutschland.
5. Diese Rutschbahn in Hälsingborg, Schweden, ist 18 m lang.

The slides shown here all follow the natural slope of the sites, which in some cases results in a much greater length than would be possible with free-standing structures because of the limited height of ladders. The British landscape architect, Mary Mitchell, designed playgrounds which connect these slides with other playing elements in a dramatic and attractive way, the steps leading upwards being formed of big stones or sections of tree trunks. The slides are specially designed "All Metal" structures with stainless steel sliding surfaces. The surface of a double water slide on a German playground is of polished concrete.
Older children will enjoy climbing on the brick wall of a playground designed for a housing development scheme in New York, whereas the built-in concrete tubes and iron handles of a climbing wall in Denmark encourage even small children. Wooden poles and tree trunks may be used to form palisade walls and interesting climbing structures. Climbing "trees" made of steel tubes and placed together in groups have projecting parts on three sides to give convenient holds.

Die hier gezeigten Rutschbahnen folgen alle dem natürlichen Gefälle von Böschungen, wobei in manchen Fällen sehr viel größere Längen erreicht werden, als es bei freistehenden Gerüstkonstruktionen wegen der begrenzten Leiterhöhe möglich wäre. Die englische Gratenarchitektin Mary Mitchell bringt die Rutschen auf ihren Plätzen in einen reizvollen spieldramatischen Zusammenhang, indem sie den Aufstieg mit groben Steinen pflastert oder Treppen aus großen Baumscheiben anlegt. Sie verwendet speziell entworfene Ganzmetallrutschen mit Gleitflächen aus rostfreiem Stahl. Bei der zweispurigen Wasserrutschbahn eines deutschen Platzes besteht die Oberfläche aus geschliffenem Beton.
Während die reliefierte Backsteinmauer eines New Yorker Siedlungsspielplatzes mehr für größere Kletterer gedacht ist, ermutigen die eingemauerten Betonröhren und Eisenklammern der dänischen Kletterwand auch die Kleineren. Pfähle und Stangen aus Holz lassen sich zu Palisadenwänden und vielteiligen Klettergerüsten zusammensetzen. Dreistrahlige Kletterbäume aus Stahlrohr bilden ganze Baumgruppen.

4

5

2

3

6. Playing wall of concrete with cut-out silhouette shapes. (Design: Parks Department of the City of Stuttgart)
7. Climbing wall on Carver Houses playground, New York. (Design: M. Paul Friedberg & Ass., New York)
8. Climbing "trees" of steel tubing. (Design: Alfred Trachsel, Zürich)
9 + 10. Simple, inexpensive climbing equipment of wood. (Design: Parks Department of the City of Stuttgart)
11. Climbing wall on a playground in Søborg, Denmark

6. Spielwand aus Beton mit silhouettenförmigen Ausschnitten. (Entwurf: Gartenbauamt der Stadt Stuttgart)
7. Kletterwand auf dem Spielplatz Carver Houses, New York. (Entwurf: M. Paul Friedberg & Ass., New York)
8. Kletterbäume aus Stahlrohr. (Entwurf: Alfred Trachsel, Zürich)
9 + 10. Einfache und billige Klettergeräte aus Holz. (Entwurf: Gartenbauamt der Stadt Stuttgart).
11. Kletterwand auf einem Spielplatz in Søborg, Dänemark.

6

7

8

9

10

11

Simple equipment for action and adventure games

Einfache Geräte für Bewegungs- und Abenteuerspiele

The technical world of the grown-ups offers great attraction to children. Simplified imitations like the railway track made of wood (see illustration 3) and climbing nets (see illustration 1) allow the child to grow into the technical world in its play. The urge to be creative and to construct is met by special equipment, especially on a number of Danish and Swedish playgrounds. There the attendants hand out large blocks of wood, boards and boxes for building. In English and Scandinavian playgrounds ships are a frequent feature. The hull is mostly of concrete (in the case of larger ships it is often filled with sand), whereas the superstructure and cabins are mostly made of wood. Only the shape in outline is simulated but the main attractions are the "real" ropes and rope ladders, the crane and lifting gear for moving boxes "on board", and the fact that one can look out "for the sea and the waves" from a porthole.

Die technische Welt der Erwachsenen übt große Anziehungskraft aus. Vereinfachte Nachbildungen wie Schienen aus Holz (Abbildung 3) und Kletternetze (Abbildung 1) lassen das Kind spielend in diese Welt hineinwachsen. Dem Drang zum Gestalten und Konstruieren kommt eine Einrichtung entgegen, wie sie vor allem auf dänischen und schwedischen Spielplätzen häufig anzutreffen ist: dort werden von den Spielplatzhelferinnen große Klötze, Bretter und Kisten zum Bauen ausgegeben. Auf englischen und skandinavischen Spiel- arealen sind Schiffe ein ständig wiederkehrendes Element. Der Schiffsrumpf besteht meist aus Beton (bei größeren Schiffen oft mit Sand gefüllt), Decksaufbauten und Kajüten meist aus Holz. Nur die Grundform ist angedeutet, aber die Hauptsache ist ja doch, daß es »echte« Taue und Strickleitern gibt, und daß man mit Flaschenzug und Kran Kisten an Bord holen und durchs Bullauge nach dem See- gang schauen kann.

1. Climbing net on a playground in Sayes Court, London.
2. Handing out building blocks on a playground in Stockholm.
3. Wooden railway track on a playground surrounded by blocks of flats in New York.
4, 5, 8. Ships of concrete and wood on playgrounds of housing estates in Copenhagen suburbs.
6. A "boat" for climbing: Sculpture of wooden beams in front of the Sporthalle Berlin-Charlottenburg, created by Brummack, Berlin.
7. Play sculptures of plastic designed by Joina Gudnadottir.

1. Kletternetz auf einem Parkspielplatz Sayes Court, London.
2. Ausgabe von Baukastenelementen auf einem Stockholmer Platz.
3. Holzschiene auf einem New Yorker Hausspielplatz.
4, 5, 8. Beton-Holzschiffe auf Siedlungsspielplätzen in Kopenhagen.
6. Ein »Schiff« zum Klettern: Balkenskulptur des Berliner Bildhauers Heinrich Brummack vor der Sporthalle Charlottenburg.
7. Spielskulpturen aus Kunststoff. Entwurf Joina Gudnadottir.

Play bowls and saddle slides

Designed and manufactured by "Playground Associates", New York, U.S.A.

Spielschale und Sattelrutsche

Entwurf und Herstellung: Playground Associates, New York, USA

A further piece of multi-purpose equipment is this translucent fibreglass bowl of different colours (1–3). It weighs only 37 pounds. A number of possibilities for play are shown here: climbing hillock, roundabout and shelter. Without the simple metal support the bowl can be used as a sandpit or paddling pool.

The saddle slide with its abstract organic shape serves as a riding horse, slide, house and tunnel (4–6). It offers children opportunities for climbing and jumping, crawling through and playing hide-and-seek. If used as a shelter, its many apertures provide surprising means of communication between outside and inside. The saddle slide is made of polished reconstructed stone. The group of designers who developed this item hire out the mould so that it can be cast in situ, thus economising manufacturing and transport costs.

Neither item restrains the child's imagination but rather they encourage him to find out for himself how to play with that "thing" which by virtue of its passive existence calls for initiative.

Ein weiteres Mehrzweckgerät stellt diese aus durchscheinendem Fiberglas in verschiedenen Farben gepreßte Schale dar (1–3), deren Gewicht nur 17 kg beträgt. Eine Reihe von Spielmöglichkeiten – Kletterberg, Karussell, Schutzhütte – zeigen die Abbildungen, und mit dem einfachen Eisengestell kann die Schale als Sandkasten oder Planschbecken verwendet werden.

Die Sattelrutsche aus Gußstein verbindet in ihrer ungegenständlich-biomorphen Gestalt Reittier, Rutschbahn, Haus und Tunnel (4–6). Sie bietet den Kindern Möglichkeiten zum Klettern und Abspringen, zum Durchkriechen und Verstecken und schafft mit ihren Durchbrüchen überraschend Kommunikationen zwischen Drinnen und Draußen. Die Sattelrutsche besteht aus poliertem Gußstein mit einer Stahlarmierung. Die Entwerfergruppe, die dieses Gerät entwickelte, verleiht die Form gegen eine gewisse Gebühr, so daß der Guß erst an Ort und Stelle zu erfolgen braucht und Herstellungs- wie Transportkosten möglichst niedrig gehalten werden können.

Beide Geräte legen die Phantasie des Kindes nicht fest, sondern regen sie an, selber zu finden, wie man mit diesem »Ding«, das durch sein Dasein passiv herausfordert, aus eigener Initiative spielen kann.

Concrete tunnel bridge

Designed and manufactured by Play Sculptures Division of Creative Playthings, Inc., Herndon, U.S.A.

Tunnelbrücke aus Beton

Entwurf und Herstellung: Play Sculptures Division of Creative Playthings, Inc., Herndon, USA

The tunnel bridge of simple concrete components can be supplied in different colours. If placed in echelon these tunnel bridges transform an area otherwise flat and offer exciting possibilities of an up-and-down hurdle game and they add spatial interest to a ground. This is a prize-winning design of a competition organised by the Museum of Modern Art in New York. With their clear and clean form and their contrasting colourful effects, these prefabricated concrete elements are well suited as equipment for playgrounds.

Die Tunnelbrücke aus einfachen Betonelementen kann in verschiedenen Farben geliefert werden. In gestaffelter Anordnung geben diese Tunnelbrücken einem flachen Platz das vorzüglich »bespielbare« Auf und Ab eines Berg- und Talgeländes, und eine plane Fläche gewinnt durch sie eine körperlich-räumliche Belebung. Ihr Entwurf wurde in einem Wettbewerb des Museum of Modern Art in New York mit einem Preis ausgezeichnet. Mit ihrer klaren, sauberen Form und ihrer wechselnden Farbigkeit sind diese prafabrizierten Betonelemente zur ästhetischen Gestaltung eines Spielgeländes gut geeignet.

Play sculptures with climbing nets

Designed by Joseph Brown, Princeton University, Princeton, U.S.A.

Spielplastiken mit Kletternetzen

Entwurf: Joseph Brown, Princeton University, Princeton, USA

The designer calls these structures "play communities", as they compel children to adjust their own interests to those of their playmates. Each "play community" consists of two elements: the massive central shape of concrete, resembling a snail or whale, and ropes suspended from the centre. The whole equipment contains the element of the "unpredictable", so that a creative quality is added to the mere physical act of playing. For instance, the concrete shape is so designed that children have to decide each time how to utilise it for climbing, sliding, crawling or jumping. The climbing net and hanging rope vibrate all other ropes with each grip and pull on any one part, and teach children to react in an elastic fashion to the movements of their own centre of gravity and those of others. They are meant to learn from their play how to adjust themselves to ever-new situations. It should become clear to them that success is no end in itself but a continuing process which can only be mastered by the combined efforts of physical and intellectual powers.

Diese neuartigen Spielgeräte werden von ihrem Entwerfer »Spielgemeinschaft« genannt, weil sie die verschiedensten Spielmöglichkeiten kombinieren und zugleich die Kinder beim gemeinschaftlichen Spiel dazu veranlassen, ihre eigenen Interessen auf die der anderen abzustimmen. Jedes Gerät besteht aus zwei Grundelementen: dem massiven Zentralkörper aus Beton, dessen Form an Tiere, Schnecke oder Walfisch, denken läßt, und aus Kletterseilen, die strahlenförmig vom Zentrum ausgehen. Der Entwerfer geht von der Überlegung aus, daß Spielgeräte das Moment des »Unvorhersehbaren« enthalten sollen, damit zur bloßen körperlichen Tätigkeit eine schöpferische Qualität hinzutritt. Das Betonelement beispielsweise ist so angelegt, daß das Kind sich immer neu entscheiden muß, wenn es alle Möglichkeiten zum Klettern, Rutschen, Kriechen oder Springen ausnutzen will. Das Kletternetz gibt jeden Druck und Zug an einer Stelle als Schwingung an alle anderen Seile weiter und lehrt die Kinder, elastisch auf die Wirkungen des eigenen Schwergewichts und das Verhalten anderer zu reagieren.

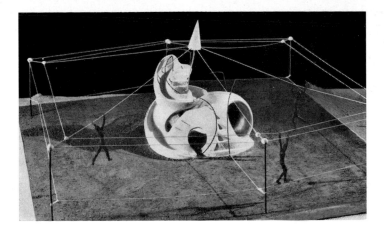

Jiggle-net and swing-ring

Designed by Joseph Brown, Princeton University,
Princeton, U.S.A.

Zappelnetz und Schwingring

Entwurf: Joseph Brown, Princeton University, Princeton, USA

The designer started with the assumption that the child should learn in his play to grasp the unpredictable and the flexible in his environment and to adjust himself within his limited sphere to the diversity of a given situation. He should understand the necessity of harmonising his individual interests with those of a group. In this dynamic process he perceives his abilities and his limitations, and learns that constant change is the principle of life. In order to achieve his aim he has to be flexible. The equipment has therefore been designed for simultaneous use by a number of children so as to present the child with such situations. The jiggle-net can be used by children of any age. It consists of semi-tight ropes with a steel core, which form knots at intersections. The children need agility and swift reaction not only for grappling with the ropes, but also for adjusting themselves to the unexpected shaking movements caused by the other children. The swing-ring consists of a ring of tubular steel which is suspended by ropes from a steel support allowing for circular movement.

Bei der Gestaltung dieser Geräte ging der Entwerfer davon aus, daß das Kind im Spiel lernen soll, die Lebendigkeit und Unberechenbarkeit seiner Umwelt zu begreifen und sich in seinem kindlichen Rahmen mit der Vielfältigkeit der jeweiligen Situation auseinanderzusetzen. Es soll die Notwendigkeit erfassen, seine Einzelinteressen auf das Gruppeninteresse abzustimmen. In diesem dynamischen Prozeß erkennt das Kind seine Fähigkeiten und Grenzen, es erfährt, daß der ständige Wechsel ein Lebensprinzip ist und daß man, um ein Ziel zu erreichen, beweglich sein muß. Um solche Situationen zu schaffen, sind die Geräte für die gleichzeitige Benutzung durch mehrere Kinder konstruiert, wobei beim Zappelnetz die Altersstufe keine Rolle spielt. Dieses Zappelnetz besteht aus ineinander verknoteten und verspannten Seilen mit einer Stahleinlage. Die Kinder brauchen ihre Geschicklichkeit nicht nur, um überhaupt mit den Hindernissen fertig zu werden, sondern vor allem, um die überraschende Wipp-, Schüttel- und Gegenbewegungen der Seile aufzufangen, die durch andere Kinder ausgelöst werden. Der Schwingring besteht aus einem Stahlrohrreifen, der mit Seilen an einer senkrecht stehenden Stahlrohrstütze drehbar aufgehängt ist.

Star-shaped balancing equipment and tents of tubular steel

Star shape designed by Joseph Brown, Princeton University, Princeton, U.S.A.
Tubular steel tents designed by the Play Sculptures Division of Creative Playthings, Inc., Herndon, U.S.A.

Balancierstern und Stahlrohrzelte

Entwurf des Balanciersterns: Joseph Brown, Princeton University, Princeton, USA
Entwurf und Herstellung der Stahlrohrzelte: Play Sculptures Division of Creative Playthings, Inc., Herndon, USA

1

2

Joseph Brown has developed a number of articles of play equipment (see pages 170 and 173) in which a stimulus for play is combined in an extraordinarily successful way with formal qualities. The star-shaped equipment (3) consists of six thin and elastic steel flats 8 feet in length which are held together at a centre and radiate in all directions. They are anchored to the ground at the ends. Every pressure and movement on any of these elastic steel bands is transmitted throughout the entire structure, thereby demanding alertness and spontaneous reaction of all children balancing or jumping at the time. The educational value of the equipment lies in the necessity imposed on the child to adapt himself quickly to unpredictable circumstances. This value is inherent in many of Joseph Brown's playthings.
The pyramid-shaped tubular steel structure (1+2) is 4 feet 3 inches high and can be used for various games. If several are grouped together they form a play encampment which can at the same time be used as climbing hillocks and crawling maze. If covered with a plastic sheet the pyramid-shaped structure becomes a Red Indian tent.

Joseph Brown hat eine Reihe von Spielgeräten entwickelt (siehe Seite 170 und 172), in denen Spielwert und formale Gestaltung auf hervorragende Weise miteinander vereinigt sind. Bei dem Balancier- oder Wackelstern (3) handelt es sich um eine Verbindung von elastischen Stahlbändern, die von einem Mittelstück sternförmig auslaufen und an ihren Enden im Boden verankert sind. Jeder Druck und jede Bewegung an einer Stelle der freigespannten Stahlbänder wird auf das ganze labile System übertragen und verlangt so beim Balancieren oder Springen von allen Mitspielenden ein spontanes Ausgleichen der Veränderung und ständige, aufmerksame Bereitschaft. Das Eingehen auf unvorhergesehene Veränderungen ist das hauptsächliche pädagogische Anliegen, das Brown in vielen seiner Spielgeräte verwirklicht.
Die Stahlrohrgestelle in Pyramidenform (1+2) lassen sich zu verschiedenen Spielen verwenden. Zu mehreren zusammengestellt ergeben sie ein Spieldorf, das zugleich Klettergebirge und Kriechlabyrinth sein kann. Mit einer Kunststoffhülle überzogen wird das Gestell zum Indianerzelt.

3

"Sandfloh" tubular steel play equipment

Designed by "Aktion Sandfloh", Ulm, Germany
Manufactured by Gerätebau Albin Grünzig, Eystrup, Germany

»Sandfloh«-Spielgeräte aus Stahlrohr

Entwurf: Aktion Sandfloh, Ulm, Deutschland
Herstellung: Gerätebau Albin Grünzig, Eystrup, Deutschland

1. The zigzag-shaped balancing rods are suspended from steel ropes supported by semi-circular "stirrups".
2. The balancing sphere of aluminium moves along a spiral track. It is attached to a steel rope which winds and unwinds itself around four poles in the centre.
3. The balancing rope is suspended between two double arches of tubular steel.
4+5. The rope of this tug-of-war runs over a wheel which is suspended from a steel spring. When in use it is pulled down until it is tight. After use the spring pulls it up again so that it cannot lie about.
6. Swings of different scale for children of varying ages separated from each other by protective barriers.
7. A swinging tower for older children. The cantilevers project a long way in order to prevent accidents.

Here the initiative for creating playgrounds originated with a working group of the Ulm Volkshochschule (a school for further education). The "Aktion Sandfloh", a name symbolising an endeavour, has been actively supported by architects and a committee formed of interested citizens. During the two-year period of experimental development, individual play structures were more and more improved until a manufacturer was ready to take over the prototypes for mass production.
Besides well established equipment like see-saws, roundabouts and climbing arches, which have been improved as a result of observation of the way they are used by children, quite new and interesting equipment was developed. Among the latter are a number of balancing gadgets which show the emphasis laid by the "Aktion Sandfloh" on the quick physical reaction and alertness of children.

Von einer Arbeitsgruppe der Ulmer Volkshochschule kam die Anregung, aus eigener Initiative Kinderspielplätze zu schaffen. Die »Aktion Sandfloh« wird durch freie Architekten und ein Gremium aus der Bürgerschaft tätig unterstützt. In zweijähriger Versuchsarbeit wurden einzelne Geräte so weit vervollkommnet, daß sie eine Spielgerätefirma zur Herstellung in Serienproduktion übernehmen konnte. Neben altbewährten Grundformen wie Wippe, Karussell und Kletterbogen, die mit beträchtlicher Einfühlung in den Spielablauf und in die Spielbedürfnisse der Kinder verbessert wurden, hat man interessante neue Geräte entwickelt. Dazu gehört vor allem eine Reihe von Balanciergeräten, die ein Grundanliegen der »Aktion Sandfloh« deutlich machen: die körperliche Geschicklichkeit der Kinder auszubilden.

1

2

3

1. Die Balancierstange in Zickzackform ist an Stahlseilen in halbmondförmigen Bügeln eingehängt.

2. Die Balancierkugel aus Aluminium bewegt sich entlang einer Schienenspirale; sie wird von einem Drahtseil gehalten, das sich um vier Pfosten im Zentrum auf- und abwickelt.

3. Das Balancierseil ist zwischen zwei Doppelbögen aus Stahlrohr verspannt.

4+5. Das Tau dieses Tauziehgerätes läuft über eine Rolle, die an einem Federzug hängt. Beim Spielen wird es so weit heruntergezogen, bis es sich strafft. Nach Gebrauch nimmt es der Federzug wieder in die Höhe, so daß es nicht herumliegen kann.

6. In den Maßen dreifach abgestufte Schaukeln für Kinder verschiedener Altersstufen, durch Schutzgeländer voneinander getrennt.

7. Ein Schwingturm für größere Kinder. Die Tragarme kragen so weit aus, daß das Gerät unfallsicher ist.

4

5

6

7

Emmy Andriesse 39 (4)
Harriet Arnold, New York 172 (2, 3), 173 (3)
Baumann 161 (6, 7)
Eva Besnyö, Amsterdam 39 (3)
Stig Billing, Hälsingborg 160 (1)
Walter Binder, Zürich 131 (3, 4), 132 (6), 133 (9, 10), 136 (23), 139 (34, 35), 146 (3)
Ernest Braun, San Anselmo, Calif. 101 (2), 102 (6)
J. Bumcke 160 (4)
Albrecht Burgger, Stuttgart 121 (2)
Horst Calles, Köln-Müngersdorf 84 (2), 85 (5, 6)
Comet, Zürich 141 (2), 142 (3)
Violette Cornelius, Amsterdam 38, 45 (5)
Creative Playthings, Inc., Herndon 169 (2, 3), 173 (1, 2)
Cugini, Zürich 143 (11), 149 (15)
Royal Danish Foreign Office, Copenhagen, Press Department
Kgl. Dänisches Außenministerium Kopenhagen, Pressebüro
110 (1, 2), 111 (3, 4), 112 (6), 113 (9)
Diamat, Zürich 151 (7, 10)
Rüdiger Dichtel, Stuttgart-Möhringen 56 (2), 160 (2), 161 (10, 11)
Kurt Eppler, Stuttgart-Vaihingen 123 (8)
Kurt Ernst, Karlsruhe 64 (4), 65 (6–8)
Charles Forberg Associates, New York 62 (2), 63 (3–5)
Fotoflight Ltd., Elstree Aerodrome, Hertfordshire 74 (2)
Gartenbauamt, Stuttgart 165 (10)
Dieter Geissler, Stuttgart-Heumaden 122 (5)
Wolgang Gerson 115 (3)
E. Glesmann, München 125 (2–5), 126 (6–8), 127 (9–12)
Peter Grünert, Zürich 71 (4), 130 (1)
Robert Häusser, Mannheim 117 (3–5), 118 (6–8), 119 (10, 11)
Ingeborg Heise, Zürich 27 (1), 68 (4, 5), 69 (7), 71 (3, 5), 72 (6–9), 73 (10), 134 (12–15), 135 (16–19), 136 (20, 21), 137 (24–27), 138 (28–32), 148 (8), 162 (3), 163 (7, 8)
Lucien Hervé, Paris 30 (4), 60 (2)
David Hirsch, New York 76 (1, 2), 77 (4, 5), 78 (6, 7), 79 (8–13), 165 (7)
Gerhard Howald, Bern 143 (8–10), 144 (12–15), 145 (16–18, 20), 148 (9) 150 (3), 151 (5, 6, 8, 9)
Interphoto Press Agency, Milano 158 (1–3)
G. Kesselbach 123 (6), 161 (8)
Kimpel, Ulm/Donau 174 (2), 175 (4, 5, 7)
Helmut Koch, Köln 84 (1)

Erwin Küenzi, Zürich 132 (5, 7)
Ed. Labhart, Zürich 150 (2)
Einar Liljeqvist, Hälsingborg 164 (5)
London County Council 166 (1)
H. Lumpe, Stuttgart-Feuerbach 57 (3, 6)
Norman Mc Grath 99 (8)
Mary Mitchell 115 (8)
M. Moor, Zürich 149 (16, 17, 19–21)
New York City Housing Authority 166 (3)
Anita Niesz 147 (4, 6), 148 (7), 165 (8)
Pal-Nils Nilsson, Lindingö 159 (3)
Cas Oorthuys 39 (2), 40
Patrick 123 (7)
J. H. Piepgrass, Odder, Danmark 160 (3), 165 (11)
Playground Associates, Inc. New York 168 (1–6)
Playscape Incorporated, New York 152 (2), 153 (5), 154 (10), 155 (14, 15)
Wolfgang Prange, Köln 85 (4)
Uwe Rau, Berlin 167 (6)
H. Sander, Ulm/Donau 174 (1)
Siegel, Ulm/Donau 174 (3)
Stadsarkivets fotografiske atelier, Kopenhagen 49 (5), 50 (1, 2), 113 (7, 8)
Stadtbildstelle, Leverkusen 161 (5)
Stadtmessungsamt, Stuttgart 122 (4)
Hans Staub, Zürich 148 (10–13), 149 (14)
Alexander von Stieger, Zürich 108 (1, 2), 109 (3–5)
Georg Ströde, Stockholm 167 (7)
Walter Studer, Bern 31 (4)
Ateljé Sundahl AB. Nacka 92 (1–3), 93 (4–6)
Thecla, New York 152 (4), 154 (11, 12), 155 (16)
Katrina Thomas, New York 156 (2–4), 157 (11, 12)
Borough of Tottenham, Public Relations Department 106
USIS Photo Unit, Bad Godesberg 94 (1, 2), 95 (6–3), 169 (1)
USIS Services Américains d'Information, Paris 28 (4), 61
Vandpytten, Holte 48 (2)
Helga Wilde, Stuttgart 31 (3), 57 (4, 5), 122 (3), 161 (9), 165 (6, 9)
Lonnie Wilson 103 (7–10)
Ludwig Windstosser, Stuttgart 120 (1)
Michael Wolgensinger, Zürich 25 (3), 30 (5), 67 (2), 69 (6), 163 (5)
Wormald Studio, London 74 (3), 75 (4–6)
Margaret Wunsch, Basel 133 (11), 139 (33)